INFLUX
Essays on Literary Influence

Kennikat Press
National University Publications
Literary Criticism Series

General Editor
John E. Becker
Fairleigh Dickinson University

INFLUX
ESSAYS ON LITERARY INFLUENCE

Edited by
Ronald Primeau

National University Publications
KENNIKAT PRESS   //   1977
Port Washington, N. Y.   //   London

Copyright © 1977 by Kennikat Press Corp. All rights reserved. No part of this publication may be reproduced, stored in a retrieval system, or transmitted, in any form or by any means, electronic, mechanical, photocopying, recording, or otherwise, without the prior written permission of the publisher.

Manufactured in the United States of America

Published by
Kennikat Press Corp.
Port Washington, N. Y./London

Library of Congress Cataloging in Publication Data
Main entry under title:

Influx.

(Literary criticism series) (Kennikat Press national university publications)
    Bibliography: p.
    CONTENTS: Introduction.—Literary history and tradition: Eliot, T. S. Tradition and the individual talent. Trilling, L. The sense of the past. Hassan, I. H. The problem of influence in literary history. [etc.]
    1. Literature—Philosophy—Addresses, essays, lectures.
2. Influence (Literary, artistic, etc.)—Addresses, essays, lectures. I. Primeau, Ronald.
PN45.I45   809   76-44836
ISBN 0-8046-9151-7

CONTENTS

INFLUX
Essays on Literary Influence

RONALD PRIMEAU

INTRODUCTION

> *A hard coming we had of it*
> *Everybody influencing everyone else*
> *And the critics chafing, rude, disorderly*
> *Cold on our tracks..*
>
> (David Wevill, from "The Poets")

Among people who take the matter at all seriously, there is considerable debate about whether an "influence study" is a legitimate critical inquiry. Perhaps as my colleague who reads science fiction as a record of the history of ideas has suggested, problems in determining literary influence will be solvable only when we have devices to collect and analyze what is now only grist for speculation. Even when explained in the most intricate critical language, an influence is always a series of irreducible experiential encounters between works and readers. Bold yet unverifiable hypotheses about what actually happens in these interactions form the core of theories about literary history, the origins of poetic creativity, and the meaning of audience response. The study of influence as the persistent flow of these dynamic interactions remains a critical inquiry of endless fascination. From *in illo tempore* to contemporary rhetorics and noncausative physics, theories of literary influence have wavered between the oversimplifications of genetic linearity and expansive yet hypothetical theories of creativity through displacement, misreading, and revisionism. The history of what poets and critics have meant by this influx reveals some predictable but nonetheless crucial insights about poetic creativity and critical sensibility.

Within this wide range from safe logics of causality to more risky ventures into the psychology of origins, the study of literary influence has

3

produced an astonishing array of detractors and advocates. At the center of shifting values throughout the history of sensibility, influence study has been overpraised, dismissed with contempt, or—in more instances than not —left to its own unexamined. But whether overvalued or too smugly cast off, source study has been essential in all theories of literary genesis and all attempts to account for the origins of creativity.

What characterizes most recent commentaries on influence is a relentless redefining of the meaning of the process itself. Traditional assumptions about what happens when A influences B have undergone massive reinterpretation. This volume is an attempt to capture some of the new thinking on an old topic. It began as a Wallace Stevens–like snapshot of "twenty-six ways of looking at" literary influence. But the album soon became too small to hold all the pictures, and space began to narrow the focus to what would fit in a collection of manageable size. There is no room for Longinus or Ben Jonson on identification with the sublime and the conversion of riches through imitation. Neither is there space for even representative samples from poems on poetry or from the journals or letters of writers who reveal conscious or unconscious influences. Nonetheless, the sheer quantity as well as the range of influence studies will be apparent in the selections reprinted here.

As all the essays collected here demonstrate, the broad inquiries of influence study go beyond one-to-one source identification to the meaning of a literary tradition—be it one writer or an entire heritage—and its role in the creation of new works of art. Significant also in all discussions of influence is the extent to which writers revise what they read and thereby create their own sources. These basic issues determine the arrangement of selections in this volume. Part 1 examines the problem of origins through a reassessment of literary history and tradition. Part 2 considers influence broadly as a species of revisionist reading. Part 3 focuses on the reader as an active participant in the shaping of his own influences. Part 4 is a brief checklist of studies touching on "influence." Although this brief summary describes a wide range of assumptions and emphases, most approaches to literary influence share their origins.

The language of literary influence originated in astrological, medical, and theological terminology taken over by literary critics. First assumed to be a primordial inflowing of undifferentiated creative energy, influx was soon systematized and absorbed into various schools of interpretation. As a critical method, source study was soon overpracticed and then distorted. Reeling from the force of corrective warnings that soon became harsh attacks, influence study took on increasingly new directions. What had degenerated from a basic vocabulary of creative origins into an abstract and highly suspect method for determining parallels has once again become today the cornerstone for new systems of critical inquiry. Study of biography has merged with investigations into the meaning of creativity and the process of poetic composition. The inspiration of the Muse and classical *inventio* updated reenact the arguments about genius vs rules. Inquiries into the meaning of literary history and the development of human consciousness call for reappraisals of the development of traditions, genres, conventions, and movements. The reciprocal nature of influx has raised new and old questions about what it means to read, to interpret, and to respond critically to a literary work. Literary influence has itself flooded the consciousness of modern criticism and is being absorbed, modified, and rechanneled as we watch it develop.

Coming down from the Latin *influere*, "to flow in," "influence" and its various derivatives have been part of English letters at least since the Renaissance. "Inflow," "influx," "influent," "influenza," "influous," "influxion," and "influxive" have all at one time or another described the flowing of a fluid or power from, into, or through a person or force. In the Renaissance the crucial humors or temperments were said to flow into (or to have influence on) men. Various astrological derivations have proved especially significant. The *O. E. D.* records:

The supposed flowing or streaming from the stars or heavens of an etherial fluid acting upon the character and destiny of men, and affecting sublunary things generally. In later times gradually viewed less literally, as an exercise of power or 'virtue,' or an occult force, and in late use chiefly a poetical or humorous reflex of earlier notions.

Other such derivations from the original astrological term include the exercise of personal power, a disposition said to flow from the astral, "the bearing of a relation," the induction of electrical fluid, the inflowing or infusion of divine power, and the "capacity or faculty of producing effects by insensible or invisible means, without the employment of material force or the exercise of formal authority."

The last two in this partial list describe the most conventional notions of literary genesis and sources. The tracing of cause-effect relationships when causes are not readily observable is the business of literary history. One writer or school or tradition exerts action which produces results in another writer, school, tradition and so on. Though any philosophy of history is more complex than my oversimplified sketch suggests, all theories of historical developments from Herodotus to Hegel to the present involve a flow of actions and reactions and some kind of ensuing interaction.

As an inflowing of divine powers, influence attaches itself to the workings of the Muse and theories of genius and inspiration. Theological treatises consistently stress the immission and influsion of immaterial powers. Thomas Hooker speaks of God's "influence into the very essence" of things: "All things are therefore partakers of God, they are his offspring, his influence is in them." The terminology as well as the procedures of influence study derive from a long and complex past that is still an essential part of what influence means in modern criticism.

In most theories of influence, imitation is a central determinant of growth and development. From Plato's artist who falls that much farther away from Ideal Forms by imitating a mere shadow to Sidney's "the poets only deliver a golden," many diverse theories of imitation are offered to explain the poet's relationship to the past. Space does not permit a review of the classical stress on converting the riches of another to one's own use through imitation. But it should at least be noted that an influence generally happens in the midst of tension and interplay between imitation and originality. To cite only one example, the classicism of Ben Jonson was energized by imitative influence. The full title of his major treatise in aesthetics reflects the latinate sense of influx—*Timber, or Discoveries Made upon Men and Matter: As They Have Flow'd out of His Daily Readings or Had Their Refluxe to His Peculiar Notion of the Times.* Jonson's famous advice to writers "to read the best authors" and "observe the best speakers" celebrates the power of creative influx. Classical imitation as well as theories of translation in which Aristotle, Horace, and Longinus were "Englished" bring together the rhetorician's *inventio* and various theories of translation and inspiration. The common denominator is always the transmission or the flow resulting from an interaction between old and new. As long as originality was not the primary criterion of aesthetic value, the pervasive linearity of literary influence was never a real threat to the imitator. Because classical imitation was a species of discipline for the purpose of liberation, the writer experienced little of the confinement that later came to be associated with staying too close to one's influences. In two selections in this volume Walter Jackson Bate and Harold Bloom examine the implications of originality as a determinant of influence and poetic creativity.

As various emphases in the study of literary history come and go, the way writers read each other and their predecessors remains intriguing. Influence study has never been able to (nor would it really want to) shake the stigma of source hunters. Any recent *PMLA* bibliography can attest to that uncontrollable mania in scholarship. Journals continue to fill up with discussions of minute source documents that often prove no more than what is self-evident from sheer chronology or cultural proximity. Invariably, arguments ensue over the authenticity or relative merits of alleged sources. Although source hunting has long been an object of scorn, it has amassed a wealth of tradition and repute. Dryden was concerned with Chaucer's "borrowing" from Boccacio, Dr. Johnson (and nearly everyone else) with Shakespeare's sources; and enough has been written about the sources of modern poetry nearly to annihilate the fresh responses of all but the most dedicated readers. When contrived and rigid or when lacking curiosity, a study of sources elicits only objections. But it is fast becoming apparent that published dissent from "source" studies has actually provided the strongest impetus for their phenomenal growth in range and importance.

Often the very questions raised in attacks against the concept of literary influence have broadened the techniques and relevance of source study. Extensive theoretical objections raised long ago in classic studies by T. S. Eliot and Lionel Trilling, in several useful guides to research techniques (the best by Richard Altick), and in systematic aesthetic reconsiderations of influence as it functioned throughout history (represented in this volume by concise yet detailed inquiries by Haskell M. Block and Ihab H. Hassan)—these objections pushed influence study into more mature methodology and more useful illuminations of the literary work.

Countering critical emphasis on linearity and priority, many poets and philosophers have expressed views of influx that transcend chronology. In "To William Wordsworth" Coleridge remarked that "The truly great / Have all one age, and from one visible space / Shed influence!" And Shelley in several places speaks of the "one great Poem" perpetually in progress and in a famous passage describes the mind in creation as "a fading coal, which some invisible influence, like an inconstant wind, awakens to transitory brightness." Of course Shelley's emphasis is always on influx as inspiration, on "the influence which is moved not, but moves." Contributions also to the loosening of the chronology at the base of influence study can be found in Hegel's dialectic, the rediscovery of Vico's primitive myth, Blake's overturning of the past in favor of his own mythic structures, Nietzsche's view of interpretation as a species of "will to power," and—to risk a vast oversimplification—the entire Romantic reassessment of the primacy of consciousness and self in the creative process. These are only a few of the issues that poised influx on the brink of what has since come into full view in more recent criticism.

Pushing off from these and other earlier inquiries, two major critical stances have reappeared in current reinterpretation of literary influence. First, source study has largely given way to a renewed interest in the broader issues of literary genesis. The Muse has returned bringing her genial inspiration, made accessible again with the help of modern interpreters. Concern has once again shifted to what classical rhetoricians called *inventio,* the sense of which is preserved in what we admire in the inventiveness of creative artists. Second, recent commentators are beginning to see the influx operating at least two ways. Writers influence readers, and readers in turn are predisposed to be influenced and, hence, help create what they read and are influenced by. Prompted by growing systematic studies of audience response as a factor of meaning, influence study is returning to questions as old as Aristotle. In ways that cannot be summarized here, recent commentators on influence have shifted from concern with sources to an examination of the origins of literary creativity itself. Genetic criticism has been transformed into a more complex examination of the writer, of literary structure, and of the reader's transforming response to what is influencing him. The two directions most apparent in recent studies of influence are first the many reinterpretations of tradition, borrowing, and revisionist reading and second, the sometimes radically altered approaches introduced by new rhetorics and physics and ventures into the psychology of influence. These major explorations are represented throughout this volume.

In modern essays on influence, borrowings have given way almost entirely to the manipulation and revision of what has gone before. The nature of the modifying process remains ever debatable. Most of the essays below explore what might be called the psychology of influence. Guillén sees influence as displacement arranged in a field and perceived as a *Gestalt.* Bloom and Bate stress the anxiety and burden felt by the latecomer. Holland interprets meaning as defense and hence influence as a similarly subjective construct. If influence is itself in psychological terms a species of delusion, then infusion of unknown power ranges from Plato's "illusion" to Oscar Wilde's "art of lying." Classical imitation is akin also to the psychological dynamics operating in identification. Finally, the psychology of influence confronts the problem of solipsism wherein the poet becomes his own influence by reading himself into all his precursors. The psychology of self-conscious influence draws a thin line between the emulation of models, the invocation of the Muse, and the revisionism of discovering the self as the measure of all. The psychological dimensions of subjectivity link all these concerns closely with the next major concern of modern studies of influence—reader response theories.

Concerned students of language and literary art have for some time been refuting source hunters, zealous but misguided biographers, and proponents of various kinds of genetic, intentionalist, and affective fallacies. But the problem is even more complex than what such old fallacies suggest. Because the influence of A on B clearly depends as much on the response of B as on the source A, questions about the creative activity of the reader further complicate an already unwieldy investigation. Reading response is by its very nature subjective. But, accustomed to feeling safe with at least the illusion of objectivity, commentary on literature has tended to be sloppy and unsystematic whenever it has ventured into the affective. It may be especially surprising, then, to find rigorous, systematic, and insightful critical commentary in recent studies of literary influence and reader-response—two areas generally considered unpromising or at best nonessential.

The most encouraging recent trend in literary criticism is the attempt on several fronts to put the reader and his experience of reading back into theories of what literature is and how it works. Interest in influence and reader response has revealed an astonishing set of curious bedfellows. Structuralists and avowed anti-structuralists, literary historians, linguists, rhetoricians, Freudians, and revisionists of every variety are reexamining questions about the origins of creativity and the dynamics of influence and audience response. How encouraging all this will turn out to be depends ultimately on the impact such critical breakthroughs will have on all of us as readers, teachers, and students of language and literature. Can what is beginning to look like a plethora of studies of influence and audience response make us more sensitive readers of literature?

Theories of audience participation heighten the tensions inherent in any present reader's relationship to the past. Imitation and creative misreading coexist in comfortable tension in the neoclassical view of imitation as a conversion one's own riches. Classical theory in any culture repeats the dictum that an artist imitates in order to be free. But as Harold Bloom has pointed out in his emphasis on belatedness, in Western culture anteriority has attained status in itself and lack of priority therefore produces great anxiety. Bloom's sustained pursuit of the meaning of literary origins has brought influence back to its earliest sense of the primordial influx of creative powers. He has returned critical exploration to questions about not only what is going on when one writer influences another but also how an interpretation of that influence—whatever one decides is happening—fits into one's overall theory of literature and criticism. Bloom provides clearly demonstrative and challenging answers of his own. Whether or not he is right, influence can never again mean what it had become in rather mechanical source studies. Reviewing *The Anxiety of Influence,* Geoffrey Hartman has concluded that "after reading Bloom the innocence of influence is lost. We enter a realm of psychic assault, spiritual imposition and quasi-astrological fatality. Nietzschean insights into the 'guilt of indebtedness' combine with Freud's vision of mediated men to show that all influence is daemonic and resistance to it heroic."

Revisionist readings come, of course, in all varieties. There are as many different kinds of creative reading as there are theories of audience involvement with a text. Current emphasis on the ways in which a writer creates his own precursors has long been inevitable. Eliot's "the pastness of the past and its presence," Trilling's transmission as creative development, Guillén on poetry as displaced influence, and Bloom on poetry as defense against the flood of precursors—all quite clearly point to renewed interest in audience as creative participant.

Recent theories of influence have begun to shift from rhetorics of representation to rhetorics of identification. The influence of A on B entails the transmission of what Kenneth Burke has called "symbolic action." Edward T. Hall and others have shown us how "space speaks." Recent models in stylistics stress the complexities of readers structuring their own experience and hence also their influences. In emerging studies of nonverbal rhetoric, a semiology of influence is in the making. But such an approach also brings its cautions. Susanne Langer warns of absurdities perpetrated by genetic criticism on a philosophy of symbolism, where "all elementary symbolic forms have their origin in something else than symbolistic interest."

If literary scholarship is now undergoing a revolution (cybernetic, McLuhanesque, or otherwise) in its consciousness of itself, the special study of literary influence seems equipped to make the transition. In many current theories of communication and perception, cause and effect are giving way to the principle of overdetermination, and the sequential is sharing its spotlight with nonlinear pattern recognition. Suppose, in other words, (with Guillén) that literary influence is itself a *Gestalt:*

Let us suppose that A resembles B and C. We are confronted with parallelisms of relations. These may be thematically restricted, like motifs, or textually minute; or they may embrace the overall structure of a genre or mode. Let us assume that we are not examining these relations as independent data, but as parts of the literary equivalent of the scientists's "field" or "system."

Although influx is by definition to some degree linear, Guillén hints at the usefulness of an epistemology of models for the student enmeshed in what literary influence is likely to become:

The notion of medium as convention, or of vehicle or genre as convention, supersedes from the start any distinction between form and content. It is a unifying, structural notion. And it encourages the literary critic who is confronted with a chaos of resemblances or relations between hopelessly scattered individual phenomena to try to recognize not merely the isolated or atomistic contacts between them, but the broader demands of a vehicle regarded as a system of conventional premises.

Historians have for a long time noted that a speed-up in changing consciousness and the collapse of a world order are often accompanied by nostalgia for a past when all was simpler and more predictable. Critical reductionists have long misread the complexities of the past so as to make it more manageable and to make its influx into the present more predictable and coherent. Neither reassessments in the workings of human consciousness nor new systems-theories of information networks preclude the dangers of reductionism in the study of influences.

Changes in the meaning of influence in literary history lead also inevitably to ongoing reinterpretations of the meaning of history itself and the relevance of the historical approach to literature. The history of literary influence is itself a history of human consciousness. Influx stubbornly latched itself on to the fundamental beliefs and modes of perception of various ages. And the term shifted or took on new meanings depending on whether imitation of models, the Longinian Sublime, decorum, enthusiasm, originality, or the synecdoche of Freudian defense formed the core of thinking.

But such warnings beg the question of what is restrictively reductionist as opposed to creatively revisionist. Whatever one's metaphysics and epistemology, influence study seems to endure in a fine adjustment or tension in the peculiarly Western dichotomy between what is external and therefore "objective" and what is internal, subjective, and imaginative. Two unlikely companions—Samuel Johnson and Vico—deserve the last words here. First, Dr. Johnson: "The truth is that no mind is much employed upon the present: recollection and anticipation fill up most of our moments." When writers are indebted to influences of their own choosing, they demonstrate Vico's contention that "We are only what we ourselves have made."

The study of literary influence must finally be judged on its usefulness for readers and critics who are in pursuit of better practical criticism. What stands revealed when the processes of influence are more thoroughly understood must bring our response to literature closer to its irreducible core-stuff. The selections reprinted here offer several alternatives. Eliot leaves us with an "objective correlative" embedded in a past that keeps on being the present. Trilling's "sense of the past" emphasizes the shaping effects of the transmission essential in the flow of influx. Bate and Bloom struggle with the question of whether influx is vitalization or blight. Bate's "Third Temple" and Bloom's "Return of the Dead" are in many ways the same place, but Bate's absorption is Bloom's drowning. Each is ultimately shamanistic and noetic, but what for Bate (after Keats) is "immortal freemasonry" and a "joining of the past" is for Bloom a flood, a "creative sorrow," and a hyperbolic evasion that is itself art. And how readers get to, and in part themselves create, literary art is also the subject of influence study and theories of reader response. What unlocks literature's indefinables is for Rosenblatt a transaction, for Holland a transformation, for Fish a linguistic response to kinetic art which he calls affective stylistics.

Each selection in this volume is the beginning of a journey toward art's core-stuff through the language of literary influence.

PART ONE

LITERARY HISTORY AND TRADITION

To answer the abuses of "source hunting," students of literary influence have rediscovered "influx" in its broadest sense. T. S. Eliot's now classic "Tradition and the Individual Talent" is a crucial document in the history of that rediscovery. "Influence" as a flexible pattern of developing traditions draws heavily on Eliot's "historical sense," involving "perception, not only of the pastness of the past, but of its presence." The pressures of tradition, the extent to which the audience participates in the creative process, and the complexities of "influence" are at the center of Eliot's theory that "what happens when a new work of art is created is something that happens simultaneously to all the works of art which preceded it." This altering of "the *whole* existing order" helps explain the relationship between a new work of art, the tradition it becomes a part of, and the responses of an audience to tradition and individual works as they shape each other. Poetry for Eliot is therefore "a living whole of all the poetry that has ever been written."

Developing Eliot's views on the interaction of past and present within a single work, Lionel Trilling adds that a critic must always look at any literary work "as it existed in history, as it has lived its life from then to now, as it is a thing which submits itself to one kind of perception in one age and another kind of perception in another age, as it exerts in each age a different kind of power." Trilling's insight for the study of influences is precisely that the modification of all varieties of theme and technique throughout "movements" or "traditions" are not coincidental with, but result from, the very transmission. Like Eliot's "something that happens" to a "whole existing order," Trilling's modification through transmission moves the study of influence farther away from source chronology and closer to later theories of how writers variously and complexly determine their own ancestors.

Ihab H. Hassan examines interactions between approaches to literary history and the study of influence. In his attempt to provide "a sharper definition" of rather "furtive" concepts, inflexible notions of "source" and "causality" in history give way to dynamic categories. Reading "similarity," "parallels," "indebtedness," "borrowings," *influence* in any sense "with reference to a developed system of norms in a tradition," Hassan recommends that *causality* be discarded in favor of "*development*, the modification of one tradition into another." Quite simply, "influence" is always a relational phenomenon. Because "every conjuction of minds, or sensibilities, or literary works prescribes its own norms and determines its own framework," the study of influence cannot be systematized. Hassan's own models for studying "the relation of an author's work to another author or another tradition" seek to avoid at once the vagueness of attempts to codify "an affective power" and the drift toward nominalism in what must always remain, by definition, relational.

T. S. ELIOT

TRADITION AND THE INDIVIDUAL TALENT

In English writing we seldom speak of tradition, though we occasionally apply its name in deploring its absence. We cannot refer to "the tradition" or to "a tradition"; at best we employ the adjective in saying that the poetry of So-and-so is "traditional" or even "too traditional." Seldom, perhaps, does the word appear except in a phrase of censure. If otherwise, it is vaguely approbative, with the implication, as to the work approved, of some pleasing archaeological reconstruction. You can hardly make the word agreeable to English ears without this comfortable reference to the reassuring science of archaeology.

Certainly the word is not likely to appear in our appreciations of living or dead writers. Every nation, every race, has not only its own creative, but its own critical turn of mind; and is even more oblivious of the short-comings and imitations of its critical habits than of those of its creative genius. We know, or think we know from the enormous mass of critical writing that has appeared in the French language, the critical method or habit of the French; we only conclude (we are such unconscious people) that the French are "more critical" than we, and sometimes even plume ourselves a little with the fact, as if the French were the less spontaneous. Perhaps they are; but we might remind ourselves that criticism is as inevitable as breathing, and that we should be none the worse for articulating what passes in our minds when we read a book and feel an emotion about it for criticizing our own minds in their work of criticism. One of the facts that might come to light in this process is our tendency to insist, when we praise a poet, upon those aspects of his work in which he least resembles any one else. In these aspects or parts of his work we pretend to find what is individual, what is the peculiar essence of the man. We dwell with satisfaction upon the poet's difference from his predecessors, especially his immediate predecessors; we endeavour to find something that can be isolated in order to be enjoyed. Whereas if we approach a poet without this prejudice we shall often find that not only the best, but the most individual parts of his work may be those in which the dead poets, his ancestors, assert their immortality most vigorously. And I do not mean the impressionable period of adolescence, but the period of full maturity.

Yet if the only form of tradition, of handing down, consisted in following the ways of the immediate generation before us in a blind or timid adherence to its successes, "tradition" should positively be discouraged. We have seen many such simple currents soon lost in the sand; and novelty is better than repetition. Tradition is a matter of much wider significance. It cannot be inherited, and if you want it you must obtain it by great labour. It involves, in the first place, the historical sense, which we may call nearly indispensable to any one who would continue to be a poet beyond his twenty-fifth year; and the historical sense involves a perception, not only of the pastness of the past, but of its presence; the historical sense compels a man to write not merely with his own generation in his bones, but with a feeling that the whole of the literature of Europe from Homer and within it the whole of the literature of his own country has a simultaneous existence and composes a simultaneous order. This historical sense, which is a sense of the timeless as well as of the temporal and of the timeless and of the temporal together, is what makes a writer traditional. And it is at the same time what makes a writer most acutely conscious of his place in time, of his own contemporaneity.

No poet, no artist of any art, has his complete meaning alone. His significance, his appreciation is the appreciation of his relation to the dead poets and artists. You cannot value him alone; you must set him, for contrast and comparison, among the dead. I mean this as a principle of aesthetic, not merely historical, criticism. The necessity that he shall conform, that he shall cohere, is not onesided; what happens when a new work of art is created is something that happens simultaneously to all the works of art which preceded it. The existing monuments form an ideal order among themselves, which is modified by the introduction of the new (the really new) work of art among them. The existing order is complete before the new work arrives; for order to persist after the supervention of novelty, the *whole* existing order must be, if ever so slightly, altered; and so the relations, proportions, values of each work of art toward the whole are readjusted; and this is conformity between the old and the new. Whoever has approved this idea of order, of the form of European, of English literature will not find it preposterous that the past should be altered by the present as much as the present is directed by the past. And the poet who is aware of this will be aware of great difficulties and responsibilities.

In a peculiar sense he will be aware also that he must inevitably be judged by the standards of the past. I say judged, not amputated, by them; not judged to be as good as, or worse or better than, the dead; and certainly not judged by the canons of dead critics. It is a judgment, a comparison, in which two things are measured by each other. To conform merely would be for the new work not really to conform at all; it would not be new, and would therefore not be a work of art. And we do not quite say that the new is more valuable because it fits in; but its fitting in is a test of its value—a test, it is true, which can only be slowly and cautiously applied, for we are none of us infallible judges of conformity. We say: it appears to conform, and is perhaps individual, or it appears individual, and may conform; but we are hardly likely to find that it is one and not the other.

To proceed to a more intelligible exposition of the relation of the poet to the past: he can neither take the past as a lump, an indiscriminate bolus, nor can he form himself wholly on one or two private admirations, nor can he form himself wholly upon one preferred period. The first course is inadmissible, the second is an important experience of youth, and third is a pleasant and highly desirable supplement. The poet must be very conscious of the main current, which does not at all flow invariably through the most distinguished reputations. He must be quite aware of the obvious fact that art never improves, but that the material of art is never quite the same. He must be aware that the mind of Europe—the mind of his own country—a mind which he learns in time to be much more important than his own private mind—is a mind which changes, and that this change is a development which abandons nothing *en route,* which does not superannuate either Shakespeare, or Homer, or the rock drawing of the Magdalenian draughtsmen. That this development, refinement perhaps, complication certainly, is not, from the point of view of the artist, any improvement. Perhaps not even an improvement from the point of view of the psychologist or not to the extent which we imagine; perhaps only in the end based upon a complication in economics and machinery. But the difference between the present and the past is that the conscious present is an awareness of the past in a way and to an extent which the past's awareness of itself cannot show.

Some one said: "The dead writers are remote from us because we *know* so much more than they did." Precisely, and they are that which we know.

I am alive to a usual objection to what is clearly part of my programme for the *métier* of poetry. The objection is that the doctrine requires a ridiculous amount of erudition (pedantry), a claim which can be rejected by appeal to the lives of poets in any pantheon. It will even be affirmed that much learning deadens or perverts poetic sensibility. While, however, we persist in believing that a poet ought to know as much as will not encroach upon his necessary receptivity and necessary laziness, it is not desirable to confine knowledge to whatever can be put into a useful shape for examinations, drawing rooms, or the still more pretentious modes of publicity. Some can absorb knowledge, the more tardy must sweat for it. Shakespeare acquired more essential history from Plutarch than most men could from the whole British Museum. What is to be insisted upon is that the poet must develop or procure the consciousness of the past and that he should continue to develop this consciousness throughout his career.

What happens is a continual surrender of himself as he is at the moment to something which is more valuable. The progress of an artist is a continual self-sacrifice, a continual extinction of personality.

There remains to define this process of depersonalization and its relation to the sense of tradition. It is in this depersonalization that art may be said to approach the condition of science. I, therefore, invite you to consider, as a suggestive analogy, the action which takes place when a bit of finely filiated platinum is introduced into a chamber containing oxygen and sulphur dioxide.

I I

Honest criticism and sensitive appreciation are directed not upon the poet but upon the poetry. If we attend to the confused cries of the newspaper critics and the *susurrus* of popular repetition that follows, we shall hear the names of poets in great numbers; if we seek not Bluebook knowledge but the enjoyment of poetry, and ask for a poem, we shall seldom find it. I have tried to point out the importance of the relation of the poem to other poems by other authors, and suggested the conception of poetry as a living whole of all the poetry that has ever been written. The other aspect of this Impersonal theory of poetry is the relation of the poem to its author. And I hinted, by an analogy, that the mind of the mature poet differs from that of the immature one not precisely in any valuation of "personality," not being necessarily more interesting, or having "more to say," but rather by being a more finely perfected medium in which special, or very varied, feelings are at liberty to enter into new combinations.

The analogy was that of the catalyst. When the two gases previously mentioned are mixed in the presence of a filament of platinum, they form sulphurous acid. This combination takes place only if the platinum is present; nevertheless the newly formed acid contains no trace of platinum, and the platinum itself is apparently unaffected; has remained inert, neutral, and unchanged. The mind of the poet is the shred of platinum. It may partly or exclusively operate upon the experience of the man himself; but, the more perfect the artist, the more completely separate in him will be the man who suffers and the mind which creates; the more perfectly will the mind digest and transmute the passions which are its material.

The experience, you will notice, the elements which enter the presence of the transforming catalyst, are of two kinds: emotions and feelings. The effect of a work of art upon the person who enjoys it is an experience different in kind from any experience not of art. It may be formed out of one emotion, or may be a combination of several; and various feelings, inhering for the writer in particular words or phrases or images, may be added to compose the final result. Or great poetry may be made without the direct use of any emotion whatever: composed out of feelings solely. Canto XV of the *Inferno* (Brunetto Latini) is a working up of the emotion evident in the situation; but the effect, though single as that of any work of art, is obtained by considerable complexity of detail. The last quatrain gives an image, a feeling attaching to an image, which "came," which did not develop simply out of what precedes, but which was probably in suspension in the poet's mind until the proper combination arrived for it to add itself to. The poet's mind is in fact a receptacle for seizing and storing up numberless feelings, phrases, images, which remain there until all the particles which can unite to form a new compound are present together.

If you compare several representative passages of the greatest poetry you see how great is the variety of types of combination, and also how completely any semi-ethical criterion of "sublimity" misses the mark. For it is not the "greatness," the intensity, of the emotions, the components, but the intensity of the artistic process, the pressure, so to speak, under which the fusion takes place, that counts. The episode of Paolo and Francesca employs a definite emotion, but the intensity of the poetry is something quite different from whatever intensity in the supposed experience it may give the impression of. It is no more intense, furthermore, than Canto XXVI, the voyage of Ulysses, which has not the direct dependence upon an emotion. Great variety is possible in the process of transmutation of emotion: the murder of Agamemnon, or the agony of Othello, gives an artistic effect apparently closer to a possible original than the scenes from Dante. In the *Agamemnon*, the artistic emotion approximates to the emotion of an actual spectator; in *Othello* to the emotion of the protagonist himself. But the difference between art and the event is always absolute; the combination which is the murder of Agamemnon is probably as complex as that which is the voyage of Ulysses. In either case there has been a fusion of elements. The ode of Keats contains a number of feelings which have nothing particular to do with the nightingale, but which the nightingale, partly, perhaps, because of its attractive name, and partly because of its reputation, served to bring together.

The point of view which I am struggling to attack is perhaps related to the metaphysical theory of the substantial unity of the soul: for my meaning is, that the poet has, not a "personality" to express, but a particular medium, which is only a medium and not a personality, in which impressions and experiences combine in peculiar and unexpected ways. Impressions and experiences which are important for the man may take no place in the poetry, and those which become important in the poetry may play quite a negligible part in the man, the personality.

I will quote a passage which is unfamiliar enough to be regarded with fresh attention in the light—or darkness—of these observations.

> And now methinks I could e'en chide myself
> For doating on her beauty, though her death
> Shall be revenged after no common action.
> Does the silkworm expend her yellow labours
> For thee? For thee does she undo herself?
> Are lordships sold to maintain ladyships
> For the poor benefit of a bewildering minute?
> Why does yon fellow falsify highways,
> And put his life between the judge's lips,
> To refine such a thing—keeps horse and men
> To beat their valours for her? . . .

In this passage (as is evident if it is taken in its context) there is a combination of positive and negative emotions: an intensely strong attraction toward beauty and an equally intense fascination by the ugliness which is contrasted with it and which destroys it. This balance of contrasted emotion is in the dramatic situation to which the speech is pertinent, but that situation alone is inadequate to it. This is, so to speak, the structural emotion, provided by the drama. But the whole effect, the dominant tone, is due to the fact that a number of floating feelings, having an affinity to this emotion by no means superficially evident, have combined with it to give us a new art emotion.

It is not in his personal emotions, the emotions provoked by particular events in his life, that the poet is in any way remarkable or interesting. His particular emotions may be simple, or crude, or flat. The emotion in his poetry will be a very complex thing, but not with the complexity of the emotions of people who have very complex or unusual emotions in life. One error, in fact, of eccentricity in poetry is to seek for new human emotions to express; and in this search for novelty in the wrong place it discovers the perverse. The business of the poet is not to find new emotions, but to use the ordinary ones and, in working them up into poetry, to express feelings which are not in actual emotions at all. And emotions which he has never experienced will serve his turn as well as those familiar to him. Consequently, we must believe that "emotion recollected in tranquillity" is an inexact formula. For it is neither emotion, nor recollection, nor, without distortion of meaning, tranquillity. It is a concentration, and a new thing resulting from the concentration, of a very great number of experiences which to the practical and active person would not seem to be experiences at all; it is a concentration which does not happen consciously or of deliberation. These experiences are not "recollected," and they finally unite in an atmosphere which is "tranquil" only in that it is a passive attending upon the event. Of course this is not quite the whole story. There is a great deal, in the writing of poetry, which must be conscious and deliberate. In fact, the bad poet is usually unconscious where he ought to be conscious, and conscious where he ought to be unconscious. Both errors tend to make him "personal." Poetry is not a turning loose of emotion, but an escape from emotion; it is not the expression of personality, but an escape from personality. But, of course, only those who have personality and emotions know what it means to want to escape from these things.

III
ὁ δὲ νοῦς ἴσως θειότερόν τι καὶ ἀπαθές ἐστιν

This essay proposes to halt at the frontier of metaphysics or mysticism, and confine itself to such practical conclusions as can be applied by the responsible person interested in poetry. To divert interest from the poet to the poetry is a laudable aim: for it would conduce to a juster estimation of actual poetry, good and bad. There are many people who appreciate the expression of sincere emotion in verse, and there is a smaller number of people who can appreciate technical excellence. But very few know when there is an expression of *significant* emotion, emotion which has its life in the poem and not in the history of the poet. The emotion of art is impersonal. And the poet cannot reach this impersonality without surrendering himself wholly to the work to be done. And he is not likely to know what is to be done unless he lives in what is not merely the present, but the present moment of the past, unless he is conscious, not of what is dead, but of what is already living.

LIONEL TRILLING

THE SENSE OF THE PAST

In recent years the study of literature in our universities has again and again been called into question, chiefly on the ground that what is being studied is not so much literature itself as the history of literature. John Jay Chapman was perhaps the first to state the case against the literary scholars when in 1927 he denounced the "archaeological, quasi-scientific, and documentary study of the fine arts" because, as he said, it endeavored "to express the fluid universe of many emotions in terms drawn from the study of the physical sciences." And since Chapman wrote, the issue in the universities has been clearly drawn in the form of an opposition of "criticism" to "scholarship." Criticism has been the aggressor, and its assault upon scholarship has been successful almost in proportion to the spiritedness with which it has been made; at the present time, although the archaeological and quasi-scientific and documentary study of literature is still the dominant one in our universities, it is clear to everyone that scholarship is on the defensive and is ready to share the rule with its antagonist.

This revision of the academic polity can be regarded only with satisfaction. The world seems to become less and less responsive to literature; we can even observe that literature is becoming something like an object of suspicion, and it is possible to say of the historical study of literature that its very existence is an evidence of this mistrust. De Quincey's categories of *knowledge* and *power* are most pertinent here; the traditional scholarship, in so far as it takes literature to be chiefly an object of knowledge, denies or obscures that active power by which literature is truly defined. All sorts of studies are properly ancillary to the study of literature. For example, the study of the intellectual conditions in which a work of literature was made is not only legitimate but sometimes even necessary to our perception of its power. Yet when Professor Lovejoy in his influential book, *The Great Chain of Being,* tells us that for the study of the history of ideas a really dead writer is better than one whose works are still enjoyed, we naturally pull up short and wonder if we are not in danger of becoming like the Edinburgh body-snatchers who *saw to it* that there were enough cadavers for study in the medical school.

Criticism made its attack on the historians of literature in the name of literature as power. The attack was the fiercer because literary history had all too faithfully followed the lead of social and political history, which, having given up its traditional connection with literature, had allied itself with the physical sciences of the nineteenth century and had adopted the assumption of these sciences that the world was reflected with perfect literalness in the will-less mind of the observer. The new history had many successes and it taught literary study what it had itself learned, that in an age of science prestige is to be gained by approximating the methods of science. Of these methods the most notable and most adaptable was the investigation of genesis, of how the work of art came into being. I am not concerned to show that the study of genesis is harmful to the right experience of the work of art: I do not believe it is. Indeed, I am inclined to suppose that whenever the genetic method is attacked we ought to suspect that special interests are being defended. So far is it from being true that the genetic method is in itself inimical to the work of art, that the very opposite is so; a work of art, or any human thing, studied in its genesis can take on an added value. Still, the genetic method can easily be vulgarized, and when it is used in its vulgar form, it can indeed reduce the value of a thing; in much genetic study the implication is clear that to the scholar the work of art is nothing but its conditions.

One of the attractions of the genetic study of art is that it seems to offer a high degree of certainty. Aristotle tells us that every study has its own degree of certainty and that the well-trained man accepts that degree and does not look for a greater one. We may add that there are different kinds as well as different degrees of certainty, and we can say that the great mistake of the scientific-historical scholarship is that it looks for a degree and kind of certainty that literature does not need and cannot allow.

The error that is made by literary scholars when they seek for a certainty analogous with the certainty of science has been so often remarked that at this date little more need be said of it. Up to a point the scientific study of art is legitimate and fruitful; the great thing is that we should recognize the terminal point and not try to push beyond it, that we should not expect that the scientific study of, say, literature will necessarily assure us of the experience of literature; and if we wish as teachers to help others to the experience of literature, we cannot do so by imparting the fruits of our scientific study. What the partisans of the so-called New Criticism revolted against was the scientific notion of the fact as transferred in a literal way to the study of literature. They wished to restore autonomy to the work of art, to see it as the agent of power rather than as the object of knowledge.

The faults of these critics we know. Perhaps their chief fault they share with the scientific-historical scholars themselves—they try too hard. No less than the scholars, the critics fall into an error that Chapman denounced, the great modern illusion "that anything whatever . . . can be discovered through hard intellectual work and concentration." We often feel of them that they make the elucidation of poetic ambiguity or irony a kind of intellectual calisthenic ritual. Still, we can forgive them their strenuousness, remembering that something has happened to our relation with language which seems to require that we make methodical and explicit what was once immediate and unformulated.

But there is another fault of the New Critics of which we must take notice. It is that in their reaction from the historical method they forget that the literary work is ineluctably a historical fact, and, what is more important, that its historicity is a fact in our aesthetic experience. Literature, we may say, must in some sense always be a historical study, for literature is a historical art. It is historical in three separate senses.

In the old days the poet was supposed to be himself a historian, a reliable chronicler of events. Thucydides said that he was likely to be an inaccurate historian, but Aristotle said that he was more accurate, because more general, than any mere analyst, and we, following Aristotle, suppose that a large part of literature is properly historical, the recording and interpreting of personal, national, and cosmological events.

Then literature is historical in the sense that it is necessarily aware of its own past. It is not always consciously aware of this past, but it is always practically aware of it. The work of any poet exists by reason of its connection with past work, both in continuation and in divergence, and what we call his originality is simply his special relation to tradition. The point has been fully developed by T. S. Eliot in his well-known essay "Tradition and the Individual Talent." And Mr. Eliot reminds us how each poet's relation to tradition changes tradition itself, so that the history of literature is never quiet for long and is never merely an additive kind of growth. Each new age makes the pattern over again, forgetting what was once dominant, finding new affinities; we read any work within a kaleidoscope of historical elements.

And in one more sense literature is historical, and it is with this sense that I am here chiefly concerned. In the existence of every work of literature of the past, its historicity, its *pastness,* is a factor of great importance. In certain cultures the pastness of a work of art gives it an extra-aesthetic authority which is incorporated into its aesthetic power. But even in our own culture with its ambivalent feeling about tradition, there inheres in a work of art of the past a certain quality, an element of its aesthetic existence, which we can identify as its pastness. Side by side with the formal elements of the work, and modifying these elements, there is the element of history, which, in any complete aesthetic analysis, must be taken into account.

The New Critics exercised their early characteristic method almost exclusively upon lyric poetry, a genre in which the historical element, although of course present, is less obtrusive than in the long poem, the novel, and the drama. But even in the lyric poem the factor of historicity is part of the aesthetic experience; it is not merely a negative condition of the other elements, such as prosody or diction, which, if they are old enough, are likely to be insufficiently understood—it is itself a positive aesthetic factor with positive and pleasurable relations to the other aesthetic factors. It is a part of the *given* of the work, which we cannot help but respond to. The New Critics imply that this situation *should* not exist, but it cannot help existing, and we have to take it into account.

We are creatures of time, we are creatures of the historical sense, not only as men have always been but in a new way since the time of Walter Scott. Possibly this may be for the worse; we would perhaps be stronger if we believed that Now contained all things, and that we in our barbarian moment were all that had ever been. Without the sense of the past we might be more certain, less weighted down and apprehensive. We might also be less generous, and certainly we would be less aware. In any case, we have the sense of the past and must live with it, and by it.

And we must read our literature by it. Try as we will, we cannot be like Partridge at the play, wholly without the historical sense. The leap of the imagination which an audience makes when it responds to *Hamlet* is enormous, and requires a comprehensive, although not necessarily a highly instructed, sense of the past. This sense does not, for most artistic purposes, need to be highly instructed; it can consist largely of the firm belief that there really is such a thing as the past.

In the New Critics' refusal to take critical account of the historicity of a work there is, one understands, the impulse to make the work of the past more immediate and more real, to deny that between Now and Then there is any essential difference, the spirit of man being one and continuous. But if is only if we are aware of the reality of the past as past that we can feel it as alive and present. If, for example, we try to make Shakespeare literally contemporaneous, we make him monstrous. He is contemporaneous only if we know how much a man of his own age he was; he is relevant to us only if we see his distance from us. Or to take a poet closer to us in actual time, Wordsworth's Immortality Ode is acceptable to us only when it is understood to have been written at a certain past moment; if it had appeared much later than it did, if it were offered to us now as a contemporary work, we would not admire it; and the same is true of *The Prelude,* which of all works of the Romantic Movement is closest to our present interest. In the pastness of these works lies the assurance of their validity and relevance.

The question is always arising: What is the real poem? Is it the poem we now perceive? Is it the poem the author consciously intended? Is it the poem the author intended and his first readers read? Well, it is all these things, depending on the state of our knowledge. But in addition the poem is the poem as it has existed in history, as it has lived its life from Then to Now, as it is a thing which submits itself to one kind of perception in one age and another kind of perception in another age, as it exerts in each age a different kind of power. This makes it a thing we can never wholly understand—other things too, of course, help to make it that—and the mystery, the unreachable part of the poem, is one of its aesthetic elements.

To suppose that we can think like men of another time is as much of an illusion as to suppose that we can think in a wholly different way. But it is the first illusion that is exemplified in the attitude of the anti-historical critics. In the admirable poetry textbook of Cleanth Brooks and Robert Penn Warren, the authors disclaim all historical intention. Their purpose being what it is, they are right to do so, but I wonder if they are right in never asking in their aesthetic analysis the question: What effect is created by our knowledge that the language of a particular poem is not such as would be uttered by a poet writing now? To read a poem of even a hundred years ago requires as much translation of its historical circumstance as of its metaphors. This the trained and gifted critic is likely to forget; his own historical sense is often so deeply ingrained that he is not wholly conscious of it, and sometimes, for reasons of his own, he prefers to keep it merely implicit. Yet whether or not it is made conscious and explicit, the historical sense is one of the aesthetic and critical faculties.

What more apposite reminder of this can we have than the early impulse of the New Critics themselves to discover all poetic virtue in the poetry of the seventeenth century, the impulse, only lately modified, to find the essence of poetic error in the poetry of Romanticism? Their having given rein to this impulse is certainly not illegitimate. They were doing what we all do, what we all must and even should do: they were involving their aesthetics with certain cultural preferences, they were implying choices in religion, metaphysics, politics, manners. And in so far as they were doing this by showing a preference for a particular period of the past, which they brought into comparison with the present, they were exercising their historical sense. We cannot question their preference itself; we can only question the mere implicitness of their historical sense, their attitude of making the historical sense irrelevant to their aesthetic.

But if the historical sense is always with us, it must, for just that reason, be refined and made more exact. We have, that is, to open our minds to the whole question of what we mean when we speak of causation in culture. Hume, who so shook our notions of causation in the physical sciences, raises some interesting questions of causation in culture. "There is no subject," he says, "in which we must proceed with more caution than in tracing the history of the arts and sciences; lest we assign causes which never existed and reduce what is merely contingent to stable and universal principles." The cultivators of the arts, he goes on to say, are always few in number and their minds are delicate and "easily perverted." "Chance, therefore, or secret and unknown causes must have great influence on the rise and progress of all refined arts." But there is one fact, he continues, which gives us the license to speculate—this is the fact that the choice spirits arise from and are related to the mass of the people of their time. "The question, therefore, is not altogether concerning the taste, genius, and spirit of a few, but concerning those of a whole people; and may, therefore, be accounted for, in some measure, by general causes and principles." This gives us our charter to engage in cultural history and cultural criticism, but we must see that it is a charter to deal with a mystery.

The refinement of our historical sense chiefly means that we keep it properly complicated. History, like science and art, involves abstraction: we abstract certain events from others and we make this particular abstraction with an end in view, we make it to serve some purpose of our will. Try as we may, we cannot, as we write history, escape our purposiveness. Nor, indeed, should we try to escape, for purpose and meaning are the same thing. But in pursuing our purpose, in making our abstractions, we must be aware of what we are doing; we ought to have it fully in mind that our abstraction is not perfectly equivalent to the infinite complication of events from which we have abstracted. I should like to suggest a few ways in which those of us who are literary scholars can give to our notion of history an appropriate complication.

It ought to be for us a real question whether, and in what way, human nature is always the same. I do not mean that we ought to settle this question before we get to work, but only that we insist to ourselves that the question is a real one. What we certainly know has changed is the *expression* of human nature, and we must keep before our minds the problem of the relation which expression bears to feeling. E. E. Stoll, the well-known Shakespearean critic, has settled the matter out of hand by announcing the essential difference between what he calls "convention" and what he calls "life," and he insists that the two may have no truck with each other, that we cannot say of Shakespeare that he is psychologically or philosophically acute because these are terms we use of "life," whereas Shakespeare was dealing only with "convention." This has the virtue of suggesting how important is the relation of "convention" to "life," but it misses the point that "life" is always expressed through "convention" and in a sense always *is* "convention," and that convention has meaning only because of the intentions of life. Professor Stoll seems to go on the assumption that Shakespeare's audiences were conscious of convention; they were aware of it, but certainly not conscious of it; what they were conscious of was life, into which they made an instantaneous translation of all that took place on the stage. The problem of the interplay between the emotion and the convention which is available for it, and the reciprocal influence they exert on each other, is a very difficult one, and I scarcely even state its complexities, let alone pretend to solve them. But the problem with its difficulties should be admitted, and simplicity of solution should always be regarded as a sign of failure.

A very important step forward in the complication of our sense of the past was made when Whitehead and after him Lovejoy taught us to look not for the expressed but for the assumed ideas of an age, what Whitehead describes as the "assumptions which appear so obvious that people do not know that they are assuming them because no other way of putting things has ever occurred to them."

But a regression was made when Professor Lovejoy, in that influential book of his, assured us that "the ideas in serious reflective literature are, of course, in great part philosophical ideas in dilution." To go fully into the error of this common belief would need more time than we have now at our disposal. It is part of our suspiciousness of literature that we undertake thus to make it a dependent art. Certainly we must question the assumption which gives the priority in ideas to the philosopher and sees the movement of thought as always from the systematic thinker, who thinks up the ideas in, presumably, a cultural vacuum, to the poet who "uses" the ideas "in dilution." We must question this even if it means a reconstruction of what we mean by "ideas."

And this leads to another matter about which we may not be simple, the relation of the poet to his environment. The poet, it is true, is an effect of environment, but we must remember that he is no less a cause. He may be used as the barometer, but let us not forget that he is also part of the weather. We have been too easily satisfied by a merely elementary meaning of environment; we have been content with a simple quantitative implication of the word, taking a large and literally cnvironing thing to be always the environment of a smaller thing. In a concert room the audience and its attitude are of course the environment of the performer, but also the performer and his music make the environment of the audience. In a family the parents are no doubt the chief factors in the environment of the child; but also the child is a factor in the environment of the parents and himself conditions the actions of his parents toward him.

Corollary to this question of environment is the question of influence, the influence which one writer is said to have had on another. In its historical meaning, from which we take our present use, "influence" was a word intended to express a mystery. It means a flowing-in, but not as a tributary river flows into the main stream at a certain observable point; historically the image is an astrological one and the meanings which the Oxford Dictionary gives all suggest "producing effects by *insensible* or *invisible* means"—"the infusion of any kind of divine, spiritual, moral, immaterial, or *secret* power or principle." Before the idea of influence we ought to be far more puzzled than we are; if we find it hard to be puzzled enough, we may contrive to induce the proper state of uncertainty by turning the word upon ourselves, asking, "What have been the influences that made me the person I am, and to whom would I entrust the task of truly discovering what they were?"

Yet another thing that we have not understood with sufficient complication is the nature of ideas in their relation to the conditions of their development and in relation to their transmission. Too often we conceive of an idea as being like the baton that is handed from runner to runner in a relay race. But an idea as a transmissible thing is rather like the sentence that in the parlor game is whispered about in a circle; the point of the game is the amusement that comes when the last version is compared with the original. As for the origin of ideas, we ought to remember that an idea is the formulation of a response to a situation; so, too, is the modification of an existing idea. Since the situations in which people or cultures find themselves are limited in number, and since the possible responses are also limited, ideas certainly do have a tendency to recur, and because people think habitually ideas also have a tendency to persist when the situation which called them forth is no longer present; so that ideas do have a certain limited autonomy, and sometimes the appearance of a complete autonomy. From this there has grown up the belief in the actual perfect autonomy of ideas. It is supposed that ideas think themselves, create themselves and their descendants, have a life independent of the thinker and the situation. And from this we are often led to conclude that ideas, systematic ideas, are directly responsible for events.

A similar feeling is prevalent among our intellectual classes in relation to words. Semantics is not now the lively concern that it was a few years ago, but the mythology of what we may call political semantics has become established in our intellectual life, the belief that we are betrayed by words, that words push us around against our will. "The tyranny of words" became a popular phrase and is still in use, and the semanticists offer us an easier world and freedom from war if only we assert our independence from words. But nearly a century ago Dickens said that he was tired of hearing about "the tyranny of words" (he used that phrase); he was, he said, less concerned with the way words abuse us than with the way we abuse words. It is not words that make our troubles, but our own wills. Words cannot control us unless we desire to be controlled by them. And the same is true of the control of systematic ideas. We have come to believe that some ideas can betray us, others save us. The educated classes are learning to blame ideas for our troubles, rather than blaming what is a very different thing—our own bad thinking. This is the great vice of academicism, that it is concerned with ideas rather than with thinking, and nowadays the errors of academicism do not stay in the academy; they make their way into the world, and what begins as a failure of perception among intellectual specialists finds its fulfillment in policy and action.

In time of war, when two different cultures, or two extreme modifications of the same culture, confront each other with force, this belief in the autonomy of ideas becomes especially strong and therefore especially clear. In any modern war there is likely to be involved a conflict of ideas which is in part factitious but which is largely genuine. But this conflict of ideas, genuine as it may be, suggests to both sides the necessity of believing in the fixed, immutable nature of the ideas to which each side owes allegiance. What gods were to the ancients at war, ideas are to us. Thus, in the last war, an eminent American professor of philosophy won wide praise for demonstrating that Nazism was to be understood as the inevitable outcome of the ideas of Schopenhauer and Nietzsche, while the virtues of American democracy were to be explained by tracing a direct line of descent from Plato and the Athenian polity. Or consider a few sentences from a biography of Byron, written when, not so long ago, the culture of Nazism was at its height. The author, a truly admirable English biographer, is making an estimate of the effort of the Romantic Movement upon our time. He concludes that the Romantic Movement failed.

Well, we have all heard that before, and perhaps it is true, although I for one know less and less what it means. Indeed, I know less and less what is meant by the ascription of failure to any movement in literature. All movements fail, and perhaps the Romantic Movement failed more than most because it attempted more than most; possibly it attempted too much. To say that a literary movement failed seems to suggest a peculiar view of both literature and history; it implies that literature ought to settle something for good and all, that life ought to be progressively completed. And according to our author, not only did the Romantic Movement fail— it left a terrible legacy:

> Nationalism was essentially a Romantic movement, and from nationalism springs the half-baked racial theorist with his romantic belief in the superiority of "Aryan" blood and his romantic distrust of the use of reason. So far-reaching were the effects of the Romantic Revival that they still persist in shapes under which they are no longer recognized. . . . For Romantic literature appeals to that strain of anarchism which inhabits a dark corner of every human mind and is continually advancing the charms of extinction against the claims of life—the beauty of all that is fragmentary and youthful and half-formed as opposed to the compact achievement of adult genius.

It is of course easy enough to reduce the argument to absurdity—we have only to ask why Germany and not ourselves reponded so fiercely to the romantic ideas which, if they be indeed the romantic ideas, were certainly available to everybody. The failure of logic is not however what concerns us, but rather what the logic is intended to serve: the belief that ideas generate events, that they have an autonomous existence, and that they can seize upon the minds of some men and control their actions independently of circumstance and will.

Needless to say, these violations of historical principle require a violation of historical fact. The Schopenhauer and the Nietzsche of the first explanation have no real reference to two nineteenth-century philosophers of the same names; the Plato is imaginary, the Athens out of a storybook, and no attempt is made to reconcile this fanciful Athens with the opinion of the real Athens held by the real Plato. As for the second explanation, how are we to connect anarchism, and hostility to the claims of life, and the fragmentary, and the immature, and the half-formed, with Kant, or Goethe, or Wordsworth, or Beethoven, or Berlioz, or Delacroix? And how from these men, who *are* Romanticism, dare we derive the iron rigidity and the desperate centralization which the New Order of the Nazis involved, or the systematic cruelty or the elaborate scientism with which the racial doctrine was implicated?

The two books to which I refer are of course in themselves harmless and I don't wish to put upon them a weight which they should not properly be made to bear. But they do suggest something of the low estate into which history has fallen among our educated classes, and they are of a piece with the depreciation of the claims of history which a good many literary people nowadays make, a depreciation which has had the effect of leading young students of literature, particularly the more gifted ones, to incline more and more to resist historical considerations, justifying themselves, as it is natural they should, by pointing to the dullness and deadness and falsifications which have resulted from the historical study of literature. Our resistance to history is no doubt ultimately to be accounted for by nothing less than the whole nature of our life today. It was said by Nietzsche—the real one, not the lay figure of cultural propaganda—that the historical sense was an actual faculty of the mind, "a sixth sense," and that the credit for the recognition of its status must go to the nineteenth century. What was uniquely esteemed by the nineteenth century is not likely to stand in high favor with us: our coldness to historical thought may in part be explained by our feeling that it is precisely the past that caused all our troubles, the nineteenth century being the most blameworthy of all the culpable centuries. Karl Marx, for whom history was indeed a sixth sense, expressed what has come to be the secret hope of our time, that man's life in politics, which is to say, man's life in history, shall come to an end. History, as we now understand it, envisions its own extinction—that is really what we nowadays mean by "progress"—and with all the passion of a desire kept secret even from ourselves, we yearn to elect a way of life which shall be satisfactory once and for all, time without end, and we do not want to be reminded by the past of the considerable possibility that our present is but perpetuating mistakes and failures and instituting new troubles.

And yet, when we come to think about it, the chances are all in favor of our having to go on making our choices and so of making our mistakes. History, in its meaning of a continuum of events, is not really likely to come to an end. There may therefore be some value in bringing explicitly to mind what part in culture is played by history of in its other meaning of an ordering and understanding of the continuum of events. There is no one who is better able to inform us on this point than Nietzsche. We can perhaps listen to him with the more patience because he himself would have had considerable sympathy for our impatience with history, for although he thought that the historical sense brought certain virtues, making men "unpretentious, unselfish, modest, brave, habituated to self-control and self-renunciation," he also thought that it prevented them from having the ability to respond to the very highest and noblest developments of culture, making them suspicious of what is wholly completed and fully matured. This ambivalent view of the historical sense gives him a certain authority when he defines what the historical is and does. It is, he said, "the capacity for divining quickly the order of the rank of the valuation according to which a people, a community, or an individual has lived." In the case of a people or of a community, the valuations are those which are expressed not only by the gross institutional facts of their life, what Nietzsche called "the operating forces," but also and more significantly by their morals and manners, by their philosophy and art. And the historical sense, he goes on to say, is "the 'divining instinct' for the relationships of these valuations, for the relation of the valuations to the operating forces." The historical sense, that is, is to be understood as the critical sense, as the sense which life uses to test itself. And since there never was a time when the instinct for divining—and "quickly"! —the order of rank of cultural expressions was so much needed, our growing estrangement from history must be understood as the sign of our desperation.

Nietzsche's own capacity for quickly divining the order of rank of cultural things was, when he was at his best, more acute than that of any other man of his time or since. If we look for the explanation of his acuity, we find it in the fact that it never occurred to him to separate his historical sense from his sense of art. They were not two senses but one. And the merit of his definition of the historical sense, especially when it is taken in conjuction with the example of himself, is that it speaks to the historian and to the student of art as if they were one person. To that person Nietzche's definition prescribes that culture be studied and judged as life's continuous evaluation of itself, the evaluation being understood as never finding full expression in the "operating forces" of a culture, but as never finding expression at all without reference to these gross, institutional facts.

IHAB H. HASSAN

THE PROBLEM OF INFLUENCE IN LITERARY HISTORY: NOTES TOWARDS A DEFINITION

Few problems can prove more vexing to the critic or historian of literature than the problem of influence. In its pursuit, rank aversions and irrepressible enthusiasms seem to be equally rife. Even among informed students of literature the subject has acquired a certain ambivalence, an ambivalence which is not entirely resolved by enclosing the word "influence" within guarded or ironic quotes. And perhaps none is more aware of the difficulty than the scholarly critic who is bound to illuminate the relation of writer to writer, and writer to tradition, without yielding to a facile claim of influence. The dilemma which confronts him is often disagreeably concrete; for should he remain content to indicate the similarities between two authors, his efforts are deemed superficial, and should he be rash enough to discover an influence, his efforts are eyed with the suspicion due to a mountebank.

It is precisely because the issue of influences is so genuinely problematic that a sharper definition of its character, and of its implications, is needed. Such a definition may be achieved by engaging the issue in four related steps. It will be first necessary to delimit the legitimate province of an influence, susceptible as the term is to varied applications. The notion will then be allowed to reveal its dependency on those ontological conceptions of literature which have so largely contributed to its apparent anomalies. A possible resolution of these anomalies will require that the question of influences be considered as one of intracultural significance, articulating itself with equal vigor in the historical, social, psychological, and aesthetic contexts of a literary work. (To some extent, the last two views of the problem are complementary: they explore the intrinsic and extrinsic elements of the same issue.) And finally, it will be possible to suggest that the ideas of Tradition and of Development provide, in most cases, a sounder alternative to the concept of Influence in any comprehensive scheme of literature.

The uses to which the word "influence" has lent itself recommend a sharper definition of what appears to be a rather furtive concept. Now learned and meticulous essays have been written to demonstrate the influence of everything on anything. Instead of subjecting these altruistic efforts to general censure, it may be wiser to find out what common and coherent idea of influence they possibly share.

Upon inspection, the *sources* of plausible influences prove to be diverse indeed. Such agents as can be said to have exerted an influence on literature include the climate, mores, or locale of a people, to witness the Anglo-Saxon *kenning* in such poems as the *Widsith* and *The Seafarer;* a historical event, like the Black Death, the destruction of the Armada, or the Chartist Movement; some particular style or literary convention, for instance that of the Ciceronian oration or Petrarchan sonnet; a social and cultural tradition, like Courtly Love; a particular theory or idea, be it that of Platonic essences or Natural Selection; a thinker, like Aristotle, Rousseau, or Nietzsche; a literary movement, say Romanticism or Dadaism; an author, like Donne or Hemingway; some specific literary work, such as Montaigne's *Essays,* Percy's *Reliques,* or Eliot's *The Waste Land*—include, in fact, many other agents, equally conceivable and equally affective. The *forms* which an influence may take are no less diverse: the forgeries of Chatterton, the borrowings of Shakespeare from Holinshed, the interactions between Coleridge and Wordsworth, and the effects of Boccaccio on Chaucer, or Laforgue on Eliot, show well the different degrees to which a writer may be indebted to another. And if variety is to be seen in the source as well as in the form of influences, it is no less obvious in the *recipients* of it. An age, a tradition, a literary movement, a single author, and a particular work, have been all considered, at one time or another, as legitimate objects of some influence.

It would be rather pointless to ferret more instances of heterogeneity in the field of influence. The concept is obviously called upon to account for any relationship, running the gamut of incidence to causality, with a somewhat expansive range of intermediate correlations. And despite unavoidable confusions, there is something indicative in this lack of method. For the idea of influence is at bottom a problem in relationships, and it would be as unreasonable to expect method and uniformity in literary or intellectual relationships as it would be to expect them in social inter-course. Every conjuction of minds, or sensibilities, or literary works, pre-scribes its own norms and determines its own framework. The responsi-bility of the influence scholar lies in the full exploration of these, and his success depends on both his clarification of, and adherence to, the assump-tions of his case.

But to surrender the problem completely to relativism is to err on the side of caution. A good deal may be said about the idea of influence with-out violating the individuality of any given case. It is to one type of in-fluence that we must now address ourselves if we are to grasp the import of our subject to a systematic view of literature.

Of the various types of influence none seems to be more central to liter-ary history, or more challenging to the literary scholar, than that type which seeks to define the relation of an author's work to another author or another tradition. And since biography has been the traditional cyno-sure of scholarly interest, it is in relation to the individual writer that we must begin to examine the idea of influence. The question which im-mediately rises can be framed simply enough: What do we precisely mean when we say that a certain writer has been the object of a demonstrable influence? Presumably, we mean that he has been affected by some other writer in a particular way. But then, authors are affected by a great many things which become part of their vast hoard of experience; they are affected by a sunset or the loss of a daughter, addiction to a drug or a love affair. The effect of a literary work on our hypothetical author may be certainly considered as part of his general experience; it is trans-formed, together with the impression of a sunset and the phantasies of opium, into something different, a literary work in its own rights. The notion of an affective power is therefore too vague to throw much light on the concept of literary influences.

That concept, I believe, can be more usefully resolved, for the time being, into the two principles of similarity and causality operating in a time continuum. When we say that A has influenced B, we mean that after literary or aesthetic analysis we can discern a number of significant simi-larities between the works of A and B. We may also mean that historical, social, and perhaps psychological analyses of the data available about A and B reveal similarities, points of contact, between the "lives" or "minds" of the two writers. So far we have established no influence; we have only documented what I shall call an *affinity*. For influence presupposes some manner of causality and causality has repeatedly shown itself to be the scholar's Gordian knot. The old scientism of nineteenth-century scholar-ship, stimulated no doubt by a certain predictability and a certain consistency in the findings of the great German philologists—the Grimm brothers, Max Müller, Wilhelm Scherer—and further abetted by the sociological positivism of Taine, has permitted the simple causal relationship between environment and writer, then in fashion, to extend itself after the proper amount of biographical research to the relationship between writer and writer. The modern scholar, though conscious that from Hume to Heisenberg the idea of a strict causality has been discounted, still feels the incubus of this venerable tradition. The situation has its interest: to reach for its ontological implications is, I believe, to approach the essential problem of literary influences.

As might have been expected, the conception of literature which takes causality on assumption is also the one under whose aegis the influence hunter has battened and the influence problem has multiplied. I am referring in broadest terms to that conception which holds literature to be primarily an expression of values, ideas, and trends clearly discernible in the lives of authors or in the tempers of their age, and which concerns itself largely with correlations, often deterministic in their character, between the intentions of an "informing spirit" and the finished literary work.[1] Though it admits of certain variations, this view of literature motivated the greater part of nineteenth-century European scholarship no less than the native tradition to which Parrington's *Main Currents in American Thought* gave direction. It further underlies, though with sharper reservations, Babbitt's and More's Humanism, the *Geistesgeschichte* outlook on literature, and Professor Douglas Bush's critical stand, admirable in so many respects, in a *Kenyon Review* symposium.[2] The positions implicit in these last three instances are, to be sure, not wholly susceptible to the error of determinism: each carries, in its particular way, the "expressionist" view of literature beyond a simplified relationship between the literary work and its context. Furthermore, it now seems quite evident that both scholarship and criticism should be implanted on the sound contextualist foundation which our heritage of knowledge and patient research has laid. But one is forced to wonder if the emphasis on biography "as the root from which the history of literature has grown, the basis for narrative and interpretation ringed about an individual personality," and on the idea that "literary criticism is not an essential part of the history of literature unless it aids interpretation in relation to time and authorship,"[3] does not give sanction to the accumulation of biographical data as equivalent to a proof of influence.

The danger here is not confined to that type of determinism which forges every literary event in a causal chain. The danger equally resides in the "expressionist" tendency to consider the relationship between authors and their works as more or less of a constant, that constant being the factor of "expression" in the misleading phrase: a piece of writing is the "expression" of its author. And since no literary work can be said to influence another without the intermediacy of a human agent, that danger is always active whenever influences are in question. To locate the error more distinctly—and the error seems to be logical no less than ontological —I shall resort to a simplified symbolic illustration of the variables involved in a typical case of influence.

Let us suppose that A is the author of a literary work Wa, and B is the author of Wb, and let us further suppose that Wa and Wb reveal such close similarities as would indicate a possible influence of A on B. Now the relationship between Wb and Wa (Wb / Wa) cannot be thought equivalent to that between B and A (B / A) unless it can be also said that the relationship between Wb and B is equivalent to that between Wa and A, in which case the formula $B / A = Wb / Wa$ or $Wb / B = Wa / A$ is applicable. (In this case, A is to B what A's work is to B's work, and the relationship between the two authors is parallel to the relationship between their respective works.) Yet barring those rare instances in which plagiarism and imitation have resulted in works of art, the relationship between an author and his work is seldom analogical to that between any other author and his work, similar as the two works may be. Expressed in symbolic terms, this means that $Wb / B \neq Wa / A$. This is precisely the difficulty most often ignored by the source hunter who speaks of influences and borrowings but, to cite Collingwood, "never asks . . . what there was in A which laid it open to B's influence, or what there was in A which made it capable of borrowing from B."[4] The complexity of the problem, even with as few variables as are here introduced, is further revealed by the fact that, strictly speaking, it is Wa that has acted upon B and not A on Wb. Nor is the action of A on B the same as that of Wa on B. The truth of this is amply illustrated by Picasso, who is consummate both in eclecticism and originality. Indeed, we have it from Gertrude Stein that Picasso cared not who did, or still does, influence him as long as it was not himself. The statement has the air of a quip, though its avowal of complexity in the creative experience is serious enough.

It is this complexity in the creative process that the "expressionist" view of literature has tended to neglect in the past, and, by so neglecting it, has permitted a degree of simplification in the pursuit of influences to go unchallenged. The corrective interest in processes of the imagination, of the subconscious, and of artistic composition has followed close on the speculations of Freud and Jung, and has resulted in a growing number of studies conducted from rather special points of view.[5] These studies, in spite of the brilliant insights they have sometimes offered, have not altogether succeeded in dispelling the tentativeness which still envelops the subject. But to judge from the tenor of modern aesthetics, and from the chorus of artists' opinions on the creative process, a particular note seems to be unusually audible—it is a note which sounds a further challenge to that naive and causal expressionism on which influences have flourished. I am referring to what Herbert Read has called "the uniqueness of . . . [the artist's] mental disposition and the privateness of his experience."[6] What the idea of influence often presupposes is a causal and direct relationship between a writer's intention, traceable to his social and historical matrix, and the finished work. "That would lead," Read affirms, "to the heresy that forms are a logical expression of values, to be determined by the intellect. It is quite obvious that they are often illogical, and that their discovery is accidental."[7] The evidence of artists at work testifies to the fact that intention is as inextricable from the process of creation as the latter is from the finished work. The fact is equally confirmed by musicians, painters, and poets. It is what Stravinsky has in mind when he writes, "What we imagine does not necessarily take on a concrete form and may remain in a state of virtuality, whereas invention is not conceivable apart from its actual working out";[8] or Picasso when he says, "The picture is not thought out and determined beforehand, rather while it is being made it follows the mobility of thought";[9] or Wordsworth when in the Preface to the Second Edition of *Lyrical Ballads* he writes, "Not that I always began to write with a distinct purpose formerly conceived, but habits of meditation have, I trust, so prompted and regulated my feelings, that my descriptions of such objects as strongly excite those feelings, will be found to carry along with them a *purpose*"; or Paul Valéry when he admits, "All may be summed up in this formula: that in the making of a work, an act comes in contact with the undefinable."[10] One is therefore inclined to find it strange that while so many have accepted the fact that intention, creation, and style are indissoluble, so few have recognized the immediate bearing of that same fact on the question of influences.

But if the expressionist conception of literature has amplified the problems of influence, the neo-formalist conception, to which the earlier is in so many ways opposed, has moved little towards a solution. The lapses of the neo-formalist often appear the less flagrant, but they so appear only because he either eschews all questions of influence or else he confines himself to stylistic parallels. His attitude is in effect a gesture in the direction of "literary positivism." The attitude, however, is not without some justification. For if we believe, like Herbert Read or André Malraux, that originality is mainly discernible in technique, we might discover some merit in the neo-formalist emphasis on form, on the finished artifact, on the values and sensibility he can discover *through* that artifact. Realizing how putative and complex the elements of the creative process are, the neo-formalist declines to engage the complexities of intention or to level the literary work with its cultural matrix. His bias is therefore non-psychologistic—and psychology seems to be the current method of probing into a writer's mind and writer's intention to establish the causalities of influence, as if Jung himself had not warned us that "the present state of development of psychology does not allow us to establish rigorous causal connections which we expect of a science. . . . Any reaction to stimulus may be causally explained; but the creative act, which is the absolute antithesis of mere reaction, will forever elude human understanding."[11] It is this bias against psychological solutions that we see in Susanne Langer when she indicts, in her excellent recent study of aesthetics, the psychologistic currents that have tended, for the last fifty years at least, to force all philosophical problems of art into the confines of behaviorism and pragmatism, where they find neither development nor solution, but are assigned to vague realms of "value" and "interest," in which nothing of great value or interest has yet been done.[12]

From the foregoing juxtaposition of expressionist and neo-formalist views, it may be seen that while the idea of influence retains its causal force in the one, it is in the other so divested from causality as to become mere similarity. This is our initial, and basic, dilemma articulated in terms of ontological polarities. The risk, in short, lies in saying too much or too little where influence is concerned.

But the impasse is not so final as it may seem. We hardly need to invoke the customary "synthesis" to recognize the direction a solution must take. Such a solution would inevitably keep the contradictory claims of any given case in a state of complicated tension. It would further submit the two key concepts of intention and of causality to more viable modifications. And it would assign the idea of influence to its proper sphere of action—if not the whole, certainly a large segment of man's cultural achievement. For what Cassirer says of man's total culture is apposite to to the special case of influence:

The necessity of independent methods of descriptive analysis is generally recognized. We cannot hope to measure the depth of a special branch of human culture unless such measurement is preceded by a descriptive analysis. . . . If the term "humanity" means anything at all it means that, in spite of all the differences and oppositions existing among its various forms, these are, nevertheless, working toward a common end.[13]

If the idea of influence is to become serviceable and relevant, the neo-formalist rejection of the whole notion of artistic intention ought to be taken with some qualifications. To say that the artist's intention is often vague, incipient, and verbally unformulated is both right and chastening; but to say that no clue can suggest his particular frame of mind, can shed some indirect light on his motivation, *and* can help understand his work, is somewhat less than rigorous.[14] Coleridge's prefatory note to "Kubla Khan" is to the point. The note is certainly no equivalent to the poem, nor is it perhaps the most relevant comment that can be made about that "psychological curiosity," to use the words of Coleridge, the poem itself. And certainly the transformation of the words in "Purchas's Pilgrimage": "Here the Khan Kubla commanded a palace be built, and a stately garden thereunto. And thus ten miles of fertile ground were inclosed with a wall," to Coleridge's:

> In Xanadu did Kubla Khan
> A stately pleasure-dome decree:
> Where Alph, the sacred river, ran
> Through caverns measureless to man
>   Down to a sunless sea.
> So twice five miles of fertile ground
> With walls and towers were girdled round:
> And there were gardens bright with sinuous rills,
> Where blossomed many an incense-bearing tree;

is a radical transformation. But the note and the poem testify to the existence of an inexplicit intention, and testify beyond that to the possibility of a correlation, in certain instances, between the author's intent and the finished artifact.[15] It is by recognizing the quality of this correlation, which is neither causal nor reductive, that the idea of influence can be invested with some meaning. For the limitations of influence are those of the correlations we permit ourselves to make between one author and his work, and the same author and the work of another. The sooner these limitations are accepted the more free we shall be to avoid the error of oversimplification.

It is here that intracultural analysis reveals its merit. The close literary analysis of texts is vastly rewarding, possibly the most rewarding *single* approach that takes the realization of the literary experience for its goal. Such, however, is not our present goal. Literary analysis can reveal all the techniques of a writer and much of his sensibility. And it can provide a sound basis for comparisons between different works and different writers. But alone it can go no farther than to demonstrate similarities, and if these similarities be more than technical, literary analysis may uncover some phase of an *affinity* between two writers.

But it is only when we begin to read in symbol and metaphor those suggestions of a writer's sensibility which the better psychologists have taught us to read, when we have reflected on the quality of his mind and reconstructed the character of his personality, when we have gleaned from biographical, sociological, and philosophical research the facts which allow us to see correlations operating on several coordinate levels, that we can permit ourselves to think of influence. For in the nature of the enterprise a degree of complexity is inherent, and confirmation of the hypothesis of influence is to be sought in independent lines of analysis. We need to know what made a writer susceptible to the influence of another, and we need to know, as a matter of historical fact, the nature and extent of that writer's contact with his predecessor. (Authors have been sometimes unaware of works that were supposed to have directly influenced them, a situation painfully embarrassing to all involved.) And we also need to attune our ears to the "huge, unrecorded hum of implication"—the phrase is Trilling's—which rises from a culture or a period and insinuates itself into every literary relationship. Letters, diaries, notebooks, histories, social documents, ideological manifestoes, political tracts, are all to be considered, not simply to the degree they establish the ring and hue of a cultural context, but, more important still, to the degree they and the context they establish are contradicted by those literary works which we intend to place in meaningful apposition. For if the context modifies the literary work it is in turn by the uniqueness, the recalcitrance, of that literary work modified. This silent and constant dialectic between the literary work and its environment puts the scholar of influences to his severest test, since in the realm of his wider concern cause and effect are seldom differentiated. His unenviable task begins with the collection of varied evidence; it requires the subjection of that evidence to relentless scrutiny; it must involve analysis, evaluation, and imaginative recreation; and it will have drawn to a close when all his conclusions seem to point towards one direction, the direction of a writer's specific bearing on another. The correlation he will finally make—and it should remain a correlation though we may think of it as an influence—describes the relationship between two writers as it can be best described without the aid of omniscience.

So conceived, the idea of influence becomes tantamount, not to causality and similarity operating in time, but to multiple correlations and multiple similarities functioning in a historical sequence, functioning, that is, within that framework of assumptions which each individual case will dictate. But even so conceived, a measure of speculation and uncertainty seems ineradicable. The correlations we use can be as close and synergetic or lax and random as we choose to make them. The latter will naturally adduce no proof of influence, though often they have been considered to do so. Such tentative correlations are rather to be viewed as a phase in the general pursuit of sources and antecedents which, taken with such reservations as are necessary, offers some insight into the cardinal problem of literary relationships, and is itself an index to the historicity of literature no less than an aid to its reading.[16] As an effort to suggest pattern in variety, and as an accretion to the noble volume of human knowledge, that pursuit has its value, little as it may have to do with what we understand by influence. If nothing else, it is part of what Berdyaev has called "the triumph of memory over the spirit of corruption."

With so many qualifications attached to the idea of Influence, one is led to suspect that an approach substantially different in nature and in assumption may possibly afford a readier access to the problem of literary relationships. Such an approach is, I believe, prompted by the two concepts of Tradition and Development. Both, while unlikely to render the idea of influence in every connection superfluous, can do much to limit its extensions, so often dubious, by putting the latter under some degree of pressure.

The view of "tradition" as a fundamental category of artistic and literary description is not new. It was forcefully expressed in Heinrich Wölfflin's *Principles of Art History,* a work significant in its particular definition of the "classical" and the "baroque" traditions, not as names for specific historical periods, but as descriptions of distinct structural patterns unrestricted to any epoch. The conception of a tradition as structural pattern, as a set of norms, norms of language and of attitude, does not revoke the the essential historicity of the literary work as event. It is, on the contrary, in accord with that larger view of history which I shall now enlist to reformulate the question of influence, the view which Hegel has called Reflective History. In one type of Reflective History, "The workman approaches his task with *his own* spirit; a spirit distinct from that of the element he is to manipulate." His view, "... which aspires to traverse long periods of time ... must indeed forgo the attempt to give individual representations of the past as it actually existed."[17] From such vantage as this the critical historian may distinguish those trends and traditions whose development *is* the history of literature. These traditions, dominated as they are by norms of technique and sensibility, partake of the historical process in still another sense. Their articulation in a narrower time span is what makes a period. "A period," as Wellek perceptively remarks, "... is no metaphysical entity nor an arbitrary cross-section, but rather a time section dominated by a system of literary norms, whose introduction, spread, diversification, integration, and disappearance can be traced."[18] It is in this perspective of literary history that the problem of influence assumes a new character.

The two components of influence, which we have steadily attempted to modify, the components of similarity and of causality, can now be put forth on a different basis, one that is in accord with a more complex understanding of the ontological aspects of literature and with a more coherent view of its historicity. Similarity is taken with reference to a developed system of norms, a *tradition;* causality is discarded in the favor, not of correlation, but of the more flexible and significant notion of *development,* the modification of a tradition into another.

In adapting this particular approach to the question of influence, it may seem that all interest in the individual writer is sacrificed to the wider interest in traditions, and that the problematic relation of one writer to another is left unresolved as ever. Such misgivings are unfounded since it is only within this larger context that the personal relationship can be appraised. We need to explore the two ideas of tradition and development a little further to satisfy ourselves on this score.

Eliot's distinguished essay "Tradition and the Individual Talent" has remained at the heart of the matter since 1919. Eliot has there remarked:

No poet, no artist of any art, has his complete meaning alone. His significance, his appreciation is the appreciation of his relation to the dead poets and artists. You cannot value him alone; you must set him, *for contrast and comparison,* among the dead. I mean this as a principle of aesthetic, not merely historical, criticism. The necessity that he shall conform, that he shall cohere, is not one-sided; what happens when a new work of art is created is something that happens simultaneously to all the works of art which preceded it [italics mine].[19]

It is, then, the artist's relation to the past in general (which involves not only the pastness of literature but also its presence), and to particular traditions in that past, that defines the individual aspects of his work. For, to cite Eliot again, "True originality is merely development."[20] Similarity and contrast, tradition and experiment, continuity and development— these represent in the wider view of history the dynamics of what is otherwise termed influence. They are, in consequence, the principles which must guide and restrain us in evaluating the relation of writer to writer, period to writer, or period to period.

The case of Eliot himself is relevant and revealing. Much has been made of the influence of Laforgue on him. But what of the "influences" of Dante, Donne, Webster, Lancelot Andrewes, Baudelaire, Gourmont, Rimbaud, Corbière, T. E. Hulme, and Ezra Pound, to cite only a few? Surely the effect of these writers on Eliot cannot be taken in discrete quantities or qualities, and surely their effect on him enters into, and modifies, his relationship with Laforgue. Yet were we to examine the character of Eliot's poetry, and of the norms of the modern poetic tradition he has helped to found, in connection with the nineteenth-century tradition of French Symbolism and the seventeenth-century tradition of English Baroque (which includes the so-called Metaphysical poets), Laforgue's contribution would fall in the right order and perspective of things.[21] Insights so gained in a literary relationship are often the most valuable, and perhaps, after all, the only ones admissible. Such insights are the fruit of the comparative method which, to call upon Eliot once more, does not involve the vain study of sources and influences, but rather the definition of the poet's type through comparisons with other manifestations of the same type in other languages and other traditions.[22]

In the end, all questions of influence that are of more than anecdotal interest resolve themselves in this: a dialectic between the formal and the temporal modalities of literary works. A parallel dialectic is that which is ever in progress between tradition and development. Hence the relevance of these two concepts to influence. To the extent that literary history depends on biographical detail, questions of sources and of personal influences, always tentative and always suppositious, will continue to present themselves. But to the extent that literary history, apart from its legitimate and necessary concern with authentic details of a writer's life, depends on the ordering and interpretation of literary events, the question of influence, as it is commonly understood, will appear superfluous. Its significance will be only defined by the dialectic of type and time in which the historical process engages.

NOTES

1. I am using the term "intention" in a sense somewhat more general than that of W. K. Wimsatt and M. C. Beardsley, "The International Fallacy," *Sewanee Review* LIV (Summer 1946), 468–88.

2. Douglas Bush, "The Humanist Critic," *Kenyon Review* XIII (Winter 1951), 81–91.

3. Robert Herndon Fife, "The Basis of Literary History," *PMLA* LXVI (February 1951), 13, 19. For a divergent and keen view of the question, see W. K. Wimsatt, "History and Criticism: A Problematic Relationship," ibid., 21–31.

4. R. G. Collingwood, *The Idea of Nature* (New York, 1945), p. 128.

5. Recent illuminating essays on the topic are to be found in Brewster Ghiselin, ed., *The Creative Process: A Symposium* (Berkeley and Los Angeles, 1952); and in Phyllis Bartlett, *Poems in Process* (New York, 1951).

6. Herbert Read, "Originality," *Sewanee Review* LXI (Autumn 1953), 549.

7. Ibid. Read's statement is substantiated, from a philosophical point of view, by Samuel Alexander when he says that the poet "does not know till he has said it, either what he wants to say or how he shall say it—two things which are admittedly

one." See Samuel Alexander, "Art and the Material," *Philosophical and Literary Pieces* (London, 1939), p. 214. See also Benedetto Croce, *Aesthetic* (New York, 1909), pp. 1–25.

8. Igor Stravinsky, *Poetics of Music* (Cambridge, Mass., 1947), p. 53.

9. Christian Zervos, "Conversation with Picasso," in *The Creative Process*, p. 49.

10. Paul Valéry, "A Course in Poetics: First Lesson," in *The Creative Process*, p. 104. See also Stephen Spender, "The Making of a Poem," ibid., pp. 113–26.

11. Carl Gustav Jung, *Modern Man in Search of a Soul* (New York, 1933), p. 176.

12. Susanne K. Langer, *Feeling and Form* (New York, 1953), p. 34. See also Victor Erlich, "The Russian Formalist Movement," *Partisan Review* XX (May–June 1953), 283.

13. Ernst Cassirer, *An Essay on Man*, Doubleday Anchor Books (New York, 1953), pp. 94, 96.

14. Needless to say, the best among the New Critics—they are the older ones—make no such extravagant claims.

15. The case of Coleridge is not unique. The unformulated intention of an artist is often modified by the process of creation, and sometimes discovered in that process, but it is sufficiently present, at least as a stimulus, to allow Van Gogh to say, "The first attempts are absolutely unbearable . . . if you see something worth while in what I am doing, it is not by accident but because of real intention and purpose." See Vincent Van Gogh, "Letter to Anton Ridder Van Rappard," in *The Creative Process*, p. 47.

16. Trilling seems to be one of the few critics to recognize the fact that "there inheres in a work of art of the past a certain quality, an element of its aesthetic existence, which we can identify as it pastness. Side by side with the formal elements of the work, and modifying these elements, there is the element of history, which, in any complete aesthetic analysis, must be taken into account." See Lionel Trilling, *The Liberal Imagination*, Doubleday Anchor Books (New York, 1953), p. 182.

17. Georg W. F. Hegel, *The Philosophy of History*, trans. J. Sibree (New York, (1944), pp. 4, 5.

18. René Wellek, "Periods and Movements in Literary History," *English Institute Annual, 1940* (New York, 1941), p. 89. Wölfflin's and Wellek's views of a "tradition" are in no real conflict, though each presupposes a different degree of articulation in norms. The Baroque tradition, for instance, can be thought to include phases of both Metaphysical and Symbolist poetry, though the first occurs in a seventeenth-century "period" in England, and the second in a nineteenth-century "period" in France.

19. T. S. Eliot, *Selected Essays* (New York, 1950), pp. 4f.

20. Schrecker's analysis of the different branches of man's culture confirms Eliot. See Paul Schrecker, *Work and History: An Essay on the Structure of Civilization* (Princeton, 1948), ch. 7.

21. I have elsewhere argued for a certain coherence in the Symbolist-Metaphysical tradition of poetry. See Ihab H. Hassan, "Baudelaire's 'Correspondances': The Dialectic of a Poetic Affinity," *French Review* XXVII (May 1954), 437–45.

22. A paraphrase. See T. S. Eliot, "Note sur Mallarmé et Poe," trans. Ramon Fernandez, *Nouvelle Revue Francaise* XXVII (1926), 524.

PART TWO

AN AESTHETICS OF ORIGINS AND REVISIONISM

In *Literature as System* Claudio Guillén links literary influence with theories in modern physics that go beyond single cause-effect relationships. "Traditions" and "conventions" as well as "influences" function with reference not to a "genetic" but a "synthetic-analytical frame of mind." But Guillén is quick to add that "it is not geneticism alone that is being surpassed: a certain 'atomicism'—i.e., the isolation of the single parts of a system—is also under general attack." "Influx" thus goes beyond traditional cause and effect to the identification of configurations. Influence becomes a *Gestalt* wherein ordinary "genetic links" are "irrelevant" or "secondary to the existence of the field which this relation energetically condenses and reveals."

Haskell M. Block's "The Concept of Influence in Comparative Literature" begins also as a statement of dissatisfaction with narrowly defined systems of causation. Reviewing the residue from the nineteenth-century fusion of literary history, biography, and source study, Block considers the extent to which literary influence and the study of comparative literature are even now still viewed as one. The article is reprinted here for its cautions about cross cultural influences.

In a series of works about literary influence, Harold Bloom has developed a theory of literature in which poetic creativity is nurtured by the anxiety felt by a later writer when he confronts his precursors. For Bloom, influx is a flood from the past. The poet writes in order to defend himself from drowning. Bloom stops short of nothing less than an entire reinterpretation of influence wherein the "language in which poetry is already written" *is* "the language of influence, of the dialectic that governs relations between poets *as poets.*" Literary history is "indistinguishable from poetic influence, since strong poets make that history by misreading one another, so as to clear imaginative space for themselves." By "misreading" he means not "mis-taking" but rather what Lucretius called a "clinamen," or a *"swerve* of the atoms so as to make changes possible in the universe. A poet swerves away from his precursor, by so reading his precursor's poem as to execute a *clinamen* in relation to it." Following from this swerve, the poet creatively misreads his precursor. To explain this intricate process, Bloom introduces five other "revisionary ratios" that describe at once basic rhetorical tropes and Freudian mechanisms of defense.

In *The Burden of the Past and the English Poet*, Walter Jackson Bate is similarly concerned with the poet's "accumulating anxiety" over the weight of past accomplishment. As Bate had so convincingly shown in his biography of Keats, the poet is arrested by the unanswerable question "What is there left to do?" His argument is a prototype of the paths taken by various influxes into modernism: massive achievement forced to give way through various retrenchments and eventually "through the continued pressure for difference, into the various forms of anti-art." The study of "influence" emphasizes responses to this burden of the past. Bate's notion of "the late-comer" is very like Bloom's heroic ephebe who must always seek "to rally everything that remains." But whereas Bloom sees the anxiety as a falling away, a creative "sorrow" unable to match the greatness of the precursor, Bate holds out hope for the artists' "readiness" to turn to a past that might become "truly active and liberating without also becoming intimidating."

CLAUDIO GUILLÉN

THE AESTHETICS OF LITERARY INFLUENCE

A theoretical discussion such as this must confront, for better or for worse, a wealth of possibilities.[1] What Ferdinand Brunetiére once called "the nearly infinite field of comparative literature"[2] requires, to be sure, the use not of one but of many methods, as the huge range of phenomena that it covers is submitted to more than one theoretical model. Does this diversity of both object and hypothesis reflect, as some scholars have thought, the nearness of the discipline to the texture and the winding course of literary history, i.e., to the very reluctance with which this species of history yields to a unitary theory?[3] I do not deny that such might be the case. But before the pluralism of comparative studies can be evaluated, it seems necessary that it be once more surveyed and understood.

Not long ago Henri Peyre called for a reappraisal of the notion of literary influence,[4] and I believe that an examination of this problem can provide us with a central approach to the area of comparative studies as a whole and a way of charting its several provinces. Thus, most of this essay will be devoted to the preliminary analysis of the concept of literary influence.

From *Literature as System* (Princeton, N. J.: Princeton University Press, 1973). Expanded version of the earlier "The Aesthetics of Influence Studies in Comparative Literature," copyright © 1959 by *University of North Carolina Studies in Comparative Literature* (Chapel Hill, N. C.). Reprinted by permission of the publisher.

I

Any theory of influence implies an intuition, whether conscious or not, of the nature of the creative act in art. As we glance back at earlier periods in the history of comparative literature, so heavily reliant on the compilation of influences and sources, we cannot but ask ourselves what the aesthetic assumptions of our predecessors were. The question of course is very broad, and can be dealt with here only in a selective manner. I shall refer to certain ideas prevalent in France, and adopted elsewhere, during the last quarter of the nineteenth century, and use as starting point the following words by Luigi Foscolo Benedetto: *"Letteratura comparata, Storia generale della letteratura:* due aspirazioni romantiche rifiorite in un clima tainiano"[5] (two romantic aspirations that reflowered in a Tainian climate).

Benedetto's words could not be more appropriate: the discipline of comparative literary studies did indeed result from the adaptation of cer-tain romantic aspirations to an intellectual climate of which the thought of Taine remains the most powerful and representative example. As for what the "due aspirazioni romantiche" actually were, I should like to interpret Benedetto's intent somewhat freely and go on to distinguish between two different, though obviously related, historical forces: a desire for system; and an internationalist or cosmopolitan spirit.

The yearning for system, synthesis, or unity, is an aspect of the Roman-tic movement which is too often neglected or forgotten. Herder's concep-tion of culture as a mosaic of national cultures led to the Romantic nation-alism—in literary matters—with which we are so familiar. But it had its counterpart in a powerfully synthetic trend, rooted in a yearning for total experience, for the unitary vision of interconnections and interactions, for knowing, in Faust's words, "wie alles sich zum Ganzen webt": how all things are woven and joined into a whole. As far as the criteria of poetics were concerned, the writer could no longer believe that they composed a static and normative order, nor that a few great authorities continued to preside over an exquisite *temple du goût.* With the advent of new critical theories the vast edifice of neoclassical norms had come tumbling down; and the whole of European poetry, as it were, had been shattered to pieces. Thus there were a number of reasons for reviving the durable dream of an artistic macrocosm. It appears, to put it very briefly, that a renewed vision of the integrity of literature—conceived not in normative but in historical terms—found support in three basic and parallel developments: the transcendent function attributed by many to the arts; the systematic mode of scrutiny and thought in the sciences and in philosophy; and the belief in progress.

Friedrich Schlegel, at one point, had defined art as the appearance of the kingdom of God on earth; and this enthusiastic position was of course widespread.[6] But in the *Athenäum* fragments (1798) he had also used the word "Sympoesie" and commented upon "progressive Universalpoesie"— while poking fun too, in an ironic moment, at the fact that synthesis seemed to be in fashion: "Uebersichten des Ganzen, wie sie jetzt Mode sind, entstehen, wenn einer alles einzelne uebersieht, und dann summiert" (Surveys of the whole, of the kind that are in fashion now, arise when someone overlooks all the single parts and then sums them up.)[7] The tendency toward systematic thinking and writing had been strengthened immeasurably by the trajectory of the natural sciences and of philosophy since Newton and Kant. A mechanical model of system was offered by physics, but there were others as well. In the Kantian view, as Ernst Cassirer explains, experience had ceased to be an empirical bundle of sense perceptions. "Experience, declared Kant, is a system; it is not a mere 'Rhapsodie von Wahrnehmungen.' Without systematic unity there can be no experience and no science."[8] The unified cosmos of the metaphysicians made possible various modes of unified rational response, as in Kant's *Architektonik*,[9] or later in Hegel's dialectical interpretation of the indivisibility of the part from the whole. In the literary field, however, an *organic* conception of system, based on the widely accepted analogy—since Herder and Goethe—between the artistic work and the biological organism, was found to be most effectual and convincing. René Wellek stresses in the first two volumes of his *History of Modern Criticism* the historical fruitfulness of this analogy, and how the unity of all art was reconciled with an appreciation of its single components by the comparison with the relationship between a living body and its members, or between a biological order and its different species.

As for the idea of progress, it too fulfilled a unifying function. Its adaptation to literature, which goes back to the "Querelle des anciens et des modernes," and to the suspicion since the Renaissance that progress might not take place only in the sciences, was a distinctive feature of the eighteenth century. One of the first histories of world literature, published in Parma in 1782-99 by an exiled Spanish Jesuit, Juan Andrés, was entitled *Dell'origine, de'progressi e dello stato attuale d'ogni letteratura;* and Condillac had written somewhat earlier in his *Traité des systèmes* that "les beaux-arts . . . paraissent précéder l'observation, et il faut qu'ils aient fait des progrès pour pouvoir être réduits en système."[10] The notion of literary progress reappears in Friedrich Schlegel's famous vision of "progressive Universalpoesie," and in numerous other instances of overlapping during the Romantic period (notably in Adam Mueller's *Vorlesungen ueber die deutsche Wissenschaft und Literatur,* 1806) with the dominant organic or biological analogy.

That the organic analogy could be brought to bear not only on single works but on vast artistic wholes, on groups of works assembled in the memory of the critic, Goethe began to show on more than one occasion. I shall cite but the closing words of the Introduction to the *Propyläen*, published in 1798, when the impact of Napoleon's first Italian campaign (1796-97) was still strong on the thoughts of the writer. How does the removal or the destruction of single artistic masterpeices—Goethe asks—affect our appreciation of art as a whole? What is happening to that great "art body" *(Kunstkoerper)* that is Italy? What can replace it? We will be able to answer such questions, Goethe adds, only when we know more about that new "art body" that is being formed in Paris—and

what other nationalities should do, especially the German and the English, in this time of dispersion and loss, as citizens of the world in spirit, a spirit manifested perhaps most purely in the arts and sciences, to make generally available the numerous art treasures which have been casually distributed in these countries and thus help to constitute an ideal body of art which may happily compensate in time for what the present moment tears apart, if not tears away (was andere Nationen, besonders Deutsche and Engländer thun sollten, um, in dieser Zeit der Zerstreuung und des Verlustes, mit einem wahren, weltbürgerlichen Sinne, der vielleicht nirgends reiner als bei Künsten und Wissenschaften stattfinden kann, die mannichfaltigen Kunstschätze, die bei ihnen zerstreut niedergelegt sind, allgemein brauchbar zu machen, und einen idealen Kunstkörper bilden zu helfen, der uns mit der Zeit, für das was uns der gegenwärtige Augenblick zerreisst, wo nicht entreisst, vielleicht glücklich zu entschädigen vermöchte. (*Werke*, Weimar edn. [1896], XLVII, 31)

Historical and structural at once, these words anticipated the day when works of art would again compose "ideal" and supranational wholes.

The systematic impetus that I have just discussed has origins that are primarily philosophical, scientific, or literary. Our second "romantic aspiration," the cosmopolitan or internationalist tendency, on the other hand, regards literature as a *cause*—in more than one sense of the word. It presupposes the vitality of nationalism, and responds to a broader style of living, to the experiences of political or social man. Rooted in the eighteenth century, it inspired not only the contemporaries of Goethe and Mazzini but the European pioneers of comparative literature as an academic discipline, from the days of Joseph Texte (1865-1900) to those of Fernand Baldensperger (1871-1958). Texte's main book was called *Jean-Jacques Rousseau et les origines du cosmopolitisme littéraire* (1895); and it dealt with a topic that had attracted the interest of a number of his contemporaries. Brunetière had just written for the *Revue des deux mondes* a series of fighting articles on the idea of European literature. In

1890 Georg Brandes, as prestigious as he was controversial, had published the final volume of his lengthy history of European letters in the nineteenth century. The first volume bore the subtitle *Emigrant Literature (Emigrantliteraturen)*, and Brandes underlined from the start (with reference to that cosmopolitan *malgré lui*, the political exile: Chateaubriand, Madame de Staël, Benjamin Constant, and others) that a principal feature of European life during the Romantic period was the growth of internationalism: the impact of cultural events, the quick dissemination of literary movements, and the wide-ranging consequences of political developments. It should be remembered that Marx and Engels used the term "Weltliteratur" in the *Communist Manifesto,* while stressing that the intellectual production of single nations was becoming the common patrimony of all.[11] In this sense the militant liberalism of the great Danish critic, like the antinationalism of Marx, was not as distant as one might think from the French academic attitudes that are my principal concern here. It became nearly a tradition for *comparatistes* to write of the brotherhood of nations, or of the need for a rebirth of "humanism." Joseph Texte had asked for "la formation, au point de vue littéraire, des États-Unis d'Europe," and had said, further: "Ce ne sera pas trop peut-être, un jour ou l'autre, pour s'occuper d'histoire littéraire, d'avoir l'esprit international. Pour l'instant, il faut tâcher du moins d'avoir, suivant le mot de Mme. de Staël, dans notre étroite Europe, 'l'esprit européen. ' "[12] And in 1921, not long after the close of World War I, Baldensperger inaugurated the *Revue de littérature comparée* with a ringing call for a new humanism based on the comparatist's search for universals beyond change and national differences, in order to "fournir à l'humanité disloquée un fonds moins précaire de valeurs communes."[13]

Let us now turn to Taine, very briefly, and to the intellectual environment of the early comparatists. It is apparent that Taine's conception of the creative act is not as explicit as his view of the nature of art in general or of the relationship between an artistic work and the people or the conditions that produced it. To indicate a starting point and an end result, a cause and a product, is not the same as to show how the distance between the two is eliminated, that is to say, as to question the process of creation itself. We know that in Taine's thought every work of art is determined by a cause and should be explained by it; but, again, to state that A controls B is not to show how the artist proceeded from A to B. Yet this very absence of emphasis reveals the belief that the intervention of the artist is not as radical or as inventive as the term "creation" might lead one to think. That a slender "coefficient of creation" is a corollary to Taine's theory is actually made clear by his inclination for the biological metaphor: artistic criticism, he writes, is "une sorte de botanique appliquée, non aux plantes, mais aux oeuvres humaines."[14] Spiritual events are, like physical ones, based on the principle of the conservation of matter, that is, of the transmutation or reorganization of certain elements into differently structured products. Thus the creation of a poem or a painting is analogous to the process of chemical transformation that accounts for the growth of a plant.

Taine himself was so occupied with the nonartistic causes of art that he tended to underestimate the importance of those artistic causes that are usually called influences. Art imitates nature directly, and only art indirectly. When faced with a coherent group of artists such as the Flemish painters, Taine would rather point out the national forms of existence or the historical conditions which they shared as causes than observe the trajectory of strictly pictorial influences. Two of Taine's fundamental assumptions are operative in such cases, and cannot be divided: first, the idea of causality, as applied to the arts; and second, Taine's own formulation and refinement of the Romantic concept of the "character" or the "soul" of nations. For Taine a civilization is an organic system, which he defines in ways that are compatible with a modern anthropologist's "holistic" or "structural" approach to distinct cultures:

Ici, comme partout, s'applique *la loi des dépendances mutuelles.* Une civilisation fait corps, et ses parties se tiennent à la façon des parties d'un corps organique... Dans une civilisation la religion, la philosophie, la forme de famille, la littérature, les arts composent un système où tout changement local entraîne un changement général....[15]

Thus in Taine the idea of cultural system and that of cultural causality do not necessarily clash, and the impact of one poet on another, indeed the dependence of one writer on another, simply demands to be inserted within a larger network of dependences. In what ways the *"loi des dépendances mutuelles"* did or could apply to the literatures of nations or to the processes of artistic creation was, of course, an arduous question for those contemporaries of Taine who were critics of art and, particularly, comparatists. Comparatists could scarcely refrain from seeking a reconciliation between, on the one hand, Taine's approach to the work of art as document and a more substantial concern with literature for its own sake; and, on the other, between his marked emphasis on national psychologies and the cosmopolitan or synthetic aspirations of the Romantic age. The contribution of Joseph Texte is clearly representative of this convergent phase.

Joseph Texte's reliance on the idea of "le génie des peuples" and on the biological analogy dominated his thought on the subject of international influences when he published his *Jean-Jacques Rousseau et les origines du cosmopolitisme littéraire* (1895) and his *Études de littérature européenne*

(1898). The later concentration of comparative literature on influences of one nation on another, while neglecting similar phenomena within a single country, was largely due to the early blending in such works of the Romantic belief in national originalities and the evolutionary biology of the time.

Pour qu'il y ait lieu à des études du genre de celles dont nous parlons, [explained Texte], il faut en effet qu'une littérature soit conçue comme l'expression d'un état social déterminé, tribu, clan ou nation, dont elle représente les traditions, le génie et les espérances. . . . Il faut, en un mot, qu'elle constitue un *genre* bien déterminé dans la grande *espèce* de la littérature de l'humanité.[16]

Thus each single literature was regarded as a sort of subspecies, and comparative literature as the study of the cross-fertilizations and contacts between these subspecies, and of their evolution and mutations:

C'est qu'en effet, pas plus qu'un organisme animal, une littérature ou une nation ne grandissent isolées des nations et des littératures voisines. L'étude d'un être vivant est, en grande partie, l'étude des relations qui l'unissent aux êtres voisins et des influences de tous genres qui nous enveloppent comme d'un réseau invisible.[17]

Thus national and international attitudes were comfortably blended. Comparative literature, at this stage, was the fruit of a polite compromise.

Texte's biological and evolutionary approach led him to a concept of creation, although implicit, similar to Taine's. His gifts were, in fact, those of a psychological critic. And never is what one might call the "concept of transfer" as clear as when criticism tries to deal with both an author's states of mind and his works, or to show how the substance of the former is incorporated in the latter. In his essay on Wordsworth, Texte is interested above all in asking how happy poetry could be written by any but a happy man; and in his essay on *Aurora Leigh,* in demonstrating how the author, Elizabeth Barrett Browning, "s'y est révélée tout entière."[18] The idea of transfer implied by such biographical criticism precludes the question which is central to this essay: When speaking of an influence on a writer, do we make a psychological or a literary statement? To which the psychological critic would have answered that states of mind and works of art are not only indivisible, but two stages of an uninterrupted process of formal reorganization; as the work of art, to recall Taine's definition, "a pour but de manifester quelque caractère essentiel ou saillant . . . , plus clairement et plus complètement que ne le font les objets réels, . . . en employant un ensemble de parties liées, *dont elle modifie systématiquement les rapports.* "[19]

The nineteenth-century idea of influence sprang from this notion of literature as the product of a direct reorganization of human experience into art. It was as if literary scholars selected their own targets without altering the view of the creative process which was expressed by historians and social philosophers. These scholars went about looking for literary causes instead of human ones—a natural thing to do, since the two kinds of phenomena were in their opinion practically interchangeable. One inspected the fact that literary works transmit not only the substance of experience, but that of previous literary works. The etymological image of flow *(fluere)* was taken to mean that an influence represents the undisturbed passage of certain elementary substances from one poem to another.

I I

The aim of this essay being methodological, I do not propose to recall the vicissitudes of literary theory since the days of Taine and Texte. My examples are intended not to be exhaustive, but to serve for a theoretical discussion and a summary of a large section of contemporary criticism. It will suffice, then, simply to consider briefly a view that is representative and has the merit of providing us with a different approach to our problem.

Artistic creation, according to this view, may be found somewhere between two poles: the process of transfer and reorganization mentioned above; and at the other end, the religious concept of absolute creation. Both notions are incompatible with the peculiar nature of art. The former appears to be based on an unsatisfactory biological analogy. The emergence of a work of art is not comparable to the appearance of a new member of a species as only a variation of that species, or to the gradual unfolding of embryonic elements, or to a simple mutation of structure—implying a separation of "form" and "content." Life, or the biological, or what is not fully shaped or formed by man (or, if you wish, that total environment or locus of my life, which encloses so much that is man-invented but is not a unitary form), yields precisely where art begins, in order to give place to an inorganic entity or process endowed with formal qualities and expressive virtualities and thus capable of stimulating in turn a kind of experience that is vital (that is "life" too) but must be distinguished from other classes of experience. As for the other pole, total creation, it seems, in the artistic area, to be a requirement of the mind rather than a fact: a "limit-idea" to which other ideas of creation should be referred.[20] Creation is a term particularly adaptable to art insofar as one excludes from it both the extreme of *creatio ex nihilo* and the supposition that the creative process represents a passage from one thing to another within the same order of reality (the same "unity," that is to say) without a contrast, an effort, and a change of *kind*. The movement from one sort of experience to another *(not* from life to nonlife, or vice versa) is what the idea of creation can reasonably mean and what the artist is precisely able to achieve. For he makes possible the emergence of a form which is sui generis, not preexistent, yet entitled to a vital status of its own. The "un-formed" environment is separated from the completed artistic product by a difference of being or "ontological gap." From Kant to Croce, the premise of modern aesthetics has been that action, ethics, logic, art belong to different (though mutually dependent) orders of existence. Creation bridges this fundamental gap, then, and cannot be considered a sort of continuum. The poet does not merely deflect, refract, or contradict experience. He is able to displace or replace both un-formed life and previous works of art—for the sake of the reader as well as for his own sake. Negatively speaking, the poem is the result of a displaced process of experience. Positively speaking, it reveals the attempt to inform, shape, and conquer one's environment through a creative passage from one order of existence to another. Every truly great work of art, to the knowing observer is still vibrant with this triumph—with a decisive energy, with an underlying process of "formation" and form creation.

To circumscribe this process is an arduous task—and "would know no boundaries," as Goethe said to Eckermann (December 16, 1828) regarding literary influences on himself. It does not quite include the entire life of the writer, in the sense that a particular poem will be related to particular strata of experience or of personality, though the strata may run across the whole of the artist's experience. The genesis of a poem is, if not an endless process, an endlessly complex one—as extensive, within certain temporal limits, as our knowledge of the individual's inner life may be. Certain events or conditions are crucial in it, and others trivial; but of course no single event or condition controls, shapes, or elucidates the final dimensions of the work of art.

Our idea of influence would be relevant to the aesthetic context I have just indicated. It would define an influence as a recognizable and significant part of the genesis of a literary work of art. It would refer to poetry as entering the writer's experience (so that every source is a source *vécue),* and would distinguish between genuinely genetic conditions and the presence in the finished poem of those conventions and techniques which belong to the writer's equipment or to the possibilities of his medium handed down by way of tradition. The writer's life and his creative work develop, as I have just recalled, within two different orders of experience. Influences, since they develop strictly on one level, are individual experiences of a particular nature, for a number of reasons: because they represent a kind of intrusion into the writer's being or a modification of it or the occasion for such a change; because their starting point is previously existing poetry; and because the alteration they bring about, no matter how slight, has an indispensable effect on the subsequent stages of the *genesis* of the poem. They are forces that introduce themselves into the process of creation, so to speak, from the outside—élans and incitations which carry the genetic "movement" further, and allow the artist to pursue his elaboration of expressive forms. At the same time, then, influences make a poem possible and are transcended by it, as other experiences are. (Their effect often ceases or vanishes within the span of the writer's consciousness.) The poem, to repeat our terms, is also the product of a displaced series of influences. And the latter, precisely because they are displaced and make way for what is different from them, should be distinguished from the recognizable techniques which are present in the finished poem, and may or may not be comparable to the forms responsible for the original genetic incitations.[21]

If we now return to what I called the concept of transfer, the current deviation from it should be plainer. An influence, according to the old nineteenth-century idea, was the transfer and rearrangement of literary forms and themes from one work to another. I cannot dwell at length on the theoretical difficulties involved in this notion, though it seems evident that it is not only untenable from the viewpoint of modern aesthetics, but inimical to the very existence of aesthetics. Analogous difficulties are encountered by the analysis of persistent forms or themes. A form cannot be rearranged, by anyone's logic: it cannot be reformed or deformed and yet subsist. As for themes, as Benedetto Croce showed many years ago in his criticism of *Stoffgeschichte*,[22] they are conveniently misleading entities. Tirso de Molina's Don Juan does not exist outside of the *Burlador de Sevilla* any more than Hamlet does beyond *Hamlet*, or than any form or poetic feature of the *Burlador de Sevilla* does. To call "theme" both the figure in the drama, where it is uniquely formed and expressive, and the bare plot or conceptual scheme we usually associate with themes, is to strain a single word beyond reason. These are entities that cannot be approached, as I have said elsewhere,[23] through the same process of definition. Don Juan is a dramatic character, the theme of Don Juan is a sequence of situations. The former only is literary, and only the latter is a theme. Because Don Juan is inseparable from a poetic form, he first must be perceived aesthetically, while the theme is a prepoetic outline which can be defined conceptually. Prepoetic outlines, of course, belong properly to the area of poetics and rhetoric, whether they are formal or thematic, as Ernst Robert Curtius demonstrated brilliantly with regard to those microthemes called *topoi* or *loci communes*.[24] Thus the study of themes acquires its real significance in the area of poetics.

As far as practice is concerned, the "concept of transfer" has three definite disadvantages:

1. It implies that an influence is an objective connection, a tangible affair, of which some material traces ought to remain after the work is finished. This precludes all subtler phenomena, genetic or psychological, of which the critic cannot find adequate objective proof. (In some cases the positivistic critic will be satisfied with locating the proof in evidence that is external to either the source or the influenced product, such as letters, or marginal notes on the writer's copy of a book,[25] as long as this *rapport de fait* can be counterchecked later against the work.)

2. The idea of transfer ascribes to phenomena of influence, in many cases, a kind of importance, of necessity, of effectiveness as great and enviable as that of the artistic works themselves. As all influential elements are ultimately embodied in the finished poem, nothing is lost and all is well that ends well. The traditionally sanguine comparatist is not inclined to observe the arbitrariness, the absurdity, or what I should like to call the *contingency* of so many of these phenomena. He discovers and records with a light heart that, for example, the reputation of Cervantes was largely inferior for many years to those of several of his Spanish contemporaries; or that no Frenchman truly appreciated Dante before the nineteenth century;[26] or that Antonio de Guevara was translated into English from French, into German from Italian, into Hungarian from Latin, into Dutch and Swedish from German.[27] For this complacent attitude toward influences it is probable, I think, that the aesthetic theories just mentioned are responsible. Because they posit that influences are efficient, they overestimate the proximity of influences to art, or maintain them within the area in which genuine literature takes place and in which the critic is inclined to take pleasure.

3. The most remarkable consequence of this view is the persistent confusion between influences and textual similarities, or the refusal to scrutinize with some sharpness how these two groups of facts are related.[28] The notion of transfer, since it assumes that an influence leads to the presence in work B of elements in some manner comparable to others in A, as well as derived from them, is equivalent to the premise that influences and parallelisms are indivisible. Our assumption, on the contrary, is that genetic incitations are part and parcel of the writer's psychic experience, whereas textual similarities pertain to the order of literature. Hence the conviction, shared by numerous scholars in recent years,[29] that an influence need not assume the recognizable form of a parallelism, just as every

parallelism does not proceed from an influence.

The former theory (best manifested by the equally liquid metaphor of "source," which is useless within any other perspective) had the advantage of being empirically manageable and simple. In other words, it made influence studies viable. The latter theory is fraught with difficulties, both theoretical and practical, inasmuch as it approaches the riddle of the creative act. For these reasons, it might be profitable to discuss an example.

We know that the process of creation often springs from, or is decisively stimulated by, a singularly favorable emotional state that may be described as an intense disposition of the will, an urgent need to write, or, most simply, a desire: the desire, whether joyful or not, to compose a work of which only the basic or vaguest lineaments can be perceived. This is the condition which Schiller described to Christian Gottfried Körner in a letter of May 25, 1792:

Ich glaube, es ist nicht immer die lebhafte Vorstellung seines Stoffes, sondern oft nur ein *Bedürfnis* nach Stoff, ein unbestimmter Drang nach Ergiessung strebender Gefühle, was Werke der Begeisterung erzeugt. Das Musikalische eines Gedichtes schwebt mir weit öfter vor der Seele, wenn ich mich hinsetze, es zu machen, als der klare Begriff von Inhalt, über den ich oft kaum mit mir einig bin. (I believe it is not always the vivid conception of a subject, but often rather the *need* for a subject, an undefined urge to allow one's driving feelings to pour out, that produces works of enthusiasm. The musical quality of a poem hovers much more often before my soul, before I sit down to write it, than the clear notion of a content, about which I am not always so certain).[30]

Such a disposition of the will may be connected, as Schiller records, with a vision of the poem's musical quality—its tone, rhythm, or structure. It is also well known that this mood can be set off or nourished by another work of art, and it seems clear that such external support, arriving at a crucial moment, deserves to be called an influence. The work in question, moreover, need not be literary. We have learned from such writers as Alfieri, Kleist, and Fray Luis de León that the creative mood can be profitably stimulated by a musical experience.

Thus Jorge Guillén explains the influence exerted on the final poem of his *Cántico*, "Cara a cara," by Ravel's "Boléro." The stubborn, unrelenting, obsessive quality of the latter's musical rhythm—only of its rhythm—fired the poet's initial desire to write his tenacious response to the more chaotic aspects of life. Would it be correct to seek here an objective parallelism? I doubt it, and not only because such a resemblance would be very vague; but rather because we would thereby be carrying over to Ravel's work the Spanish poet's highly personal interpretation of it. Or, to be more precise, we would be applying the poet's recollection of his original experience of the piece at the moment of *Stimmung* or desire. Our conclusion, should we persist in establishing a parallelism, would be based essentially on the evidence provided not by an analytical comparison of the two works of art, but by our acquaintance with the kind of psychic state on which the music acted. The effect of the "Boléro" on Jorge Guillén is representative of the sort of influence of which no objective echo can be *expected* (the mood being important insofar as it is connected with the dynamics of the writing or the intention of the poet, and as it prepares later emotions, releases forces preserved in the poet's sensibility, etc.), although of course such an echo may *also* be present. No one-to-one relationship exists, in other words, between the influential element and the final text. Of this the "mood" influence is an extreme example.

At the other extreme we find parallelisms which are not influences, that is to say, which play such a limited role in the genetic process that we cannot assign to them a name reserved for significant repercussions of one artistic work on another. I am not referring to fortuitous resemblances or coincidences, valid only insofar as they enter the reader's or the critic's experience; for these are not the source of our problem. Certain textual correspondences are not the products of chance, could only be encountered in the writings of a particular author, and yet are not connected with the central stream of genetic development to which influences necessarily belong. (This could apply to smaller or larger elements; their function, not their extent, is relevant.) It has been noted, to return to Jorge Guillén, that a line from the poem "La Florida,"

> Todas las rosas son la rosa
>
> (All roses are the rose)

reproduces almost exactly an *endecasílabo* by Juan Ramón Jiménez:

> Todas las rosas son la misma rosa
>
> (All roses are the same rose).

A textual comparison, again, would yield a scanty result, for we can be certain that even the meanings of these lines are different within their respective contexts. Once more the comparative method cannot provide us with a valid conclusion, as the absence of a similarity may conceal a genuine influence (which was the case with the "Boléro" and "Cara a cara"). It is much more information to learn that this minute echo proceeds from an involuntary reminiscence, of which the author was not aware until several years after he had written the poem; and that Jorge Guillén's considerable debt to Juan Ramón is of the kind that affects only the initial "vocabulary" of a poet. (Juan Ramón shaped to a large extent the linguistic instrument which the poets of the following generation in Spain used perhaps more fully than he had.) This "vocabulary" is the sum of the elements preserved in the memory or the sensibility of the poet before the genesis of a particular poem begins, and which are available indifferently to all his later writing. It contains potential vehicles of sensibility, reminiscences, self-contradictions. And it includes also linguistic or formal procedures, preserved in the technical memory of the artist, and of the sort covered by the terms "conventions" and "techniques." These devices and verbal mores are conditions of the poet's production. They are the circumstances of his medium, the situation in which he finds himself linguistically. But they cannot be regarded as causes unless they touch directly the emergence of the poem. The fact is that no significant psychic state, within the limits of the genesis of "La Florida," linked "Todas las rosas son la rosa" with "Todas las rosas son la misma rosa."[31]

Thus one is led to recognize the following propositions:

1. The comparative method is insufficient in such cases. The question of the possible influence of A on B cannot be settled by a simple comparison between A and B. Every study of influences is initially a study of the genesis of a work of art, and should be predicated on the knowledge and interpretation of the components of that genesis.

2. To ascertain an *influence* is to make a value judgment, not to measure a fact. The critic is obliged to evaluate the function or the scope of the effect of A on the making of B, for he is not listing the total amount of these effects, which are legion, but ordering them. Thus "influence" and "significant influence" are practically synonymous. (The decision and the final value judgment must be the critic's. Thus a term like "borrowing" is not very helpful, since it stresses unduly the poet's own awareness of the event.)

3. An influence study, when pursued to the full, contains two very different phases, just as it bridges the gap between the origin of the creative process and the poem itself. The first step consists, as we have seen, in interpreting genetic phenomena. It deals with the influence as such, or *impact*. The second step is textual and comparative, but entirely dependent on the first for its existence and value. It deals with *parallelisms* or *echoes*. Thus our method would first ascertain that an influence has been operative; and then evaluate the relevance or *genetic function* of that effect. Then one would consider the objective result which may have been a product of the influence, and define the latter's *textual function*. The

genetic function controls the impact, and the textual function the echo or the parallelism.

4. The value of an influence is not aesthetic, but psychological. In evaluating an influence we are engaged in judging its genetic function. The added presence or absence of a parallelism is a different matter, for the order of the aesthetic—the area of the poem—is to be kept apart from the domain of influences (where function is psychological or biographical) also where values are concerned. Obviously the discovery of an influence does not modify our appreciation or evaluation of a poem (although conventions may), and the analysis of these phenomena has precious little to do with any absolute scale of aesthetic values or broad survey of literary achievements. Although the fundamental difference between *artistic value* and influential value, which I would rather call *effectiveness of impact,* seems quite simple in this context, it appears to be easily forgotten, curiously enough, when the object of consideration is extended under the aegis of literary history. It is important that comparatists should keep this distinction in mind on a broad scale, too, and that the study of a topic such as, say, Dutch poetry be encouraged not for charitable but for poetic reasons. Influence and effectiveness of impact should not affect the choice of works that is sometimes termed *Weltliteratur.* The more sensible critics, following Goethe, never intended this term to signify a sort of literary *Who's Who,* but to stress the fruitfulness of literary relations, of what Guillermo de Torre calls "diálogo de literaturas." A compilation of influential works would turn out to be, like most snobbish endeavors, a *temple du mauvais goût;* and one would be perpetuating the distasteful error of Brunetière, who regarded only those works or those literatures which had exercised an influence beyond their frontiers as worthy of being a part of "European literature."[32] The evaluation of a Dutch poet like Gerrit Achterberg should not suffer from the fact (though the actual study of his works may) that Manhattan Island was not permanently settled by his compatriots. Whenever students of influences overlook this point, they become ratifiers of success, colonialism, and international power—political historians in spite of themselves.[33]

5. The study of conventions and techniques (modes, genres, myths, themes, devices of style and structure) is distinct from the study of influences—and of parallelisms when these are viewed as related to the latter. The merit of influence studies may be that they point out how much of a writer's equipment is left untouched, in many cases, by the truly valuable influences exerted upon him. As these investigations analyze the various strands which interweave in the genesis of a poem, they are able to distinguish between what is more conventional and what is centrally opera-

tive, or to discover what conventions become particularly operative. As for echoes and parallelisms alone, they evidently increase the harvest of the student of recurrences and conventions.

I I I

In closing, I have planned to glance at some of the fundamental areas and aims of comparative studies from the point of view of literary influences as discussed and defined here. Although a number of additional subdivisions could naturally be presented, I will limit myself here to four broad perspectives, theoretically distinct though they may often converge in practice.

These perspectives all assume or advance a historical view and a historical preoccupation. But there are important differences between them, and I should like to mention at this point four basic criteria that may help to clarify the differences. (1) It will be readily apparent that the first two perspectives, which have been characteristic of comparative literature in its early stages and of the so-called French school, center on influence studies and on their particular uses of the genetic method, as opposed to a direct concern with literary works as finished forms or with literary categories. (2) Only the last perspective is synchronic, while the others are above all diachronic. (3) It is also pertinent to distinguish between history as narrative (that is, as narrative of events and processes *in illo tempore,* as story of events in the making) and history as recapitulation (as an a posteriori review of the profile of events), if I may use terms that are reminiscent of Ramon Fernandez's memorable distinction, in the field of the novel, between *roman* and *récit.*[34] (4) One may also observe the ways in which comparatists focus their attention on the individual (work, writer, process)—thus furthering some sort of *critica individualizzante,* to use Croce's term—as well as on the areas where they are likely to practice their concern with synthesis and system. It has of course been the position of Croce's followers that this dichotomy is meaningless, as the individual work of art embraces, expresses, or symbolizes, through its forms, not only universal values but those of history itself.[35] Why construct broader configurations, when this is just what the work of art accomplishes? Yet comparatists are likely to retort that the single work of art either fails to provide the critic-historian with a symbol of history as diachrony and as narrative, or obliges the critic, in order to rejoin the flow of process, of time passing and time past, to turn once more to the study of genetic and biographical phenomena.

The historical heritage of the comparatist, as I recalled earlier, is precisely the synthetic-systematic view, and the main challenge with which he is confronted is to make synthesis possible, or to draw out systems, on a genuinely literary level. "Literary history as a synthesis, literary history on a supernational scale," René Wellek and Austin Warren have said, "will have to be written again."[36] In other words, the problem is whether or how the systematic view can find within the order of literature itself the organizational principles that it requires.

Before I delineate briefly these perspectives, I should like to mention an additional kind of research, which provides the comparatist with many of the materials he needs.

Comparative studies use their own fact-finding agency, as it were, their own *Hilfswissenschaft*, whenever they rely on the preliminary gathering of all manner of data that are not intended to have a function in the interpretation of a work of art or of a category, like a genre or a style, that is both literary and historical. These data are elementary and genetic, very much as what I called earlier an "impact" (the first stage of an influence study, dealing with genetic data) is. I am referring to miscellaneous information concerning, for example, travel, the teaching of foreign languages, dictionaries, newspaper coverage, personal intermediaries, and translations when they are not regarded, which is often the case here, either as literature or as a problem in poetic theory. This information has the advantage sometimes of rescuing from oblivion the second-rate writer who made possible the first-rate work, or of supplying the positivists with what Jean-Marie Carré called "rapports de fait."[37] Actually, its status is rather puzzling, and one wonders whether it is at all literary or historical. Surely, it does not compose a branch of literary history, understood as a history *of* literature, of its works and forms. But does it pertain to general history (i.e., the history of non-art)? Let us recall some of the numberless instances that come to mind: Cervantes or Goethe in Italy, Voltaire or Chateaubriand in London, Navagero in Granada, Hemingway or Montherlant in Madrid; César Oudin, Ambrosio de Salazar, and other interpreters or teachers of Spanish in seventeenth-century France; the use made by Manzoni, while revising his *Promessi sposi*, of Cherubini's *Vocabulario milanese-italiano;* the very large part played by the press in the diffusion of Goethe's work in France, as Baldensperger proved in *Goethe en France* (1904); or, in our day, the antiparochial effects of such literary magazines as *La Nouvelle Revue française, Sur,* etc.; the crucial role played by "intermediaries" such as Charles de Villers (whose articles in the *Spectateur du nord* in 1799 revealed German literature to Madame de Staël), José María Blanco White (an essential link in the career of Spanish Romanticism), or the exiled European intellectuals in America during the second third of the twentieth century; the invitation of poetic discovery beyond ordinary frontiers offered in the work or the personal example of such critics as Charles Du Bos, Ernst Robert Curtius, Ricardo Baeza, Edmund Wilson;

exact surveys of the translations of Dostoevsky, Rilke, Valéry, or Kafka; and so forth. The character of some of these data is reminiscent of biography, and the character of others, of bibliography, that is, of research concerning first editions, reprints, recovered manuscripts, and so on. One cannot say that these topics are pertinent to any of the central regions of general history. But they are relevant to what may be regarded as a special province of social history: the career of literary communications on an international scale. They clarify not art but the literary life and its function in society. In other words, they offer the comparatist an opportunity to contribute to historical sociology.

Comparative critics, to begin with, may concentrate on influence studies and thus interpret the genesis of individual works of art, and, beyond them, of a writer's whole production, a school, a movement, a tradition. Both the origin and the result of an influence can be seen as involving a group of writers or a movement or a period, so that their scope becomes quite extensive. But critics have usually preferred, under this first perspective, to broaden only one of the two basic terms. When a single author is either the origin of an influence or its receiver, the critic can gather more readily, as in a single sheaf, the numerous forces that he wishes to observe. Sometimes the single author is the transmitter: Montaigne and his influence in England (Charles Dédéyan); or he may be the receiver: Goethe and his experience of European culture (Fritz Strich); or influences may be followed in both directions: Shelley and France, and their reciprocal contacts (Henri Peyre).

For reasons well known to all of us,[38] this class of comparative study, usually associated with the so-called French school, appears less promising and stimulates less interest today than it once did. Contemporary critics are inclined to narrow their target and to examine, when influences attract their attention, contacts between single works and single authors. It seems clear that this kind of study is an example of *critica individualizzante,* and perhaps for the very same reasons that influence studies no longer conceal their psychological bias. In this sense, it seems natural that certain comparatists in the past should have been so fond of topics like national mirages, national reputations, and other instances of the *psychologie comparée des peuples*—usually a mediocre but operative truth—or of the impact and prestige not of great works but of great writers (the legend and charisma of Rousseau, Goethe, Nietzsche, J. R. Jiménez, Gide, Hemingway, etc.). Critics with an insight into the "soul" of nations may hope to emulate Sainte-Beuve on a large scale, while others still prefer the format of the *Causeries du lundi.* Thus influence studies contribute, for good or ill, to various kinds of literary "psychology."

Comparative studies, secondly, have also stressed the global consideration of influences which French specialists call *fortune*. The term can be relied upon to evoke, in a nineteenth-century context, the bourgeois historian's appreciation of solid success. But a much earlier framework, that of the Latin goddess Fortuna, is rather more suggestive of the relations that a modern critic can hope to discover between influence studies and political or social history.

A traditional textbook, Paul Van Tieghem's *La Littérature comparée*, introduced this branch of comparative literature with the following words:

On sait qu'il faut distinguer le *succès* d'un auteur dans un pays de son *influence* sur la littérature de ce pays. Le premier ne prouve nullement la seconde; mais il la favorise, il l'aide à naître et à s'exercer. D'ailleurs, dans la pratique, l'étude de l'influence d'un écrivain à l'étranger est si étroitement liée à celle de son appréciation ou de sa *fortune*—comme l'on dit maintenant de préférence—qu'il est le plus souvent impossible de les séparer l'une de l'autre. Nous pouvons appeler ce genre d'études *doxologie* (Gr. *doxa*, opinion, gloire), puisqu'il y est question de la réputation d'un auteur ou de plusieurs auteurs, et de l'opinion qu'on se forme à leur égard.[39]

To return to the terms of this discussion, the notion of fortune, then, implies three things: that the student of influences chooses to underline their ultimate effectiveness as "echoes" or "parallelisms," rather than the preliminary stage of biographical or psychological "impact"; that he surveys broad or synthetic configurations, instead of analyzing individual parts; and, third, that he approaches history not as narrative (the "novelistic" narrative of events "under way") but as recapitulation (the "tale" of events "after the fact"). For as all literary historians are bound to remark, the patterns of literary history, indeed the shape and direction of literary history, are largely conditioned by the arbitrary sequence of events appropriately named *fortune*.

Poetry is *not* composed by unambitious writers in a peaceful universe where the greatest of literary accomplishments are freely and justly made available to the proper audience of enlightened men. Poetic phenomena do *not* unfold and disclose in history—i.e., as they become actualized in time—an ideal order of "structures" or of autonomous processes. Alexander Gillies recalled not long ago that both the influence of Shakespeare on Herder and the impact of Herder on the Romantic movements in the Slavic countries—two crucial conjunctions—were based on the misreading of literary texts.[40] As no student or theorist of influences, including myself, denies that literature breeds literature, it seems apparent that the writing of new works is prepared for not only by misreadings, legends, mirages, mistranslations, and other verbal delusions or failures of communication, but by their conjunction with political and historical circumstances like exile or national conquest. The diffusion of literature demands translation or the knowledge of foreign languages, that is to say, either the most hazardous of creative efforts or a condition notoriously dependent on political or economic power.

Comparatists are in a better position to observe these vicissitudes than specialists in the so-called national literatures, particularly in countries still burdened with romantic mythologies concerning not only the "genius" but the "sense" of their respective literary traditions.[41] I have had the opportunity to notice that a most important link in the genesis of the modern novel, the success in seventeenth-century Europe of the Spanish picaresque genre, with its portrayal of squalor and corruption, was made possible by the pleasure with which these narratives were read by the enemies of Spain, who were legion, in the heyday of the Spanish empire. Even today there are a number of critics who think that the picaresque novel was prompted by the misery and the struggle for life that were characteristic of the land of the Inquisition (even though urban poverty and delinquency were the most general of phenomena in sixteenth-century Europe), rather than by the compassion or the sheer inventiveness of individual Spaniards (or of classes of Spaniards). I have even been tempted to postulate that national antagonisms necessarily result in an increased amount of literary influence on the part of the dominant nation (for example, that the landing of American troops in Lebanon would probably bring about a rash of Lebanese novels in the manner of Faulkner or of Hemingway). But this hypothesis is bluntly disproved by the fact—recently recalled by Alda Croce[42]—that the Spanish presence in Italy for several hundreds of years hindered rather than promoted Italian acceptance of the prose and poetry of the *Siglo de oro*. Actually, the array of data collected by what I called a moment ago the comparatist's fact-finding agency is most useful insofar as it makes clear the precariousness of all literary relations, communications, and intermediary processes—the huge distance, as it were, normally separating the poetic work from the writer and the ordinary reader who were "born" to be inspired by it. Comparative literature, in short, highlights the *contingency* of our literary past and the contingent profile of literary history (though not of the single works of art). I realize of course that the term is arguable; but much more important, I also know that the concept is, i.e., that this is just the sort of argument which is likely to engage us in the theory of literary history.

Our subject now is not the usual elucidation of the connections between "history" and "literature"—as practiced, for example, by sociological criticism, *Geistesgeschichte*, the history of ideas. I am not referring here to the important and difficult area of literary theory that concerns the relations existing between historical experience and the literary work *before* it is written or completed. In this area one studies the passage from history to art. In terms of influences, the stage of "impact" would be involved, which is rather restricted and mostly psychological. The comparative study of *fortune* deals, instead, with a far more aleatory object, which is the passage from art to history. It observes how poetry fares (to take a modest contemporary example: by way of the Nobel Prize)[43] in the arena of political, social, or economic history. A sociology of literature exists which, as José F. Montesinos reminded us recently,[44] considers how a *poem* (as it emerges from the writer's workshop) becomes a *book* (something that is forgotten or read, printed or reprinted, acclaimed or condemned, and, for good or ill, translated). Thus, our first perspective embraces the genesis of the poem, and our second, the career of the book. If literary creation, as I suggested earlier, bridges the "gap" between historical experience and the poem as between two different "orders" of the real, by a kind of displacement of experience, the career of the book represents, and is a function of, the replacement of the poem in history. This branch of comparative studies contributes significantly, I think, to the theory of literary history.

The third type of investigation is so predominant today that it is all around us, and I shall limit myself to pointing to its existence. It is diachronic without being basically genetic. As it does not rely on influences, indivisible as these are from biographical-historical factors, it can and primarily does consider the history of literature as an object, a process or an interpretative construction that is primarily literary. As we all know, comparative literature is the systematic study of literature in international terms. The numerous kinds of research that are subsumed under this third perspective have, besides, two essential traits in common: they postulate the integrity of literary study, and hence of comparative literature, as an inquiry entitled to establish its own procedures and goals (without claiming necessarily the "autonomy" of literature itself in any formalistic sense); and they regard this study as a historical discipline. Obvious and fundamental though both objectives seem, their true reconciliation and joint development are continuing and demanding tasks for comparative scholarship.

Within the prevalent contemporary perspective, then, comparative studies remain historical while disengaging themselves from the automatic subservience to the nonliterary that was the burden of influence studies. The movement toward independence from other branches of history has been very clear in recent years. But whether this trend will develop such momentum as to sweep a number of critics away from or beyond history *tout court*, remains to be seen. The assumption of the third perspective is that it will not. Under the impact of Jungian psychology, or of Gaston Bachelard's anthropology of the imagination, there are gifted scholars who doubtless appear to strive for a vision of permanence and a critical neoclassicism. This is not surprising at a time when such poets, historians, art critics, anthropologists, or literary historians as Saint-John Perse, Toynbee, Malraux, Éliade, Ernst Robert Curtius, and Northrop Frye all share the very long and synthetic view. Yet the scholar usually stops short of quarreling with history, salutary though the consequences of the quarrel could be. In my opinion, the more formidable adversaries of comparative literature—that is, of its commitment to a historical humanism—are not the different versions of formalism, which have their place in literary criticism and can be assimilated by it, but such semi-temporal and elusive entelechies as the idea of "tradition" and the notion of "myth," that is, not the open rejection but the jaded, lukewarm, half-hearted exercise of the historical imagination.

It could be pointed out that comparatists investigate formal or thematic categories such as genres, modes, styles, metrics, motifs, images, types, archetypes, *topoi;* while they also examine, on the other hand, historical classes such as periods, movements, schools, generations. But this is hardly more than a practical distinction. Periods or movements are collective clusters into which critical insights become integrated. The trajectory of a genre like the pastoral or of a heroic type like Prometheus constitutes some sort of historical series. Comparative studies of this kind are not oriented basically toward other disciplines. In fact, they condition and mold literary history itself.

Finally, I should like to refer to a fourth perspective which has little practical value but is nevertheless a part of our theoretical scheme. This view questions the existence of synchronic orders in literature. Until now, every form of comparative research that I have discussed assumed a diachronic dimension, and in some cases a genetic one as well. Do literary configurations exist, we might now ask, that are neither diachronic nor genetic but merely synchronic? Moreover, I have recalled earlier the synthetic-systematic aspirations that are an essential legacy of comparative literature. These aims, one notices, are seldom realized in practice; a topic like the history of tragedy or the career of the figure of Ulysses is wide-ranging enough from a chronological point of view, but does it provide anyone with a qualitative basis for synthesis? Thus we are also led to ask: Are there literary groupings that are not merely synchronic but systematic? Though I do not possess the answers to these questions, I should like to indicate two of the levels on which one is likely to confront them. The first of these levels is historical. Following the terms of Ferdinand de Saussure, we may wish to inquire whether synchronic "states of literature" or "stages of literary development" can be profitably studied and described. Is the aesthetic organization of literature available to the cultured reader in the form of groupings or patterns? Is this what a "tradition," in T. S. Eliot's sense, really means? Or the idea of *Weltliteratur?* Is it what the concept of literary period (Renaissance, Baroque) or the notion of movement (Romanticism, Symbolism) actually accomplishes? Secondly, I have suggested elsewhere that synchronic designs are known to all insofar as they enter the reading experience.[45] Formal and semantic relations play a part in the apprehension and evaluation of the individual literary work. Poems are recalled and organized into clusters by the reading of poems. In Saussure's terms, the *langue* of universal literature becomes, as we read, the *parole* of remembered systems; and the links created by this comparative aesthetic experience are similar to the interdependence of the semantic units of a single language, which Saussure called *valeur.* On this level, literary systems, like linguistic ones, possess a mental, mnemonic existence. The synchronic view highlights problems that pertain, in the final analysis, to the area of aesthetics.

NOTES

1. The substance of this paper was presented at the Second Congress of the ICLA, held in Chapel Hill, N. C., on September 8–12, 1958; and it was published under the title "The Aesthetics of Influence Studies in Comparative Literature" in *Comparative Literature* in *Proceedings of the Second Congress of the International Comparative Literature Association,* ed. Werner P. Friederich (Chapel Hill, N. C., 1959), I, 175–92. I have expanded it somewhat, mostly by adding certain passages from the article "Perspectivas de la literatura comparada," *Boletín del Seminario de Derecho Político,* no. 27 (August 1962), 252–66.
2. Ferdinand Brunetière, "La Littérature européenne," in *Variétés littéraires* (Paris, n.d.), p. 5: "Le champ presque infini de la littérature comparée."
3. Cf. Italo Siciliano, "Quelques Remarques sur la littérature comparée," *Lettere italiane* VIII (1956), 8; and especially Alexander Gillies, "Some Thoughts on Comparative Literature," *Yearbook of Comparative and General Literature* I (1952), 17 (hereafter cited as *Yearbook).*
4. Cf. Henri Peyre, "A Glance at Comparative Literature in America," *Yearbook* I (1952), 7.
5. "La letteratura mondiale," *Il Ponte* II (1946), 129; reprinted in *Uomini e tempi* (Milan and Naples, 1953), p. 14.
6. Cf. René Wellek, *A History of Modern Criticism:* 1750-1950 (New Haven, 1955), 18, 349. Professor Wellek quotes the *Philosophische Vorlesungen:* "Die Kunst ist eine sichtbare Erscheinung des Reichs Gottes auf Erden."
7. Friedrich Schlegel, *Kritische Ausgabe,* ed. E. Behler (Munich, Paderborn, Vienna, Zurich, 1967), *Athenäum* fragment no. 72, p. 175. Cf., on "progressive Universalpoesie," no. 116, pp. 182–83, and on "Sympoesie," no. 125, pp. 185–86.
8. Ernst Cassirer, "Structuralism in Modern Linguistics," *Word* I (1945), 117.

9. Cf. Jose Ferrater Mora, "Filosofia y arquitectura," in *Cuestiones disputadas* (Madrid, 1955), pp. 43-59. In linguistics, although the comparative scrutiny of national languages would generally predominate, Wilhelm von Humboldt, in *Ueber die Verschiedenheit des menschlichen Sprachbaues* (1836), would recommend the study of not only the particular "form" of each language but the universal form underlying all languages.

10. *Ouevres philosophiques de Condillac*, ed. G. Le Roy (Paris, 1947), I, 215.

11. Cf. Karl Marx and Friedrich Engels, *Werke* (Berlin, 1964), IV, 466: "Die geistigen Erzeugnisse der einzelnen Nationen werden Gemeingut. Die national Einseitigkeit and Beschränktheit wird mehr und mehr unmöglich, und aus den vielen nationalen und lokalen Literaturen bildet sich eine Weltliteratur."

12. "L'Histoire comparée des littératures," *Etudes de littérature* (Paris, 1898), pp. 13, 23.

13. "Littérature comparée: Le Mot et la chose," *Revue de Littérature Comparée* I (1921), 29.

14. Hippolyte Taine, *Philosophie de l'art*, 8th edn., I (Paris, n.d.), 15.

15. *Histoire de la littérature anglaise* (Paris, 1866), I, XI.

16. Texte, "L'Histoire comparée des littératures," p. 3.

17. Ibid., p. 14.

18. Texte, "Elizabeth Browning et l'idéalisme," in *Études de littérature européenne*, p. 240.

19. Taine, *Philosophie de l'art*, p. 47 (italics mine).

20. Cf. Jose Ferrater Mora, *Diccionario de filosofía*, 4th edn. (Buenos Aires, 1958), p. 291.

21. I do not mean to imply that influences take place only "in the mind," as may be suggested to some readers by Haskell Block's concise summary of my article "Literatura como sistema" in his essay "The Concept of Influence in Comparative Literature (*Yearbook* VII [1958], 33): an influence would be "a part of the process by which works are created, hence located in the mind of the writer rather than in his work." My emphasis, as Professor Block also indicates, is on the fact that influences are part of the "work in progress," and that they happen *to* the writer primarily—to the whole of his being. This may take place before actual work in the artist's medium has begun, and in such cases it is clear that the artistic product is affected indirectly. Fortunately, most significant influences appear to enter just as such a part of the creative process. If actual work has started, our problem grows of course more complex, and I would be the first to recognize the difficulty of any attempt to single out the exact moment in which a work of art becomes independent of its creator and assumes an aesthetic vitality of its own. But the *existence* of such a moment must, for theoretical purposes, be accepted.

22. Cf. "Storia di temi e storia letteraria," in *Problemi di estetica*, 6th edn. (Bari, 1966), pp. 77-91.

23. Cf. my article "Problemas de tematología: *Die verführte Unschuld* de H. Petriconi," *Romanische Forschungen* LXVI (1955), 397-406.

24. Cf. *Europäische Literatur und lateinisches Mittelalter* (Bern, 1948), chs. 5, 10.

25. An example of this fallacy is discussed by Harry Levin, "La Littérature comparée: Point de vue d'outre-Atlantique," *Revue de Littérature Comparée* XXVII (1953), 20.

26. Cf. Carlo Pellegrini, "Relazioni fra la letteratura italiana e la letteratura francese," in *Letterature comparate*, ed. A. Viscardi et al. (Milan, 1948), p. 48.

27. Cf. Carlos Clavería, *Estudios hispano-suecos* (Granada, 1954), p. 12.

28. I refer the reader to some articles on the subject, which I cannot discuss within the limits of this paper (my differences with Professors Bateson and Stallman, besides, being quite clear): Louis Cazamian, "Goethe en Angleterre. Quelques réflexions sur les problèmes d'influence," *Revue Germanique* XII (1921), 371-78; F. W. Bateson, "Editorial Commentary," *Essays in Criticism* IV (1954), 436-40; Ihab H. Hassan, "The Problem of Influence in Literary History: Notes Towards a Definition," *Journal of Aesthetics and Art Criticism* XIV (1955), 66-76; R. W. Stallman, "The Scholar's Net: Literary Sources," *College English* XVII (1955), 20-27; and Haskell M. Block, "The Concept of Influence in Comparative Literature." I find myself in agreement, not only with Professor Block's criticism of the more mechanical practices of comparatists, but with his view of influences as real and indispensable to the understanding of literature itself. But when he writes that "substitution of terminology will

not alter this need" (p. 37), and that "the movement of influence is not simply from writer to writer but from work to work" (p. 34), without further analysis or explanation, it seems to me that he is dealing with questions that are different from those I raise here. Surely we can all think of influences that are genuine and convincing. But we also recognize the existence of recurrent techniques and conventions, or of noninfluential echoes and parallelisms. And what is needed today is not an empirical, haphazard approach to these differences, but concepts that will account for them. I accept the statement "influences from work to work exist." But I think it calls for clarification.

29. Cf., generally speaking, Henry W. Wells, *New Poets from Old* (New York, 1940), p. 25; Carlos Clavería, *Cinco estudios de literatura espanola moderna* (Salamanca, 1945), p. 7; Henri Peyre, "A Glance at Comparative Literature in America," 7: "an influence is almost never an imitation"; Harry Levin, "La Littérature comparée: Point de vue d'outre-Atlantique," p. 25; René Wellek, "The Concept of Comparative Literature," *Yearbook* II (1953), 1-5; Amado Alonso, "Estilistica de las fuentes literarias: Rubén Darío y Miguel Angel," in *Materia y forma en poesía* (Madrid, 1955); the practice of Mario Praz, "Rapporti tra la letteratura italiana e la letteratura ingles," in *Letterature comparate*, pp. 145-96; and, finally, Kurt Wais, "Vergleichende Literaturbetrachtung," in *Forschungsprobleme der vergleichenden Literaturgeschichte* (Tubingen, 1951), p. 11: "Es empfiehlt sich überdies, zwischen Aufnahme und Einfluss zu unterscheiden und je nachdem des Sprunghafte. . . oder das Kontinuierliche in der Art der Auswirkung festzustellen."
30. Schiller, *Briefe*, ed. G. Fricke (Munich, 1955), p. 272.
31. Cf. "Cara a cara" and "La Florida" in Jorge Guillén, *Cantico* (Buenos Aires, 1950), pp. 514-23, 352-53. Concerning the older poet's bilious reaction, cf. Enrique Diez-Canedo, *Juan Ramón Jiménez en su obra* (Mexico, 1944), p. 127.
32. Cf. Brunetière, "La Littérature européenne," p. 23: "Les productions d'une grande littérature ne nous appartiennent qu'autant qu'elles sont entrées en contact avec d'autres littératures, et que, de ce contact ou de cette rencontre, on a vu résulter des conséquences."
33. See Guillermo de Torre's distinction between "literatura universal" and "literatura cosmopolita" in *Las metamorfosis de Proteo* (Buenos Aires, 1956), p. 284.
34. Cf. *Messages* (Paris, 1926), pp. 59-77.
35. Cf. Benedetto Croce, *Nuovi saggi di estetica*, 4th edn. (Bari, 1958), p. 177; and Luigi Russo, *La critica letteraria contemporanea*, 3rd edn. (Bari, 1953), I, 100, 287.
36. *Theory of Literature* (New York, 1949), p. 42.
37. "Avant Propos" to M. F. Guyard, *La Littérature comparée* (Paris, 1951), p. 5.
38. Cf. Wellek and Warren, *Theory of Literature*, p. 40.
39. Paul Van Tieghem, *La Littérature comparée*, 4th edn. (Paris, 1951), p. 117.
40. Cf. Gillies, "Some Thoughts on Comparative Literature," pp. 17-24.
41. Cf. Russo, *La critica letteraria contemporanea*, I, 102 ff., II, 196 ff.
42. Cf. "Relazioni della letteratura italiana con la letteratura spagnuola," in *Letterature comparate*, p. 110.
43. Cf. my review article "The Problem of Juan Ramón Jiménez," *New Republic* (December 16, 1957), pp. 17-18.
44. Cf. *Introducción a una historia de la novela en España, en el siglo* XIX (Valencia, 1955).
45. Cf. my essay "Literatura como sistema," *Filologia Romanza* IV (1957), 22-27.

HASKELL M. BLOCK

THE CONCEPT OF INFLUENCE IN COMPARATIVE LITERATURE

The continuing growth of Comparative Literature in recent years, in this country and abroad, has been accompanied by a constant re-examination of aims and methods, animated by changes that have been taking place in literary study generally. Increasingly, in Europe as well as in America, there is an active dissatisfaction with the narrowness and rigidity of concepts and techniques in literary study which have been derived largely from scientific method as it developed in the nineteenth century, with its emphasis on verification by fact, on a mechanical and deterministic view of causation, on a restriction of the field of inquiry to the realm of positive phenomena whose behavior can be analyzed and explained by means of empirical observation. In all likelihood, it was out of the analogy between *Naturwissenschaft* and *Literaturwissenschaft* that the concept of influence became of primary importance. Viewed as objective data, literary works and literary history itself could be explained as a series of cause and effect relationships, that is to say, through the study of sources and influences. The vogue of biographical investigations, founded on the same view of literary causation, lent increased importance to studies of the origins of literary works in the experience of their authors and of the stages by which these works developed. It is perhaps for this reason, as Paul Van Tieghem declares, that literary history in the nineteenth century was primarily biographical in emphasis.[1] As Comparative Literature developed, largely as a historical discipline concerned with the interrelations of national literatures, it was altogether natural that the genetic approach should be employed as the most apparent means of demonstrating this interrelatedness. Indeed, the view of Comparative Literature as a province of literary history was grounded first of all on the notion that "le jeu des *influences* reçues ou exercées est un élément essentiel de l'histoire littéraire."[2]

The importance of the concept of influence in Comparative Literature is largely the result of the work of French scholars such as Baldensperger, Van Tieghem, and Carré. Not only in their methodological discussions but in their own investigations and in those of their pupils, they emphasized the study of filiations of themes, attitudes, and techniques from one writer or group of writers to another, embracing not only influences, but sources, imitations, means of diffusion, fortune, reputation, and the like. Influence, however, has been the controlling concept. It is altogether understandable, in the light of the character of comparative studies of the past fifty years, why Gustave Rudler, in his discussion of modes of critical investigation, should virtually equate Comparative Literature with "critique d'influence," a special manifestation of a technique derived from the study of national literary history.[3] One need only turn to any page of the Baldensperger-Friederich *Bibliography of Comparative Literature* for confirmation of the central role of the concept of influence in comparative studies.[4]

The recent definition of Comparative Literature of Jean-Marie Carré provides an excellent example of the continuity of the methodological assumptions of French *comparatistes* down to the present day: "La littérature comparée est une branche de l'histoire littéraire: elle est l'étude des relations spirituelles internationales, des *rapports de fait* qui ont existé... entre les oeuvres, les inspirations, voire les vies d'écrivains appartenant à plusieurs littératures."[5] The central preoccupation of Comparative Literature according to this view is the study of "rapports de fait," that is, of demonstrable influences which cut across the boundaries of national literatures. The notion of influence as the expression of direct causal relationships is for Carré, as for the great majority of his predecessors and followers, at the very core of Comparative Literature.

Within recent years there has been increasing discontent not merely with the concept of influence as here defined but with the view of literature which applications of the methods of scientific investigation impose. The attacks on the so-called "Paris School" of Comparative Literature which have proceeded to the point where some critics have spoken of an "American School," whatever that means, are really part of a larger reassessment of the nature and scope of literary study taking place in Europe as well as in America. More and more, we are coming to recognize that novels, plays, and poems are works of art, and as such, are not subject to empirical investigations. They are first and foremost embodiments of aesthetic value, partaking of a uniqueness and individuality which can be defined only through direct experience of the work itself. The great service of such introductions to literary study as Wellek and Warren's *Theory of Literature* or Kayser's *Das sprachliche Kunstwerk* has been to direct our attention to the formal values inherent in literary works, and to suggest ways by which these values may be apprehended. Fundamental to an aesthetic approach is a rejection of any view of literature which reduces the work of art to the status of a document or fact. The assault on the concept of influence is essentially a demand for a readjustment of the relationship between literary history and literary criticism, in which the traditional view of literary study as a scientific discipline is sharply qualified. Emil Staiger's viewpoint expresses that of a growing number of scholars: "Der Positivist, der sich erkundigt, was ererbt and was erlernt ist, macht vom Kausalitätsgesetz der Naturwissenschaft einen falschen Gebrauch und scheine zu vergessen, dass Schöpferisches, gerade weil es schöpferisch ist, nei abgeleitet werden kann."[6] Staiger is not suggesting that a philological approach to literature is irrelevant, but rather that any interpretation must begin with direct confrontation of the text and must depend first of all on the sensitivity of the reader to aesthetic values. Philology gives direction to critical interpretation and confirms or modifies its findings, but any attempt to divorce literary history from literary criticism is in opposition to the nature of literature itself.

It is from this standpoint that the concept of influence and the view of Comparative Literature on which it rests have been attacked. René Wellek has declared that influence as an expression of "rapports de fait," is necessarily restricted to externals and militates against a meaningful understanding of the nature of literature itself. "There is no methodological distinction," he insists, "between a study of the influence of Ibsen on Shaw and a study of the influence of Wordsworth on Shelley. There is no distinction between a study of the influence of Shakespeare in eighteenth-century England and of Shakespeare in eighteenth-century France. Comparative literature thus narrowly defined, never allows us to analyze an individual work of art, or even to explain its total genesis, as this will never be found merely in its foreign relations."[7] Clearly, for Wellek the analysis of the individual work of art is of primary importance in any literary study, whether from a comparative or a national point of view. Harry Levin has similarly objected to a concept of influence based on documentary evidence and limited to "rapports extérieurs": ". . . des signes de plus en plus nombreux indiquent que la chasse aux sources et aux influences ne rapporte plus grande chose. En ce moment les traditions et les mouvements l'attirent de plus en plus intérêt."[8] Not only for Levin but for many others, the concept of influence is of little or no value in Comparative Literature, and should be discarded in favor of a broader concept, free of the restrictions of the old factualism, such as the notion of tradition. It is precisely this notion which is advanced by Ihab Hassan in terms derived primarily from T. S. Eliot's "Tradition and the Individual Talent."[9] Hassan contends that any concept of influence limited to causality is bound to be inadequate, and should be replaced by "multiple correlations and multiple similarities functioning in a historical sequence," multiple in their derivation from symbol and metaphor, "from biographical, sociological, and philosophical research . . . which allow us to see correlations operating on several coordinate levels."[10] In this sense Hassan redefines the notion of influence by replacing causality with the interrelations of traditions. Here again, the primary aim is to bring the concept of influence into nearer accord with the demands of scholarship and criticism.

The most recent assault on the concept of influence and perhaps the most far-reaching is by Claudio Guillén.[11] Raising the same objections that we have seen in earlier discussions, Guillén defines influence primarily as a part of the process by which works are created, hence located in the mind of the writer rather than in his work: "Toda crítica de influencias tiende a ser un estudio de génesis" and as such, Guillén adds, cannot serve as a means of "comparación de índole estética entre textos literarios, considerados como objetos artísticos."[12] The concept of influence, according to Guillén, is simply too limited in scope to provide a way of conciliating the claims of literary criticism with the traditional historical orientation of Comparative Literature. Literary relationships are defined not as influences but as the convergence of text and tradition, and in this sense enter directly into aesthetic experience. Guillén, like Hassan, defines tradition in Eliot's terms, but unlike Eliot, he derives it not from the activity of the writer, but from the experience of the reader confronted with the work of art: the reader provides a context of interrelations in the very act of reading. The function and obligation of the student of Comparative Literature is to organize the infinite possibilities of aesthetic experience out of which literary relations arise, and which Guillén would pattern on the linguistic system of Ferdinand de Saussure. Literary history would then depend on the totality of the relationships of a work with all other works, not on mechanical causation or similarity. Artistic experience, Guillén asserts, is per se made up of interrelational situations which provide the groundwork of the study of Comparative Literature, in that they express the multiplicity of traditions present within the literary work. In Guillén's attempt at a systematization of literary study, the concept of influence is virtually discarded, limited to a part of the psychological background of aesthetic expression and of no direct interest to Comparative Literature.

The scope and vigor of the recent attacks on the concept of influence would suggest that its use is rapidly becoming discredited. Clearly, the objections we have observed are based not merely on methodological grounds, but on discontent with the results of investigations of influence in literary relationships. There are too many examples of vain or trivial attempts to demonstrate causal relationships where none exist, and too often such studies have magnified the importance of mediocre works out of all proportion to their aesthetic value. If part of the discontent stems from the mechanical definition of influence employed by orthodox theoreticians and investigators, much of the dissatisfaction is due in the first instance to the fact that the concept of influence has been obliged to bear more than it can properly carry. One should add that in the minds of some critics, the very notion of influence is illicit, suggesting undue dependence or a lack of originality. For a variety of reasons, a re-examination of the concept of influence is a primary need for Comparative Literature today.

The first point to be made in any reconsideration of influence is that it is an essential part of the way literature comes about. The literature of the past is surely not the whole of a writer's experience, but it is at least a part of it, and can serve, like any other experience, as the inspiration of his art. No one will deny that writers learn from other writers, just as painters learn from other painters, and what they learn is often not merely a matter of technique, but of total experience, of life and of art as a part of life. As is often the case, Paul Valéry's personal observation is at the same time a general commentary on the writer's situation: "Rien de plus original, rien de plus *soi* que de se nourrir des autres. Mais il faut les digérer. Le lion est fait de mouton assimilé."[13] It is true, of course, that literary influences are often nominal and incidental, but it is also true that at times influences are operative forces which shape and direct subsequent artistic activity.

If the study of the influence of one writer on another or on a group of writers can provide direct illumination of the creative process, it is also true that such study can serve as a means of direct insight into literary works. For influences which do not find expression in literature itself are hardly worth mentioning at all. The primary object of the study of influences should not be "rapports extérieurs" as has been too frequently the case, but "rapports intérieurs," in which the movement of influence is not simply from writer to writer but from work to work. External data may supplement and perhaps reinforce such relationships, and if so, should not be neglected, but of primary importance is the aesthetic interaction in which influence plays a vital and intrinsic role. In such significant instances of influence, this concept, rightly used, can provide insight into the aesthetic character of individual works and at the same time clarify and define their historical relationships. There are, of course, innumerable instances of works mutually illuminating one another where there is absolutely no possibility of influence, but there are also abundant examples of relationships between novels, plays, and poems, in which influence is an appropriate and valuable concept.

An illustration or two will help to bear this out. We could speak of the influence of *Don Quixote* on *Joseph Andrews* or *Tom Jones* even more readily than of the influence of Cervantes on Fielding, and without necessary recourse to the title page of *Joseph Andrews*. Not only in scattered allusions, parallel situations, and similarities in character relationships do Fielding's works reflect the adventures of the Knight of La Mancha, but in the structure of the novels, in the novelistic form which gives order and purpose to characters and events, there can be no question of a vital and significant internal relationship. This is not to argue against the originality of Fielding's novels or of Fielding himself; indeed, the unique aesthetic value which makes his novels worth reading and discussing in the first place depends in part on the aesthetic resources—the tremendous accretion to the art of the novel—provided by *Don Quixote*. I see no reason why we should define the relationship between these novels in terms of tradition when it is far more accurate to speak of influence. An equally familiar illustration is provided by the relationship of Mallarmé and Valéry. René Wellek might not allow an investigation of this influence to rest within the province of Comparative Literature; yet there is a tremendous difference between the study of—let us say—the influence of Ibsen on Shaw from a comparative standpoint and a study of the influence of Wordsworth on Shelley wholly from the standpoint of the student of English literature. In the former case the student of Comparative Literature should approach the subject with a comprehensiveness of insight that will make it possible for him to develop the full implications of this relationship for both the art and the history of the drama. I do not see how the student occupied with but a single literature can provide this comprehensiveness and richness of implication. There is furthermore no reason why the *comparatiste*, from his own point of view, should not deal with literary relationships within the same literature as well as between literatures. Certainly no one could write a study of the Symbolist movement, as a movement in European literature or indeed as part of the whole of Western literature, without some attention to the influence of Mallarmé on Valéry. This influence can be reduced to a simple biographical relationship for which all kinds of factual evidence is available, but it can also be viewed as an influence residing in the interrelations of works as well as in the personal association of their authors: of *Hérodiade* and *La Jeune Parque*, of *Divagations* and *Variété*, and so on. I strongly doubt that in this instance the personal influence is wholly separable from the literary, and I do not see why the notion of influence must be assigned wholly to the area of biographical experience or to the psychology of literary creation as opposed to the interrelational character of individual works. Should we speak of the influence of *The Aeneid* on *The Divine Comedy*, to choose a celebrated instance, or would not this be a major part of a proper discussion of the influence of Virgil on Dante? A last example of a less familiar character: the influence of Strindberg on Kafka. Here we have all the external documentation for which the most orthodox investigator of influences could wish.

Ich lese ihn [Kafka wrote of Strindberg in his diary in 1915], nicht um ihn zu lesen sondern um an seiner Brust zu liegen. Er hält mich wie ein Kind auf seinem linken Arm. Ich sitze dort wie ein Mensch auf einer Statue. Bin zehnmal in Gefahr abzugleiten, beim elften Versuch sitze ich aber fest, habe Sicherheit und grosse Übersicht.

The following day Kafka's diary contains the brief but arresting statement: "Strindberg gelesen, der mich nährt."[14] Now to hold that information of this kind is of no value to the student of literature is to suggest that the best person capable of interpreting a work of art is he who has least in his head. On the other hand, we would not discuss Kafka at all were we not primarily concerned with his fiction, and if the works of Strindberg do not illuminate those of Kafka and share a reciprocal relationship with them, there is no point in talking about influence. As the study of Maurice Gravier has recently shown, there is no doubt that we have here not only an instance of affinity and of works belonging to a common tradition, but of influence as well, and I see no reason why we should not use this concept where it is applicable.

It is of course true that all too often the study of influences has been an end where it should have been a means, and too frequently influence has been employed in a simple and simple-minded way as the determining cause and unique source of a literary creation. Concepts are bound in time to be abused, and it may well be that influence lends itself to abuse more readily than most. Yet as we have come to recognize that an awareness of the historicity of literature does not preclude a simultaneous awareness of the aesthetic character of the individual work of art, we should be prepared to modify, to sharpen and direct the concept of influence if it can enhance and enlarge this awareness. We have had studies of influence that have been neither trivial nor merely factual, and there is room for many more. Henri Peyre has suggested that the best subjects for investigations of influence have not yet been touched.[15] Of immediate importance, especially in view of the direction of recent discussion, is the need for clarification and redefinition of this concept. As Peyre remarks: "The most essential task which faces the comparative scholar at the present time is to renovate and broaden his methods and to acquire a fresh conception of the essential notion of influence in literature."[16] The character of studies of influence must be changed so as to provide direct insight into both the individuality and the interrelatedness of literary works. For this to be possible, we need imaginative and sensitive reading, coupled with a live conception of literary history grounded on an awareness of the interdependence of history and criticism. Substitution of terminology will not alter this need. The concept of influence needs redefinition. It should be used with a precise understanding of its scope and limits; but it is an intrinsic part of literary experience, and is too valuable, too essential a notion to be discarded.

NOTES

1. Paul Van Tieghem, *La Littérature comparée* (Paris, 1946), p. 10.
2. Ibid., 12.
3. Gustave Rudler, *Les Techniques de la critique et de l'histoire littéraires* (Oxford, 1923), p. 160.
4. A convenient list of recent studies is provided by Paul Van Tieghem in his "Bibliographie Sommaire," op. cit., pp. 217-22.
5. Jean-Marie Carré, "Avant Propos," in M. F. Guyard, *La Littérature comparée* (Paris, 1951), p. 5.
6. Emil Staiger, *Die Kunst der Interpretation* (Zurich, 1955), pp. 9-10.
7. René Wellek, "The Concept of Comparative Literature," *Yearbook of Comparative and General Literature* II (1953), 1-2.
8. Harry Levin, "La Littérature comparée: Point de vue d'Outre-Atlantique," *Revue de Littérature Comparée* XXVII (1953), 25.
9. Ihab H. Hassan, "The Problem of Influence in Literary History: Notes towards a Definition," *Journal of Aesthetics and Art Criticism* XIV (1955), 66-76.
10. Ibid., 73.
11. Claudio Guillén, "Literatura como sistema," *Filologia Romanza* IV (1957), 1-29.
12. Ibid., 11.
13. Paul Valéry, *Tel Quel* (Paris, 1941), I, 18.
14. I owe this example and the following remarks to Maurice Gravier, "Strindberg et Kafka," *Etudes Germaniques* VIII (1953), 118-40.
15. Henri Peyre, "A Glance at Comparative Literature in America," *Yearbook of Comparative and General Literature* I (1952), 5-7.
16. Ibid., 7.

HAROLD BLOOM

CLINAMEN, OR POETIC MISPRISION

Shelley speculated that poets of all ages contributed to one Great Poem perpetually in progress. Borges remarks that poets create their precursors. If the dead poets, as Eliot insisted, constituted their successors' particular advance in knowledge, that knowledge is still their successors' creation, made by the living for the needs of the living.

But poets, or at least the strongest among them, do not read necessarily as even the strongest of critics read. Poets are neither ideal nor common readers, neither Arnoldian nor Johnsonian. They tend not to think, as they read: "This is dead, this is living, in the poetry of X." Poets, by the time they have grown strong, do not read the poetry of X, for really strong poets can read only themselves. For them, to be judicious is to be weak, and to compare, exactly and fairly, is to be not elect. Milton's Satan, archetype of the modern poet at his strongest, becomes weak when he reasons and compares, on Mount Niphates, and so commences that process of decline culminating in *Paradise Regained,* ending as the archetype of the modern critic at his weakest.

Let us attempt the experiment (apparently frivolous) of reading *Paradise Lost* as an allegory of the dilemma of the modern poet, at his strongest. Satan is that modern poet, while God is his dead but still embarrassingly potent and present ancestor, or rather, ancestral poet. Adam is the potentially strong modern poet, but at his weakest moment, when he has yet to find his own voice. God has no Muse, and needs none, since he is dead, his creativity being manifested only in the past time of the poem. Of the living poets in the poem, Satan has Sin, Adam has Eve, and Milton has only his Interior Paramour, an Emanation far within that weeps incessantly for his sin, and that is invoked magnificently four times in the poem. Milton has no name for her, though he invokes her under several; but, as he says, "the meaning, not the Name I call." Satan, a stronger poet even than Milton, has progressed beyond invoking his Muse.

Why Satan a modern poet? Because he shadows forth gigantically a trouble at the core of Milton and of Pope, a sorrow that purifies by isolation in Collins and Gray, in Smart and in Cowper, emerging fully to stand clear in Wordsworth, who is the exemplary Modern Poet, the Poet proper. The incarnation of the Poetic Character in Satan begins when Milton's story truly begins, with the Incarnation of God's Son and Satan's rejection of *that* incarnation. Modern poetry begins in two declarations of Satan: "We know no time when we were not as now" and "To be weak is miserable, doing or suffering."

Let us adopt Milton's own sequence in the poem. Poetry begins with our awareness, not of a fall, but that *we are falling*. The poet is our chosen man, and his consciousness of election comes as a curse; again, not "I am a fallen man," but "I am Man, and I am falling"—or rather, "I *was* God, I *was* Man (for to a poet they were the same), and I *am* falling, from myself." When this consciousness of self is raised to an absolute pitch, *then* the poet hits the floor of Hell, or rather, comes to the bottom of the abyss, and by his impact there creates Hell. He says, "I seem to have stopped falling; now I *am fallen,* consequently, I lie here in Hell."

There and then, in this bad, he finds his good; he chooses the heroic, to know damnation and to explore the limits of the possible within it. The alternative is to repent, to accept a God altogether other than the self, wholly external to the possible. This God is cultural history, the dead poets, the embarrassments of a tradition grown too wealthy to need anything more. But we, to understand the strong poet, must go further still than he can go, back into the poise before the consciousness of falling came.

When Satan or the poet looks around him on the floor of fire his falling self had kindled, he sees first a face he only just recognizes, his best friend, Beelzebub, or the talented poet who never quite made it, and now never shall. And, like the truly strong poet he is, Satan is interested in the face of his best friend only to the extent that it reveals to him the condition of his own countenance. Such limited interest mocks neither the poets we know, nor the truly heroic Satan. If Beelzebub is that scarred, if he looks that unlike the true form he left behind on the happy fields of light, then Satan himself is hideously bereft of beauty, doomed, like Walter Pater, to be a Caliban of Letters, trapped in essential poverty, in imaginative need, where once he was all but the wealthiest, and needed next to nothing. But Satan, in the accursed strength of the poet, refuses to brood upon this, and turns instead to his task, which is to tally everything that remains.

That task, comprehensive and profoundly imaginative, includes everything that we could ascribe as motivation for the writing of any poetry that is not strictly devotional in its purposes. For why do men write poems? To rally everything that remains, and not to sanctify nor propound. The heroism of endurance—of Milton's post-lapsarian Adam, and of the Son in *Paradise Regained*—is a theme for Christian poetry, but only barely a heroism for poets. We hear Milton again, celebrating the strong poet's natural virtue, when Samson taunts Harapha: "bring up thy van,/My heels are fetter'd, but my fist is free." The poet's final heroism, in Milton, is a spasm of self-destruction, glorious because it pulls down the temple of his enemies. Satan, organizing his chaos, imposing a discipline despite the visible darkness, calling his minions to emulate his refusal to mourn, becomes the hero as poet, finding what must suffice, while knowing that nothing can suffice.

This is a heroism that is exactly on the border of solipsism, neither within it, nor beyond it. Satan's later decline in the poem, as arranged by the Idiot Questioner in Milton, is that the hero retreats from this border into solipsism, and so is degraded; ceases, during his soliloquy on Mount Niphates, to be a poet and, by intoning the formula: "Evil be thou my good," becomes a mere rebel, a childish inverter of conventional moral categories, another wearisome ancestor of student non-students, the perpetual New Left. For the modern poet, in the gladness of his sorrowing strength, stands always on the farther verge of solipsism, having just emerged from it. His difficult balance, from Wordsworth to Stevens, is to maintain a stance just there, where by his very presence he says: "What I see and hear come not but from myself" and yet also: "I have not but I am and as I am I am." The first, by itself, is perhaps the fine defiance of an overt solipsism, leading back to an equivalent of "I know no time when I was not as now." Yet the second is the modification that makes for poetry instead of idiocy: "There are no objects outside of me because I see into their life, which is one with my own, and so I am that I am, which is to say, 'I too will be present wherever and whenever I choose to be present.' I am so much in process, that all possible movement is indeed possible, and if at present I explore only my own dens, at least I *explore*." Or, as

Satan might have said: "In doing and in suffering, I shall be happy, for even in suffering I shall be strong."

It is sad to observe most modern critics observing Satan because they never do observe him. The catalog of unseeing could hardly be more distinguished, from Eliot who speaks of "Milton's curly haired Byronic hero" (one wants to reply, looking from side to side: "Who?") to the astonishing backsliding of Northrop Frye, who invokes, in urbane ridicule, a Wagnerian context (one wants to lament: "A true critic, and of God's party without knowing it"). Fortunately we have had Empson, with his apt rallying cry: "Back to Shelley!" Whereto I go.

Contemplating Milton's meanness towards Satan, towards his rival poet and dark brother, Shelley spoke of the "pernicious casuistry" set up in the mind of Milton's reader, who would be tempted to weigh Satan's flaws against God's malice towards him, and to excuse Satan because God had been malicious beyond all measure. Shelley's point has been twisted by the C. S. Lewis or Angelic School of Milton Criticism, who proceed to weigh up the flaws and God's wrongs, and find Satan wanting in the balance. This pernicious casuistry, Shelley would have agreed, would not be less pernicious if we were to find (as I do) Milton's God wanting. It would still be casuistry, and as discourse upon poetry it would still be moralizing, which is to say, pernicious.

Even the strongest poets were at first weak, for they started as prospective Adams, not as retrospective Satans. Blake names one state of being Adam, and calls it the Limit of Contraction, and another state Satan, and calls it the Limit of Opacity. Adam is given or natural man, beyond which our imaginations will not contract. Satan is the thwarted or restrained desire of natural man, or rather the shadow or Specter of that desire. Beyond this spectral state, we will not harden against vision, but the Specter squats in our repressiveness, and we are hardened enough, as we are contracted enough. Enough, our spirits lament, not to live our lives, enough to be frightened out of our creative potential by the Covering Cherub, Blake's emblem (out of Milton, and Ezekiel, and Genesis) for that portion of creativity in us that has gone over to constriction and hardness. Blake precisely named this renegade part of Man. Before the Fall (which for Blake meant before the Creation, the two events for him being one and the same) the Covering Cherub was the pastoral genius Tharmas, a unifying process making for undivided consciousness; the innocence, pre-reflective, of a state without subjects and objects, yet in no danger of solipsism, for it lacked also a consciousness of self. Tharmas is a poet's (or any man's) power of realization, even as the Covering Cherub is the power that blocks realization.

No poet, not even one so single-minded as Milton or Wordsworth, is a

Tharmas, this late in history, and no poet is a Covering Cherub, though Coleridge and Hopkins both allowed themselves, at last, to be dominated by him, as perhaps Eliot did also. Poets this late in tradi.ion are both Adams and Satans. They begin as natural men, affirming that they will contract no further, and they end as thwarted desires, frustrated only that they cannot harden apocalyptically. But, in between, the greatest of them are very strong, and they progress through a natural intensification that marks Adam in his brief prime and a heroic self-realization that marks Satan in his brief and more-than-natural glory. The intensification and the self-realization alike are accomplished only through language, and no poet since Adam and Satan speaks a language free of the one wrought by his precursors. Chomsky remarks that when one speaks a language, one knows a great deal that was never learned. The effort of criticism is to teach a language, for what is never learned but comes as the gift of a language is a poetry already written—an insight I derive from Shelley's remark that every language is the relic of an abandoned cyclic poem. I mean that criticism teaches not a language of criticism (a formalist view still held in common by archetypalists, structuralists, and phenomenologists) but a language in which poetry already is written, the language of influence, of the dialectic that governs the relations between poets *as poets.* The poet *in every reader* does not experience the same disjunction from what he reads that the critic in every reader necessarily feels. What gives pleasure to the critic in a reader may give anxiety to the poet in him, an anxiety we have learned, as readers, to neglect, to our own loss and peril. This anxiety, this mode of melancholy, is the anxiety of influence, the dark and daemonic ground upon which we now enter.

How do men become poets, or to adopt an older phrasing, how is the poetic character incarnated? When a potential poet first discovers (or is discovered by) the dialectic of influence, first discovers poetry as being both external and internal to himself, he begins a process that will end only when he has no more poetry within him, long after he has the power (or desire) to discover it outside himself again. Though all such discovery is a self-recognition, indeed a Second Birth, and ought, in the pure good of theory, to be accomplished in a perfect solipsism, it is an act never complete in itself. Poetic Influence is the sense—amazing, agonizing, delighting —of *other poets,* as felt in the depths of the all-but-perfect solipsist, the potentially strong poet. For the poet is condemned to learn his profoundest yearnings through an awareness of *other selves.* The poem is *within* him, yet he experiences the shame and splendor of *being found by* poems— great poems—*outside* him. To lose freedom in this center is never to forgive, and to learn the dread of threatened autonomy forever.

"Every young man's heart," Malraux says, "is a graveyard in which are inscribed the names of a thousand dead artists but whose only actual denizens are a few mighty, often antagonistic, ghosts." "The poet," Malraux adds, "is haunted by a voice with which words must be harmonized." As his main concerns are visual and narrative, Malraux arrives at the formula: "from pastiche to style," which is not adequate for poetic influence, where the movement towards self-realization is closer to the more drastic spirit of Kierkegaard's maxim: "He who is willing to work gives birth to his own father." We remember how for so many centuries, from the sons of Homer to the sons of Ben Jonson, poetic influence had been described as a filial relationship, and then we come to see that poetic *influence*, rather than *sonship*, is another product of the Enlightenment, another aspect of the Cartesian dualism.

The word "influence" had received the sense of "having a power over another" as early as the Scholastic Latin of Aquinas, but not for centuries was it to lose its root meaning of "inflow," and its prime meaning of an emanation or force coming in upon mankind from the stars. As first used, to be influenced meant to receive an ethereal fluid flowing in upon one from the stars, a fluid that affected one's character and destiny, and that altered all sublunary things. A power—divine and moral—later simply a secret power—exercised itself, in defiance of all that had seemed voluntary in one. In our sense—that of *poetic* influence—the word is very late. In English it is not one of Dryden's critical terms, and is never used in our sense by Pope. Johnson in 1755 defines influence as being either astral or moral, saying of the latter that it is "Ascendant power; power of directing or modifying"; but the instances he cites are religious or personal, and not literary. For Coleridge, two generations later, the word has substantially our meaning in the context of literature.

But the anxiety had long preceded the usage. Between Ben Jonson and Samuel Johnson filial loyalty between poets had given way to the labyrinthine affections of what Freud's wit first termed the "family romance," and moral power had become a legacy of melancholy. Ben Jonson still sees influence as health. Of *imitation*, he says he means: "to be able to convert the substance or riches of another poet to his own use. To make choice of one excellent man above the rest, and so to follow him till he grow very he, or so like him as the copy may be mistaken for the original." So Ben Jonson has no anxiety as to imitation, for to him (refreshingly) art is *hard work*. But the shadow fell, and with the post-Enlightenment passion for Genius and the Sublime, there came anxiety too, for art was beyond hard work. Edward Young, with his Longinian esteem for *Genius,* broods on the baneful virtues of the poetic fathers and anticipates the Keats of the letters and the Emerson of *Self-Reliance* when he laments, of the great precursors: "They *engross* our attention, and so prevent a due inspection of ourselves; they *prejudice* our judgment in favor of their abilities, and so lessen the sense of our own; and they *intimidate* us with this splendor of their renown." And Dr. Samuel Johnson, a sturdier man and with more classical loyalties, nevertheless created a complex critical matrix in which the notions of indolence, solitude, originality, imitation, and invention are most strangely mixed. Johnson barked: "The case of Tantalus, in the region of poetick punishment, was somewhat to be pitied, because the fruits that hung about him retired from his hand; but what tenderness can be claimed by those who though perhaps they suffer the pains of Tantalus will never lift their hands for their own relief?" We wince at the Johnsonian bow-wow, and wince the more because we know he means himself as well, for as a poet he was another Tantalus, another victim of the Covering Cherub. In this respect, only Shakespeare and Milton escaped a Johnsonian whipping; even Virgil was condemned as too much a mere imitator of Homer. For, with Johnson, the greatest critic in the language, we have also the first great diagnostician of the malady of poetic influence. Yet the diagnosis belongs to his age. Hume, who admired Waller, thought Waller was saved only because Horace was so distant. We are further on, and see that Horace was not distant enough. Waller is dead. Horace lives. "The burden of government," Johnson brooded, "is increased upon princes by the virtues of their immediate predecessors," and he added: "He that succeeds a celebrated writer, has the same difficulties to encounter." We know the rancid humor of this too well, and any reader of *Advertisements For Myself* may enjoy the frantic dances of Norman Mailer as he strives to evade his own anxiety that it is, after all, Hemingway all the way. Or, less enjoyably, we can read through Roethke's *The Far Field* or Berryman's *His Toy, His Dream, His Rest,* and discover the field alas is too near to those of Whitman, Eliot, Stevens, Yeats, and the toy, dream, veritable rest are also the comforts of the same poets. Influence, for us, is the anxiety it was to Johnson and Hume, but the pathos lengthens as the dignity diminishes in this story.

Poetic Influence, as time has tarnished it, is part of the larger phenomenon of intellectual revisionism. And revisionism, whether in political theory, psychology, theology, law, poetics, has changed its nature in our time. The ancestor of revisionism is heresy, but heresy tended to change received doctrine by an alteration of balances, rather than by what could be called creative correction, the more particular mark of modern revisionism. Heresy resulted, generally, from a change in emphasis, while revisionism follows received doctrine along to a certain point, and then deviates, insisting that a wrong direction was taken at just that point, and no other. Freud, contemplating his revisionists, murmured: "You have only to think of the strong emotional factors that make it hard for many people to fit themselves in with others or to subordinate themselves," but Freud was too tactful to analyze just those "strong emotional factors." Blake, happily free of such tact, remains the most profound and original theorist of revisionism to appear since the Enlightenment and an inevitable aid in the development of a new theory of Poetic Influence. To be enslaved by any precursor's system, Blake says, is to be inhibited from creativity by an obsessive reasoning and comparing, presumably of one's own works to the precursor's. Poetic Influence is thus a disease of self-consciousness; but Blake was not released from his share in that anxiety. What plagued him, a litany of evils, came to him most powerfully in his vision of the greatest of his precursors:

> . . . the Male-Females, the Dragon Forms,
> Religion hid in War, a Dragon red & hidden Harlot.

> All these are seen in Milton's Shadow, who is the Covering
> Cherub. . . .

We know, as Blake did, that Poetic Influence is gain and loss, inseparably wound in the labyrinth of history. What is the nature of the gain? Blake distinguished between States and Individuals. Individuals passed through States of Being, and remained Individuals, but States were always in process, always shifting. And only States were culpable, Individuals never. Poetic Influence is a passing of Individuals or Particulars through States. Like all revisionism, Poetic Influence is a gift of the spirit that comes to us only through what could be called, dispassionately, the perversity of the spirit, or what Blake more accurately judged the perversity of States.

It does happen that one poet influences another, or more precisely, that one poet's poems influence the poems of the other, through a generosity of the spirit, even a shared generosity. But our easy idealism is out of place here. Where generosity is involved, the poets influenced are minor or weaker; the more generosity, and the more mutual it is, the poorer the poets involved. And here also, the influencing moves by way of misapprehension, though this tends to be indeliberate and almost unconscious. I arrive at my argument's central principle, which is not more true for its outrageousness, but merely true enough:

Poetic Influence—when it involves two strong, authentic poets,—always proceeds by a misreading of the prior poet, an act of creative correction that is actually and necessarily a misinterpretation. The history of fruitful poetic influence, which is to say the main tradition of Western poetry since the Renaissance, is a history of anxiety and self-saving caricature, of

*distortion, of perverse, wilful revisionism without which modern poetry as
such could not exist.*

My own Idiot Questioner, happily curled up in the labyrinth of my own
being, protests: "What is the use of such a principle, whether the argument
it informs be true or not?" Is it useful to be told that poets are not common readers, and particularly are not critics, in the true sense of critics,
common readers raised to the highest power? And what *is* Poetic Influence
anyway? Can the study of it really be anything more than the wearisome
industry of source-hunting, of allusion-counting, an industry that will soon
touch apocalypse anyway when it passes from scholars to computers? Is
there not the shibboleth bequeathed us by Eliot, that the good poet steals,
while the poor poet betrays an influence, borrows a voice? And are there
not all the great Idealists of literary criticism, the deniers of poetic influence, ranging from Emerson with his maxims: "Insist on yourself: never
imitate" and "Not possibly will the soul deign to repeat itself" to the
recent transformation of Northrop Frye into the Arnold of our day, with
his insistence that the Myth of Concern prevents poets from suffering the
anxieties of obligation?

Against such idealism one cheerfully cites Lichtenberg's grand remark:
"Yes, I too like to admire great men, but only those whose works I do not
understand." Or again from Lichtenberg, who is one of the sages of Poetic
Influence: "To do just the opposite is also a form of imitation, and the
definition of imitation ought by rights to include both." What Lichtenberg
implies is that Poetic Influence is itself an oxymoron, and he is right. But
then, so is Romantic Love an oxymoron, and Romantic Love is the closest
analogue of Poetic Influence, another splendid perversity of the spirit,
though it moves precisely in the opposite direction. The poet confronting
his Great Original must find the fault that is not there, and at the heart
of all but the highest imaginative virtue. The lover is beguiled to the heart
of loss, but is found, as he finds, within mutual illusion, the poem that is
not there. "When two people fall in love," says Kierkegaard, "and begin to
feel that they are made for one another, then it is time for them to break
off, for by going on they have everything to lose and nothing to gain."
When the ephebe, or figure of the youth as virile poet, is found by his
Great Original, then it is time to go on, for he has everything to gain, and
his precursor nothing to lose; if the fully written poets are indeed beyond
loss.

But there is the state called Satan, and in that hardness poets must
appropriate for themselves. For Satan is a pure or absolute consciousness
of self compelled to have admitted its intimate alliance with opacity. The
state of Satan is therefore a constant consciousness of dualism, of being
trapped in the finite, not just in space (in the body) but in clock-time as

well. To be pure spirit, yet to know in oneself the limit of opacity; to assert that one goes back before the Creation-Fall, yet be forced to yield to number, weight, and measure; this is the situation of the strong poet, the capable imagination, when he confronts the universe of poetry, the words that were and will be, the terrible splendor of cultural heritage. In our time, the situation becomes more desperate even than it was in the Milton-haunted eighteenth century, or the Wordsworth-haunted nineteenth, and our current and future poets have only the consolation that no certain Titanic figure has risen since Milton and Wordsworth, not even Yeats or Stevens.

If one examines the dozen or so major poetic influencers before this century, one discovers quickly who among them ranks as the great Inhibitor, the Sphinx who strangles even strong imaginations in their cradles: Milton. The motto to English poetry since Milton was stated by Keats: "Life to him would be Death to me." This deathly vitality in Milton is the state of Satan in him, and is shown us not so much by the character of Satan in *Paradise Lost* as by Milton's editorializing relationship to his own Satan, and by his relationship to all the stronger poets of the eighteenth century and to most of those in the nineteenth.

Milton is the central problem in any theory and history of poetic influence in English; perhaps more so even than Wordsworth, who is closer to us as he was to Keats, and who confronts us with everything that is most problematic in modern poetry, which is to say in ourselves. What unites this ruminative line—of which Milton is the ancestor; Wordsworth the great revisionist; Keats and Wallace Stevens, among others, the dependent heirs— is an honest acceptance of an actual dualism as opposed to the fierce desire to overcome all dualisms, a desire that dominates the visionary and prophetic line from the relative mildness of Spenser's temperament down through the various fiercenesses of Blake, Shelley, Browning, Whitman, and Yeats.

This is the authentic voice of the ruminative line, the poetry of loss, and the voice also of the strong poet accepting his task, rallying what remains:

> Farewell happy fields
> Where joy for ever dwells: Hail horrors, hail
> Infernal world, and thou profoundest Hell
> Receive thy new Possessor: One who brings
> A mind not to be chang'd by Place or Time,
> The mind is its own place, and in it self
> Can make a Heav'n of Hell, a Hell of Heav'n,
> What matter where, if I be still the same . . . ?

These lines, to the C. S. Lewis or Angelic School, represent moral idiocy, and are to be met with laughter, if we have remembered to start the day with our Good Morning's Hatred of Satan. If, however, we are not so morally sophisticated, we are likely to be very much moved by these lines. Not that Satan is not mistaken; of course he is. There is terrible pathos in his "if I be still the same," since he is not the same, and never will be again. But he knows it. He is adopting an heroic dualism, in this conscious farewell to Joy, a dualism upon which almost all post-Miltonic poetic influence in the language founds itself.

To Milton, all fallen experience had its inevitable foundation in loss, and paradise could be regained only by One Greater Man, and not by any poet whatsoever. Yet Milton's own Great Original, as he confessed to Dryden, was Spenser, who allows his Colin a Poet's Paradise in Book VI of *The Faerie Queene*. Milton—as both Johnson and Hazlitt emphasize—was incapable of suffering the anxiety of influence, unlike all of his descendants. Johnson insisted that, of all the borrowers from Homer, Milton was the least indebted, adding: "He was naturally a thinker for himself, confident of his own abilities, and disdainful of help or hindrance: he did not refuse admission to the thought or images of his predecessors, but he did not seek them." Hazlitt, in a lecture heard by Keats—an influence upon Keats's subsequent notion of Negative Capability—remarked upon Milton's positive capability for ingesting his precursors: "In reading his works, we feel ourselves under the influence of a mighty intellect, that the nearer it approaches to others, becomes more distinct from them." What then, we are compelled to inquire, did Milton mean by nominating Spenser as his Great Original? At least this: that in his Second Birth, Milton was reborn into Spenser's romance world, and also that when he replaced what he came to regard as the unitary illusion of Spenserian romance by an acceptance of an actual dualism as the pain of being, he retained his sense of Spenser as the sense of the Other, the dream of Otherness that all poets must dream. In departing from the unitary aspiration of his own youth Milton may be said to have fathered the poetry that we call post-Enlightenment or Romantic, the poetry that takes as its obsessive theme the power of the mind over the universe of death, or as Wordsworth phrased it, to what extent the mind is lord and master, outward sense the servant of her will.

No modern poet is unitary, whatever his stated beliefs. Modern poets are necessarily miserable dualists, because this misery, this poverty is the starting point of their art—Stevens speaks appropriately of the "profound poetry of the poor and of the dead." Poetry may or may not work out its own salvation in a man, but it comes only to those in dire imaginative need of it, though it may come then as terror. And this need is learned first through the young poet's or ephebe's experience of another poet, of the

Other whose baleful greatness is enhanced by the ephebe's seeing him as a burning brightness against a framing darkness, rather as Blake's Bard of Experience sees the Tyger, or Job the Leviathan and Behemoth, or Ahab the White Whale or Ezekiel the Covering Cherub, for all these are visions of the Creation gone malevolent and entrapping, of a splendor menacing the Promethean Quester every ephebe is about to become.

For Collins, for Cowper, for many a Bard of Sensibility, Milton was the Tyger, the Covering Cherub blocking a new voice from entering the Poet's Paradise. The emblem of this discussion is the Covering Cherub. In Genesis he is God's Angel; in Ezekiel he is the Prince of Tyre; in Blake he is fallen Tharmas, and the Specter of Milton; in Yeats he is the Specter of Blake. In this discussion he is a poor demon of many names (as many names as there are strong poets) but I summon him first namelessly, as a final name is not yet devised by men for the anxiety that blocks their creativeness. He is that something that makes men victims and not poets, a demon of discursiveness and shady continuities, a pseudo-exegete who makes writings into Scriptures. He cannot strangle the imagination, for nothing can do that, and he in any case is too weak to strangle anything. The Covering Cherub may masquerade as the Sphinx (as the Specter of Milton masqueraded, in the nightmares of Sensibility) but the Sphinx (whose works are mighty) must be a female (or at least a female male). The Cherub is male (or at least a male female). The Sphinx riddles and strangles and is self-shattered at last, but the Cherub only covers, he only appears to block the way, he cannot do more than conceal. But the Sphinx *is* in the way, and must be dislodged. The unriddler is in every strong poet when he sets out upon his quest. It is the high irony of poetic vocation that the strong poets can accomplish the greater yet fail the lesser task. They push aside the Sphinx (else they could not be poets, not for more than one volume), but they cannot uncover the Cherub. More ordinary men (and sometimes weaker poets) can uncover enough of the Cherub so as to live (if not quite to choose Perfection of the Life), but approach the Sphinx only at the risk of death by throttling.

For the Sphinx is natural, but the Cherub is closer to the human. The Sphinx is sexual anxiety, but the Cherub is creative anxiety. The Sphinx is met upon the road back to origins, but the Cherub upon the road forward to possibility, if not to fulfillment. Good poets are powerful striders upon the way back—hence their profound joy as elegists—but only a few have opened themselves to vision. Uncovering the Cherub does not require power so much as it does persistence, remorselessness, constant wakefulness; for the blocking agent who obstructs creativity does not lapse into "stony sleep" as readily as the Sphinx does. Emerson thought that the poet unriddled the Sphinx by perceiving an identity in nature, or else yielded to the Sphinx, if he was merely bombarded by diverse particulars he could never hope to integrate. The Sphinx, as Emerson saw, is nature and the riddle of our emergence from nature, which is to say that the Sphinx is what psychoanalysts have called the Primal Scene. But what is the Primal Scene, for a poet *as pcet?* It is his Poetic Father's coitus with the Muse. There he was begotten? No—there they failed to beget him. He must be self-begotten, he must engender himself upon the Muse his mother. But the Muse is as pernicious as Sphinx or Covering Cherub, and may identify herself with either, though more usually with the Sphinx. The strong poet fails to beget himself—he must wait for his Son, who will define him even as he has defined his own Poetic Father. To beget here means to usurp, and is the dialectical labor of the Cherub. Entering here into the center of our sorrow, we must look clearly at him.

What does the Cherub cover, in Genesis? in Ezekiel? in Blake? Genesis 3:24—"So He drove out the man; and He placed at the east of the Garden of Eden the cherubim, and the flaming sword which turned every which way, to keep the way to the tree of life." The rabbis took the cherubim here to symbolize the terror of God's *presence;* to Rashi they were "Angels of destruction." Ezekiel 28:14–16 gives us an even fiercer text:

Thou waste the far-covering [*mimshach,* "far-extending," according to Rashi] cherub; and I set thee, so that thou wast upon the holy mountain of God; thou hast walked up and down in the midst of the stones of the fire. Thou wast perfect in thy ways from the day that thou wast created, till unrighteousness was found in thee. By the multitude of thy traffic they filled the midst of thee with violence, and thou hast sinned; therefore have I cast thee as profane out of the mountain of God; and I will destroy you, O Covering Cherub, in the midst of the stones of the fire.

Here God denounces the Prince of Tyre, who is a cherub because the cherubim in the tabernacle and in Solomon's Temple spread their wings over the ark, and so protected it, even as the Prince of Tyre once protected Eden, the garden of God. Blake is a still fiercer prophet against the Covering Cherub. To Blake, Voltaire and Rousseau were Vala's Covering Cherubim, Vala being the illusory beauty of the natural world, and the prophets of naturalistic enlightenment being her servitors. In Blake's "brief epic," called *Milton,* the Covering Cherub stands between the achieved Man who is at once Milton, Blake, and Los, and the emanation or beloved. In Blake's *Jerusalem* the Cherub stands as blocking agent between Blake-Los and Jesus. The answer to what the Cherub covers is therefore: in Blake, everything that nature itself covers; in Ezekiel, the richness of the earth, but by the Blakean paradox of *appearing to be those riches;* in Genesis, the Eastern Gate, the Way to the Tree of Life.

The Covering Cherub separates then? No—he has no power to do so. Poetic Influence is not a separation but a victimization—it is a destruction of desire. The emblem of Poetic Influence is the Covering Cherub because the Cherub symbolizes what came to be the Cartesian category of *extensiveness;* hence it is described as *mimshach*—"far-extending." It is not accidental that Descartes and his fellows and disciples are the ultimate enemies of poetic vision in the Romantic tradition, for the Cartesian *extensiveness* is the root category of modern (as opposed to Pauline) dualism, of the dumbfoundering abyss between ourselves and the object. Descartes saw objects as localized space; the irony of Romantic vision is that it rebelled against Descartes, but except in Blake did not go far enough—Wordsworth and Freud alike remain Cartesian dualists, for whom the present is a precipitated past, and nature a continuum of localized spaces. These Cartesian reductions of time and space brought upon us the further blight of the negative aspect of poetic influence, of *influenza* in the realm of literature, as the influx of an epidemic of anxiety. Instead of the radiation of an aetherial fluid we received the poetic flowing in of an occult power exercised by humans, rather than by stars upon humans; "occult" because invisible and insensible. Cut mind as *intensiveness* off from the outer world as *extensiveness,* and mind will learn—as never before—its own solitude. The solitary brooder moves to deny his sonship and his brotherhood, even as Blake's Urizen, a satire upon Cartesian *Genius,* is the archetype of the strong poet afflicted by the anxiety of influence. If there are two, disjunctive worlds—one a huge mathematical machine extended in space, and the other made up of unextended, thinking spirits—then we will start locating our anxieties back along that continuum extended into the past, and our vision of the Other will become magnified when the Other is placed in the past.

The Covering Cherub then is a demon of continuity; his baleful charm imprisons the present in the past, and reduces a world of differences into a grayness of uniformity. The identity of past and present is at one with the essential identity of all objects. This is Milton's "universe of death" and with it poetry cannot live, for poetry must leap, it must locate itself in a discontinuous universe, and it must make that universe (as Blake did) if it cannot find one. Discontinuity is freedom. Prophets and advanced analysts alike proclaim discontinuity; here Shelley and the phenomenologists are in agreement: "To predict, to really foretell, is still a gift of those who own the future in the full unrestricted sense of the word, the sense of what is coming toward us, and not of what is the result of the past." That is J. H. Van den Berg in his *Metabletica*. In Shelley's *A Defence of Poetry,* which Yeats rightly considered the most profound discourse upon poetry in the language, the prophetic voice trumpets the same freedom: "Poets are the hierophants of an unapprehended inspiration; the mirrors of the gigantic shadows which futurity casts upon the present."

"He proves God by exhaustion" is Samuel Beckett's own note on "So I'm not my son" in his poem *Whoroscope,* a dramatic monologue spoken by Descartes. The triumph of Descartes came in a literal vision, not necessarily friendly to imaginations other than his own. The protests against Cartesian reductiveness never cease, in constant involuntary tribute to him. Beckett's fine handful of poems in English are too subtle to protest overtly, but they are strong prayers for discontinuity.

Yet there is no overt Cartesian prejudice against poets, no analogue to the Platonic polemic against their authority. Descartes, in his *Private Thoughts,* could even write:

> It might seem strange that opinions of weight are found in the works of poets rather than philosophers. The reason is that poets wrote through enthusiasm and imagination; there are in us seeds of knowledge, as of fire in a flint; philosophers extract them by way of reason, but poets strike them out by imagination, and then they shine more bright.

The Cartesian myth or abyss of consciousness nevertheless took the fire from the flint, and trapped poets in what Blake grimly called a "cloven fiction," with the alternatives, both antipoetic, of Idealism and Materialism. Philosophy, in cleansing itself, has rinsed away this great dualism, but the whole of the giant line from Milton down to Yeats and Stevens had only their own tradition, Poetic Influence, to tell them that "both Idealism and Materialism are answers to an improper question." Yeats and Stevens, as much as Descartes (or Wordsworth), labored to see with the mind and not with the bodily eye alone; Blake, the one genuine anti-Cartesian, found such labor too a cloven fiction, and satirized the Cartesian Dioptrics by opposing his Vortex to that of the Mechanist. That the Mechanism had its desperate nobility we grant now; Descartes wished to save the phenomena by his myth of *extensiveness.* A body took definite shape, moved within a fixed area, and was divided within that area; and thus maintained an integrity in its strictly limited becoming. This established the world or manifold of sensation *given* to the poets, and from it the Wordsworthian vision could begin, rising from this confinement to the enforced ecstasy of the further reduction Wordsworth chose to call Imagination. The manifold of sensation in *Tintern Abbey* initially is further isolated, and then dissolved into a fluid continuum, with the edges of things, the fixities and definites, fading out into a "higher" apprehension. Blake's protest against Wordsworthianism, the more effective for its praise of Wordsworth's poetry, is founded on his horror of this enforced illusion, this ecstasy that is a reduction. In the Cartesian theory of vortices all motion had to be circular (there being no vacuum for matter to move through) and all matter had to be capable of further reduction (there were thus no atoms). These, to Blake, were the circlings of the Mills of Satan, grinding on vainly in their impossible task of reducing the Minute Particulars, the Atoms of Vision that will not further divide. In the Blakean theory of vortices, circular motion is a self-contradiction; when the poet stands at the apex of his own Vortex the Cartesian-Newtonian circles resolve into the flat plain of Vision, and the Particulars stand forth, each as itself, and not another thing. For Blake does not wish to save the phenomena, any more than he joins the long program of those who seek "to save the appearances," in the sense that Owen Barfield (taking the phrase from Milton) has traced. Blake is the theorist of the saving or revisionary aspect of poetic influence, of the impulse that attempts to cast out the Covering Cherub into the midst of the stones of the fire.

French visionaries, because so close to the spell of Descartes, to the Cartesian Siren, have worked in a different spirit, in the high and serious humor, the apocalyptic irony, that culminates in the work of Jarry and his disciples. The study of Poetic Influence is necessarily a branch of 'Pataphysics, and gladly confesses its indebtedness to "... *the* Science, of Imaginary Solutions." As Blake's Los, under the influence of Urizen, the master Cartesian, comes crashing down in our Creation-Fall, he *swerves,* and this parody of the Lucretian *clinamen,* this change from destiny to slight caprice, is, with final irony, *all* the individuality of Urizenic creation, of Cartesian vision as such. The *clinamen* or swerve, which is the Urizenic equivalent of the hapless errors of re-creation made by the Platonic demiurge, is necessarily the central working concept of the theory of Poetic Influence, for what divides each poet from his Poetic Father (and so saves, by division) is an instance of creative revisionism. We must understand that the *clinamen* stems always from a 'Pataphysical sense of the arbitrary. The poet so stations his precursor, so swerves his context, that the visionary objects, with their higher intensity, fade into the continuum. The poet has, in regard to the precursor's heterocosm, a shuddering sense of the arbitrary—of the equality, or equal haphazardness, of all objects. This sense is *not reductive,* for it is the continuum, the stationing context, that is reseen, and shaped into the visionary; it is brought up to the intensity of the crucial objects, which then "fade" into it, in a manner opposite to the Wordsworthian "fade into the light of common day." 'Pataphysics proves to be truly accurate; in the world of poets all regularities are indeed "regular exceptions"; the *recurrence* of vision is itself a law governing exceptions. If every act of vision determines a particular law, then the basis for the splendidly horrible paradox of Poetic Influence is securely founded; the new poet *himself* determines the precursor's *particular* law.

If a creative interpretation is thus necessarily a misinterpretation, we must accept this apparent absurdity. It is absurdity of the highest mode, the apocalyptic absurdity of Jarry, or of Blake's entire enterprise.

Let us make then the dialectical leap: most so-called accurate interpretations of poetry are worse than mistakes; perhaps there are only more or less creative or interesting misreadings, for is not every reading necessarily a *clinamen?* Should we not therefore, in this spirit, attempt to renew the study of poetry by returning yet again to fundamentals? No poem has sources, and no poem merely alludes to another. Poems are written by men, and not by anonymous Splendors. The stronger the man, the larger his resentments, and the more brazen his *clinamen.* But at what price, as readers, are we to forfeit our own *clinamen?*

I propose, not another new poetics, but a wholly different practical criticism. Let us give up the failed enterprise of seeking to "understand" any single poem as an entity in itself. Let us pursue instead the quest of learning to read any poem as its poet's deliberate misinterpretation, *as a poet,* of a precursor poem or of poetry in general. Know each poem by its *clinamen* and you will "know" that poem in a way that will not purchase knowledge by the loss of the poem's power. I say this in the spirit of Pater's rejection of Coleridge's famous organic analogue. Pater felt that Coleridge (however involuntarily) slighted the poet's pain and suffering in achieving his poem, sorrows at least partly dependent upon the anxiety of influence, and sorrows not separate from the poem's meaning.

Borges, commenting on Pascal's sublime and terrifying sense of his Fearful Sphere, contrasts Pascal to Bruno, who in 1584 could still react with exultation to the Copernican revolution. In seventy years, senescence sets in—Donne, Milton, Glanvill see decay where Bruno saw only joy in the advance of thought. As Borges sums it, "In that dispirited century, the absolute space which had inspired the hexameters of Lucretius, the absolute space which had meant liberation to Bruno, became a labyrinth and an abyss for Pascal." Borges does not lament the change, for Pascal too achieves the Sublime. But strong *poets,* unlike Pascal, do not exist to accept griefs; they cannot rest with purchasing the Sublime at so high a price. Like Lucretius himself, they opt for *clinamen* as freedom. Here is Lucretius:

When the atoms are travelling straight down through empty space by their own weight, at quite indeterminate times and places they *swerve* ever so little from their course, just so much that you can call it a change of direction. If it were not for this swerve, everything would fall downwards like rain-drops through the abyss of space. No collision would take place and no impact of atom on atom would be created. Thus nature would never have created anything. . . .

But the fact that the mind itself has no internal necessity to determine its every act and compel it to suffer in helpless passivity—this is due to the slight swerve of the atoms at no determinate time or place.

Contemplating the *clinamen* of Lucretius, we can see the final irony of Poetic Influence, and come full circle to end where we began. This *clinamen* between the strong poet and the Poetic Father is made by the whole being of the later poet, and the true history of modern poetry would be the accurate recording of these revisionary swerves. To the pure 'Pataphysician, the swerve is marvelously gratuitous; Jarry, after all, was capable of considering the Passion as an uphill bicycle race. The student of Poetic Influence is compelled to be an impure 'Pataphysician: he must understand that the *clinamen* always must be considered as though it were simultaneously intentional and involuntary, the Spiritual Form of each poet *and* the gratuitous gesture each poet makes as his falling body hits the floor of the abyss. Poetic Influence is the passing of Individuals through States, in Blake's language, but the passing is done ill when it is not a swerving. The strong poet indeed says: "I seem to have stopped falling; now I *am fallen,* consequently, I lie here in Hell," but he is thinking, as he says this, "As I fell, *I swerved,* consequently I lie here in a Hell improved by my own making."

WALTER JACKSON BATE

THE SECOND TEMPLE

Our subject could be expressed by a remark Samuel Johnson quotes from Pliny in one of the *Rambler* essays (No. 86): "The burthen of government is increased upon princes by the virtues of their immediate predecessors." And Johnson goes on to add: "It is, indeed, always *dangerous* to be placed in a state of unavoidable comparison with excellence, and the danger is still greater when that excellence is consecrated by death.... He that succeeds a celebrated writer, has the same difficulties to encounter." That word "dangerous" deserves a moment's reflection. In its original, rather ominous sense, it means "having lost one's freedom," having become "dominated" and turned into the position of a household thrall: being placed in jeopardy, subjected to the tyranny of something outside one's own control as a free agent. A cognate is our word "dungeon."

I have often wondered whether we could find any more comprehensive way of taking up the whole of English poetry during the last three centuries—or for that matter the modern history of the arts in general—than by exploring the effects of this accumulating anxiety and the question it so directly presents to the poet or artist: *What is there left to do?* To say that this has always been a problem, and that the arts have still managed to survive, does not undercut the fact that it has become far more pressing in the modern world. Of course the situation is an old one. We need not even start with Rome or Alexandria, those exemplars of what it can mean to the artist to stand in competition with an admired past. We could go back to an almost forgotten Egyptian scribe of 2000 B.C. (Khakheper-resenb), who inherited in his literary legacy no Homer, Sophocles, Dante, Shakespeare, Milton, Goethe, or Dickens—no formidable variety of literary genres available in thousands of libraries—yet who still left the poignant epigram: "Would I had phrases that are not known, utterances that are strange, in new language that has not been used, free from repetition, not an utterance which has grown stale, which men of old have spoken." But a problem can become more acute under some conditions than others. And, whatever other generalizations can be made about the arts since the Renaissance, a fact with which we can hardly quarrel—though we instinctively resist some of the implications—is that the means of preserving and distributing the literature (and more recently the other arts) of the past have immeasurably increased, and to such a point that we now have confronting the artist—or have *in potentia*—a vast array of varied achievement, existing and constantly multiplying in an "eternal present."

We could, in fact, argue that the remorseless deepening of self-consciousness, before the rich and intimidating legacy of the past, has become the greatest single problem that modern art (art, that is to say, since the later seventeenth century) has had to face, and that it will become increasingly so in the future. In comparison, many of the ideas or preoccupations (thematic, social, formal, or psychoanalytic) that we extract as aims, interests, conflicts, anxieties, influences, or "background," and then picture as so sharply pressing on the mind of the artist, are less directly urgent. In our own response to a constantly expanding subject matter, we forget that what provides opportunity for us, as critics and historians, may be simultaneously foreclosing—or at least appearing to foreclose—opportunity for the artist, and that, as T. S. Eliot said, "Not only every great poet, but every genuine, though lesser poet, fulfills once for all some possibility of the language, and so leaves one possibility less for his successors." Whatever he may say, or not say, about his predecessors, the poet from Dryden to Eliot has been unavoidably aware of them, and never so much as when he has tried to establish a difference; and he has been keenly and very personally aware of them in a way that he was not, for example (if he was writing in the early eighteenth century), of Newton, Locke, or Shaftesbury. Of course Newtonian philosophy, formal ideals of order and decorum, Shaftesburian benevolence, and many other concepts or interests that we ourselves pursue may all have concerned eighteenth-century poets. It is taken for granted that they have an important place in our consideration of what the English poetry of the eighteenth century became. The point is merely that these poets also had one very direct and practical problem that was at least as absorbing to them, and often far more so: the stark problem of what and how to write.

So with the English Romantics. Keats, who certainly faced enough personal difficulties, would become really despondent only (except after his fatal illness began) when, as he told his friend Richard Woodhouse, he felt that "there was nothing original to be written in poetry; that its riches were already exhausted—and all its beauties forestalled." Goethe rejoiced that he was not born an Englishman and forced to compete with the achievement of Shakespeare. Even if one is writing in another language, said Goethe, "a productive nature ought not to read more than one of Shakespeare's dramas in a year if he would not be wrecked entirely." Direct imitation is obviously not the answer. (Shakespeare, as he says elsewhere, "gives us golden apples in silver dishes." By careful study we may acquire the silver dishes while discovering that we have "only potatoes to put in them.") But attempting—after one knows his works—to proceed differently for the sake of mere difference is even less satisfactory. Goethe became increasingly frank about the matter as he grew older:

We spoke about English literature [said Eckermann, 2 January 1824], about the greatness of Shakespeare, and what an unlucky position all English dramatic writers have, coming after that poetic giant. "A dramatic talent," Goethe continued, "if it were significant, could not help taking notice of Shakespeare; indeed, it could not help studying him. But to study him is to become aware that Shakespeare has already exhausted the whole of human nature in all directions and in all depths and heights, and that for those who come after him, there remains nothing more to do. And where would an earnest soul, capable of appreciating genius, find the courage even to set pen to paper, if he were aware of such unfathomable and unreachable excellence already in existence! In that respect I was certainly better off in my dear Germany fifty years ago. I could very soon come to terms with the literature already in existence. It could not impose on me for long, and it could not much hold me back. . . . Thus gradually advancing I followed my own natural development. . . . And in each stage of my life and development my idea of excellence was never much greater than I was able to attain.

"But had I been born an Englishman, and had those manifold masterworks pressed in upon me with all their power from my first youthful awakening, it would have overwhelmed me, and I would not have known what I wanted to do! I would never have been able to advance with so light and cheerful a spirit, but would certainly have been obliged to consider for a long time and look about me in order to find some new expedient."

The situation is the same when we move on to the Victorians and especially to the first half of the twentieth century. These writers, we say, were faced with a difficult situation, which we then proceed to document —the decline of faith, the lack of certainty in moral as well as religious values. All this is true (and is true of certain earlier eras). But the pessi-

mism we explain with such a cumbersome machinery of ideas has often
an even sharper, more immediate spur: the nagging questions, what is there
left to write? and how, as craftsmen, do we get not only new subjects
but a new idiom? A great deal of modern literature—and criticism—is
haunted, as Stephen Spender says, by the thought of a "Second Fall of
Man," and almost everything has been blamed: the Renaissance loss of
the medieval unity of faith, Baconian science, British empiricism, Rousseau, the French Revolution, industrialism, nineteenth-century science,
universities and academicism, the growing complexity of ordinary life,
the spread of mass media. But whatever else enters into the situation, the
principal explanation is the writer's loss of self-confidence as he compares
what he feels able to do with the rich heritage of past art and literature.
Scientists, we notice, are not affected by this despondency, at least not
yet. And we do not account for that very interesting difference, or for
any number of other differences, if we try to attribute it to mere in-
sensitivity.

II

Yet this is not a subject we have been much tempted to pursue, at least
during the last century—though it is precisely during this period, and
particularly the last fifty years, that the psychological complexities we
have in mind have begun to thicken in Malthusian progression.

Why is it that we fight shy of the problem, and, in our vast annual
output of commentary on the arts, prefer to devote our energies to almost
any or every other topic or approach? There seem to me several explana-
tions. The critic, biographer, or historian, in his consideration of the arts,
has by definition a different vocation (though we need not remind ourselves of the fact itself, we occasionally need to remind ourselves of some
of its implications); and in his own personal experience the situation we
mention does not press home to him to the same degree or in the same
way. He may have his own anxieties and competitions in the face of
previous achievement, and these may certainly cripple rather than inspire
him in his own range and magnanimity as a humanist. But the accumulation of past work from which he may feel tempted or even forced to
differ in order to secure identity (whether through increasing specialism
in smaller corners, through more general forms of reinterpretation, or
through mere quibble) is chronologically far more limited. It is primarily
the product of the last fifty years. Moreover, there is a difference in kind
as well as degree. In one way especially the "literature of knowledge"
—of fact and expository discussion—will always differ, as De Quincey

said, from the "literature of power" and the other arts. The discovery of even a handful of new facts, the correction of some others, or even the mere ability to rearrange details or arguments with some ingenuity for debate or supplement, will permit the writing, again and again, of a new work. In short, the "literature of knowledge" with its expository discussion is, even at its best, "provisional" and can always be superseded. But the *Iliad* or *King Lear* will not be dislodged with the same ease or excuse. They are, as De Quincey said, "finished and unalterable"—like every other work of art, however minor. To feel constraints in competition with even the greatest scholars and critics of the last fifty years is not, in other words, the same thing as to be in competition with Michelangelo, Shakespeare, Rembrandt, Bach, Beethoven, Dickens, or Mann and with the finalities that the works of such men present.

Relatively free from immediate personal experience of the same sort, we continue to remain oblivious because of the natural pride and embarrassed silence of the writer himself. The writer or artist may be self-revealing enough in other ways. But when his anxiety has to do with the all-important matter of his craft, and his achievement or fear of impotence there, he naturally prefers to wrestle with it privately or to express it only indirectly. The subject, in other words, is not one for which we can compile a clean-cut reading list. We begin to sense its importance only when we look between the lines, or follow closely the life of writer after writer, or weigh the context of self-defensive manifestoes or fatalistic excuses in eras of militant transition in style, and, above all, when we note the nagging apprehension, from generation to generation, that the poet is somehow becoming increasingly powerless to attain (or is in some way being forbidden to try to attain) the scope and power of the earlier poetry that he so deeply admires.

But there is something else, to which we are quick to apply the word "taboo" when we confront it in others instead of ourselves. The confidence of the artist and the humanist generally has not been at one of its historical peaks during our own period. We have become very defensive, and to that extent participate in the rigidities of defense. We become especially disturbed at any speculation that would even suggest, at first glance, that what we value so highly, what we spend so much time discussing and teaching, may have taken the turns it has in the past, and may be assuming the forms that it does in our own period, because of an essential (possibly inevitable) retrenchment. We can take in our stride general theories of decline. If they are extreme enough, as in Spengler's *Decline of the West*, we are confident that we can pick holes in them. And if we find them current in some earlier period, we do not stop to ask whether they had some objective justification but deal with them as curious asides, fashionable notions, or the result of reading some earlier theorist. (Goldsmith and others in the English eighteenth century who thought the arts were moving into a less vital stage had—we say—read Vico, or had at least read or talked with someone else who h. d read Vico.) Or if, as biographers, we are considering writers like Coleridge or Keats, we dissolve their inner anxieties about what the poet is still able to do, within other, more personal forms of reductionism: Coleridge was struggling again with opium or his neuroses generally; Keats was having trouble with Fanny Brawne or memories of his dead parents, and was therefore having his own pessimistic moments.

But if we are confronted with the suggestion that one age of achievement in the arts may necessarily—because of its greatness, and because of the incorrigible nature of man's mind—force a search for difference, even though that difference means a retrenchment, we become uneasy. When the change in the arts since the Renaissance is attributed to the loss of religious faith, to the growth of science, to commercialism, or to the development of mass media, we are always at liberty to feel that those circumstances may conceivably change again. But the deepest fear we have is of the mind of man itself, primarily because of its dark unpredictabilities, and with them the possiblity that the arts could, over the long range, be considered as by definition suicidal: that, given the massive achievement in the past, they may have no further way to proceed except toward progressive refinement, nuance, indirection, and finally, through the continued pressure for difference, into the various forms of anti-art.

The speculation that this may be so—or that the modern spirit is beginning, rightly or wrongly, to believe that it is so—is a major theme of one of the most disturbing novels of our century, Thomas Mann's *Dr. Faustus.* We find the implications so unsettling, in this modern version of the Faust legend, that we naturally prefer—if we can be brought to linger on the book rather than forget it—to stress other themes, other implications that can be more localized (for instance, the condition of Germany between the two World Wars). For Mann's twentieth-century Faustus, a German composer of genius, all the most fruitful possibilities in music have already been so brilliantly exploited that nothing is now left for the art except a parody of itself and of its past—a self-mockery, technically accomplished but spiritually dead in hope, in short, an "aristocratic nihilism." It is "anti-art" in the sense of art turning finally against itself. And this modern Dr. Faustus, so cerebral and self-conscious before the variety and richness of what has already been done, sells his soul to the devil—as in the old Faust legend—in order to be able once again to produce great art. The special horror is that this involves the willing, the deliberately chosen, destruction of part of his brain in order to free himself from the crippling inhibitions of self-consciousness—a partial destruction of the brain that is to be followed, after the agreed lapse of years, by what he knows beforehand will be a complete disintegration.

The universality of the problem lies in the fact that the arts, in addition to everything else that can be said of them, are also the sensitive antennae of human life generally; that as with them so, in time, with everything else that we still subsume by the word "culture" (however inadequate the word—but we have no other shorthand term). If what is implied in Mann's fable is or even could be true, or half-true, then what of man's situation in general as he is now beginning to face, and will face increasingly, the potential self-division forced upon him by his growing literacy and sophistication—his knowledge about himself, his past, the immense variety of what has been done and said, all brought with immediate focus and pressure, like a huge inverted pyramid, upon the naked moment, the short flicker, of any one individual life? The self-division arises because, except in the cumulative sciences, where a step-by-step use of deliberately specialized effort can be harnessed, the weight of everything else that has been done, said, or exemplified cannot, in conscience, be wholly denied, though on the other hand there is the natural desire of every human being to assert himself in such time as he has—to contribute in some respect, however small, or, if he cannot contribute, to leave his mark in some other way.

III

We may feel less naked, less prey to existential *Angst* and helplessness, if we know that we have not been condemned by history to be the first to face this frightful challenge, unique though it is, in scale, to the modern world. There may be some comfort to our feeling of historical loneliness—and not only comfort but some spur to both our courage and potentialities for good sense—to know we have a predecessor in the eighteenth century, a century that serves as the essential crossroad between all that we imply when we use the word "Renaissance" and much of what we mean when we speak of the "modern." We are only beginning to understand this about the eighteenth century, and to realize how much, in our approach to it and to all that which, in Johnson's phrase, can be "put to use," we have still lingered in the suburbs of its significance—above all, its significance for us now as contrasted with that which it had, or seemed to have, for the nineteenth century. With the nineteenth and the greater part of the twentieth century behind us, the eighteenth has long ceased to be something from which we need to disengage ourselves. We are now free to concentrate less on what differentiates it from ourselves and more on what we share. For us now, looking back on the last four centuries as a whole, the central interest of the eighteenth century is that it is the first period in modern history to face the problem of what it means to come *immediately* after a great creative achievement. It was the first to face what it means to have already achieved some of the ends to which the modern (that is, the Renaissance) spirit had at the beginning aspired. Simultaneously, we have the start of almost everything else we associate with the modern world—the attempted Europeanization of the globe, with some of its new embarrassments; the American and French revolutions; the rapid spread of literacy; the beginning of industrialization, urbanization, and the sudden rapid increase of population; and, in its later half, the creation of most of what we associate with the premises of the modern effort not only in the arts but in philosophy.

What is so reassuring to us, as we look back on this astonishing century now and begin to learn more about it with the kind of perspective just mentioned, is its union of strength (good sense, even shrewdness and worldliness) with openness and generous empathy for all that William James implied when he spoke of literature and the arts as the "tender-minded pursuits." What is so reassuring is that here, if nowhere else, all that we ourselves prize (or should, like, if we were bold enough, to say that we prize) in the "tender-minded" is taken for granted as valuable, as indeed supremely valuable, while at the same time we have as "tough-minded" a group of champions for the sympathetic and the humane as, in our most desperate moments, we could ever have hoped for. As we look further into this century, which produced, in David Hume, the greatest skeptic in the history of philosophy but which also produced Mozart and Beethoven and Burke, we feel a growing confidence about what can be "put to use."

This is also true of our special problem here—the whole problem of the "burden of the past" as it applies to the arts (and, by implication, to humanistic interests and pursuits as a whole). My thought, in these lectures, is twofold: to pose for us, in general, this central problem—to express the hope that we can pluck it out into the open and to try to see it for what it is—and, second, to help us reground ourselves, to get a clearer idea of our bearings, by looking back with a fresh eye to the beginning drama of what we ourselves are now living with and feel so deep a need to bring into perspective. In using the word "drama" I am thinking not only of the variety in voice and stance (realistic, sentimental, nostalgic, prejudiced, imaginative, worldly, analytic, sociological, aesthetic, moral) but also of the trauma—and there was one in this massive self-reconsideration—and of its uneasy but brilliantly creative resolutions.

IV

But first we must narrow our focus, and, leaving broader generalities aside, concentrate on what the eighteenth-century poet inherited. This involves lingering, at least for a moment, on what for half a century we have called "neoclassicism." In what I am saying now, I am trying to focus especially on England, and not merely on England but on the poet and the situation of the poet. And this further involves freeing ourselves from some of the tyranny of abstractions and labels, and of our post-Hegelian urge to give them body, so that we can use them rather than be used by them.

If we took up English neoclassicism solely in the light of what we call the history of ideas, it could still remain one of the great unresolved puzzles of literary history. No explanation for it—at least no explanation why it caught on so quickly and firmly after 1660—would satisfy anyone for very long except the person who provided it.

Let me hurry to say that I am not speaking of English neoclassic *theory* —that is, of neoclassic *critical* writing. It is only too easy, if we confine ourselves to the history of critical theory, to trace an ancestral line through Sir Philip Sidney and Ben Jonson down to the Restoration (the history of critical theory is by definition a history of ideas). And if we want more help, we have merely to turn to the intellectual history of England during the sixteenth and seventeeenth centuries and we can find any number of ideas, if not ancestral, at least collateral, to enrich our genealogical chart. But once the glow of discovery has faded, the result is not really very persuasive except to the confirmed Hegelian, of whom we should remember that there are twentieth- as well as nineteenth-century varieties. Our consciences begin to remind us that, as historians of ideas, we are naturally swayed by special interest. We have a vocational interest in presupposing that there is a relatively clean-cut influence of ideas on artists— meaning, by "ideas," concepts that we, as historians, have abstracted from a large, diverse period of human life, which may very well have struck our attention only because they are so susceptible of genealogy. Of course we all say—and say it quite sincerely—that what we are really interested in is the *reciprocal* influence of ideas and art. But it is so difficult to put neatly the influence of art, in all its diversity, on the climate of ideas! To the orderly mind of the historian, this task is as elusive, or as unmanageably messy, as having to describe and categorize the influence of people on ideas. We find ourselves feeling that it is better to leave all that for some future, more leisurely consideration. Hence, in our actual practice if not in ultimate ideal, we lean toward the simplicities of thinking in terms of a one-way traffic.

A sense of all this begins to nag the conscience after we trace our genealogies of ideas in order to explain English neoclassicism: the rephrasing, by sixteenth- and seventeenth-century critics, of classical ideals; the premium on decorum, refinement, regularity, and the ways in which they are particularized; the confidence in method; the influence of mathematics. Are these ideas, these concepts and values that we have abstracted, not progenitors after all of the actual neoclassic literature to come but only midwives, escorts, even (to quote Eliot) "attendant persons"? Putting it another way: would these particular concepts and ideas have been left undeveloped, have fallen on deaf ears, unless there had also been *other* considerations, equally or perhaps more important?

We know very well, for example, that English literature itself, from the time of Elizabeth down into the mid-seventeenth century, showed a diversity that had been unrivaled since the most fertile days of Athens. We also know that at its best it showed a power or intensity in its diversity (in idiom, in metaphor, in cadence) that has haunted English literature ever since that time. And this literature was written at exactly the same time as those theoretical works to which we are looking for the ancestry of English neoclassicism. We know that the intensity and diversity of that literature (or, putting it more truthfully, an intensity both of and within diversity) far outweigh our thin sketch of theoretical or merely critical concepts through the Elizabethan and Jacobean eras. To put it bluntly: it is not at all from English life and English experience in its widest sense, from the time of Elizabeth through that of Cromwell, that a really developed neoclassicism came so suddenly. We know perfectly well that systematized and pervasive neoclassicism is very much a French product, and that it was in fact viewed as that (whether with respect, restiveness, or antagonism) by the English themselves, from Dryden, Rymer, and Temple down to Hazlitt and Francis Jeffrey a century and a half later.

Then why did English neoclassicism occur? We are always being reminded that these values of the "new classicism" of France never sat too easily on the English mind. Of course they did not. In fact, they were always being qualified by native English attitudes; and (though we have recently tended to exaggerate the amount) there was a good deal of open dissent. But this makes the matter all the more curious: why should it have flourished so rapidly when there was this much tendency to dissent and qualify?

There is, in fact, nothing else in the whole of the long literary history of England quite like this brisk transition. There is no other instance, after the invention of printing, where you find a settled group of literary premises and aims imported almost bodily, adopted with such dispatch, and then transformed into orthodoxy, or near-orthodoxy, for so long a time (a full seventy or eighty years), despite a large undercurrent that runs counter to it. Of the three really great transitions in English poetry since the Elizabethans and Jacobeans, this is the first. The second is found in the large shift that took place in the late eighteenth and early nineteenth centuries, and the third is the radical change of idiom and mode during the first half of the twentieth century. But the second of these transitions, to which we apply the loose word "Romantic," was the reverse in almost every way of what we are considering now. To begin with, it was slower and longer prepared for in the actual writing (as distinct from critical theory) that preceded it. It emerged from within the neoclassic stronghold, opening the walls one by one. To a large extent it was demonstrably—even dramatically—a nationalistic movement in England (as it was in another, more pronounced way in Germany). When we turn to our own era, we have to admit that the transition to the new poetic idiom of the early and middle twentieth century was almost as rapid, and that it was analogous to the neoclassic transition in speed as well as in other ways. On the other hand, this radical modern change was less metaphysically rationalized; in some ways it was closer to its own immediate past (the English Romantics) than Pope ever was to Shakespeare or Milton; nor was it—despite the influence of the French Symbolists and others—a Continental importation: too much else, by that time, was already going on within the English-speaking world generally.

V

To the England of the Restoration and the early eighteenth century, the mature and sophisticated neoclassicism of France had an irresistible appeal. It gave the English poet a chance to be different from his immediate predecessors while at the same time it offered a counter-ideal that was impressively, almost monolithically, systematized. French neoclasicism appeared to have answers ready for almost any kind of objection to it. And most of the answers had this further support: they inevitably referred—or pulled the conscience back—to the premises of "reason" and of ordered nature that the English themselves were already sharing, though not perhaps in the same spirit as the French. To dismiss an argument that led directly back to "reason" was something they were not at all prepared to do. It was like attacking virtue itself. Even the most articulate writers who might feel hesitations (for example the group appropriately called, in England as well as France, the *je ne sais quoi* critics) still lacked the vocabulary to express any effective alternative. And in any case, had not England's own Sir Isaac Newton already helped to disclose the universal architecture, and to an extent that no Frenchman had done?—Newton, as James Thomson later said, "whom God / To mortals lent to trace his boundless works."

In addition they had ready to hand the central neoclassic concept of *decorum*—of "propriety" or "what is fitting." In almost every way (ancestry, centrality, potential range of application) its credentials as both an aim and working premise were superb. Its origin was the ancient Greek and specifically Aristotelean conception of the function of art as a unified, harmonious imitation of an ordered nature. As, in the process of nature itself, the parts interrelate through universal, persisting forms and principles, so art in its own particular medium (words, sounds, or visual shapes) seeks to duplicate that process, but at the same time to stress or to highlight it. Hence art concentrates, even more than we in our ordinary experience do, on the general form—selecting only what contributes directly to the particular end (or form) and rejecting what does not. As such, poetry is more "philosophical," as Aristotle said, than a straightforward factual narrative. It is, in short, closer to the "ideal," but "ideal" in the original sense in Greek—in the intellectual perception of pattern, form, and general meaning. *Decorum* applies to the *relevance* or *fitness* of every part to the whole in this "ideal" and admittedly foreshortened selection, which permits a finished and rounded totality. Given its success in art, we have not only unity and cleanliness of form (and with them finish and completeness) but intellectual range and pertinence: cousinship at least (in its best moments something approaching the fraternal) to the process of nature itself when nature is viewed with a philosophical selectivity that focuses not on its accidental details but on its persisting forms.

Extensively and ingeniously developed throughout two centuries of critical thinking, and applied to every aspect of subject and style, the neoclassic concept of decorum was—at least in its more general significance— one of the most difficult premises in the history of art with which to quarrel theoretically. Never before in the West since classical antiquity (hardly at any time even then), and certainly never again after the mid-eighteenth century, has there been available for the poet or artist generally and also for the critic or philosopher, or for anyone who wanted to say anything about the arts, a concept that could potentially fulfill so many functions. It not only could serve as an active hinge between the theory of art and the actual practice of it, but could lead directly to moral and social values and, further, to nature itself and the cosmic order.

Yet in one important way the neoclassic conception of decorum, however theoretically persuasive, carried with it an historical, if not logical, limitation, though we should remember that limitation need not be synonymous with disadvantage or weakness. It was itself an extrapolation that had been made, argued, and embellished, first of all, in the face of the challenge of an admired past, and then contemporaneously in competition with a brilliantly creative present. It had evolved in the early 1500s as a by-product of the more general effort of the European Renaissance to rival the challenge it found in its haunting dream of classical antiquity, and, in this particular case, to do so by concentrating, strictly and analytically, upon what seemed to be the formal essentials in the classical achievement. Moreover, within a generation it was also in active rivalry (which did not of course preclude occasional and even fruitful agreement) with the inventive originality and diversity of Renaissance art and literature themselves. As with almost any ideal extrapolated and militantly defended, it quickly became centripetal rather than centrifugal or diluted. This process seems especially to occur with ideals that have to do with combination and balance of different elements. (One thinks of what has happened to the classical ideal of "temperance," meaning harmonious or rhythmic proportion—"keeping time [*tempus*] " as in music. It has not meant that to most people for quite a while.) If the premise is that every part of a work of art should contribute directly to the whole—that what is especially wanted is unity of impact, unity of focus and significance—it is always tempting to proceed to such an end (at least the "unity" if not the "impact" and "significance") by exclusion. Indeed, for frail human nature the use of exclusion or denial is immensely seductive as the answer to most problems, including moral and social ones. It is always easier, as Johnson said, to throw out or forbid than to incorporate—"to take away superfluities than to supply defects." In the title of George Granville's *Essay upon Unnatural Flights in Poetry* (1701), with all that it suggests, we sense the relief that neoclassic theory could provide: something still remained to be done, and the difficulties were not insuperable.

In the very limitation, in other words, lay much of the attraction. ("No one unable to limit himself," said Boileau, "has ever been able to write.") If in our quick summary we appear to belittle, we should remind ourselves that what we are saying can apply to any formalism that is deliberately exclusive (as opposed to the necessary exclusions in primitive arts), and especially if it is a formalism trying to free itself from, or establish itself after, a strongly emotional and richly mimetic (that is, "realistic") art. We have only to think of the immense effort of the arts, including music, of the early and middle twentieth century to get the nineteenth century off their backs. So strenuous—at times single-minded—was the effort that, during the childhood and youth of those of us now middle-aged, many of us began to assume that the first requirement of the sophisticated poet, artist, or composer was to be as unlike his nineteenth-century predecessors as possible. We even had moments when we suspected that the principal influence on modern poetry, for example, was not so much the array of abstractions cited in the recondite search for aim or justification, but rather the poetry of Tennyson. What we are trying desperately to be unlike can tell a great deal about not only what we are doing but why, and a movement may often be better understood by what it concretely opposes than by its theoretical slogans. In short, this is a situation in which we ourselves have directly shared, and when we confront something like it in other periods we should be able to approach it with some empathy if not with the most fervent applause.

VI

If Restoration England, through its delayed but now ready embrace of the neoclassic mode, at once secured standards that permitted it to avoid competition with the literature of the immediate past, this was especially because it could do so with that authority (in this case classical antiquity) which is always pleasing to have when you can invoke it from a distant (and therefore "purer") source; pleasing because it is not an authority looming over you but, as something ancestral rather than parental, is remote enough to be more manageable in the quest for your own identity—more open to what the heart wants to select or the imagination to remold. For that matter, the ancestral permitted one—by providing a "purer," more time-hallowed, more conveniently malleable example—even to disparage the parent in the name of "tradition." And in the period from 1660 to about 1730 there were plenty of people ready to snatch this opportunity. If their ranks did not include the major minds and artists, there were enough of them to justify us in recognizing this as the first large-scale example, in the modern history of the arts, of the "leapfrog" use of the past for authority or psychological comfort: the leap over the parental—the principal immediate predecessors—to what Northrop Frye calls the "modal grandfather." (So the English Romantics later invoked the Elizabethans and Jacobeans against their own immediate predecessors. Another century later T. S. Eliot was to invoke the "metaphysical poets" as the prototype of the genuine English "tradition" from which poetry had since strayed.)

It should be emphasized that we are not speaking of the taste of the reading public generally. For example, Milton was probably the most popular major poet for eighteenth-century England. The period saw over a hundred editions of *Paradise Lost,* and over seventy of the complete poems. This very fact could illustrate our argument that the neoclassic mode, in its stricter and more organized sense, was not the response to a general and popular shift of taste that it is sometimes described as being, but rather an elitist movement in which the incentives were primarily applicable to the condition of the writer himself. We have seen the same thing in twentieth-century formalism. Despite the enormous critical effort to ground it on premises and values that human beings generally—or at least the more educated—are said to be in need of appreciating, the fact remains that the essential appeals of the movement have been to the artist or to those who professionally consider themselves his guardians. (The split between "popular" and "sophisticated" art has always existed in cultivated societies, but it has become progressively greater since the seventeenth century. Of special interest is the growth since then, among intellectuals, of the number that deplore this split, look back nostalgically to happier and simpler eras before it occurred, and yet, while championing the "popular" so long as it is remote enough—Yeats's Celtic mythology, for example—side with the elitist or sophisticated against the "popular" as soon as we come to anything post-Renaissance and above all post-romantic.)

But to return to the situation: it was possible to go still further than reducing your immediate predecessors to size or manageability. You could turn, if you wished, against the ancestral source itself and demonstrate—methodically, indeed legalistically—that even classical antiquity had failed sufficiently to develop its own premises. This is precisely what happened in the still famous "quarrel of the Ancients and the Moderns" that flourished in seventeenth-century France and then seeded itself in Restoration England, though there the soil proved less promising. With the Ancients themselves being weighed in the balance and found wanting because they were not "correct" enough, the liberals began to align themselves in defense of the Ancients. So, in Swift's burlesque of the quarrel in his *Battle of the Books,* he uses the bee as the symbol of the Ancients and the spider of the Moderns. The bee, turning directly to what is outside of us (nature), brings home honey and wax, thus furnishing man with both "sweetness and light." The spider, by contrast, is a domestic creature, working within a shorter radius, indeed preferring a corner. The tireless weaving of rule and regulation that Swift is attacking in the Moderns, far from being the product of a direct and far-ranging use of "nature," is spun subjectively from the spider's own body, and the web—at once systematic and flimsy—is capable only of catching dirt and insects. The interest of the "quarrel of the Ancients and the Moderns" is that of all good comedy—potential universality (if possible, a relevance close enough to threaten) and, for the audience, detachment. The detachment is provided for us by historical distance: the *particular* issues, taking this particular form, are no longer there and we can view them without partisanship and self-defense. The universality lies in the fact that, though the special issues are now distant to the point of triviality, the motives, the procedures, are not. Human nature, as Johnson said, is in general more inclined to censure than to praise. Add to this that almost every writer finds it "not only difficult but disagreeable" to dwell on things "really and naturally great." He becomes "degraded in his own eyes by standing in comparison with his own subject, to which he can hope to add nothing." If he cannot contribute his mite, he feels that he can at least secure importance by withholding it.

But the major writers, to repeat, are found in neither group—those who turned against the parental or (least of all) against the ancestral. It was not Dryden but the almost forgotten Charles Gildon who wrote "For the Modern Poets against the Ancients" (1694) and described the new spirit of strict regulation and analysis as "more essential to Poetry than any other Art or Science"—more essential since poetry, left to itself, is so incorrigibly open to varied human interests. Nor was it Pope but poor William Guthrie who boasted of modern "dramatic poetry"—especially tragedy—that it at last "stands upon the same footing as our noble system of Newtonian philosophy." Pope, so quick to ridicule such remarks, had himself simply turned to other forms of writing, and, however self-defensive in more personal ways, without militance.

Indeed, one of the paradoxes of what we have been describing is that the pressure of the "burden of the past" was felt most sharply by the major writers and artists, if only because they had the intelligence to see where their opportunities lay; and it is they who set the tone for the new formal style, the new mode, and the genres associated with the period, especially satire and the verse essay. Yet it was also they who were least blithe or slapdash in disposing of, or downgrading, their predecessors. True, they might occasionally, forgivably, cluck the tongue or shake the finger about particular details. But this was not the same thing. In a deeper way than others, they knew how much was involved.

It was not at all the confidence of "superiority" so loudly proclaimed by others that sustained them as they developed one of the greatest formal poetic styles the English language has yet seen, the finest comic and satiric writing in modern literature, and a prose never excelled in English before and rarely since. It was, as we said, a realization of where the opportunities lay at this particular time. Had the circumstances been different, they took it for granted that they would have written differently. As Dryden said about the use of rhyme in dramatic tragedy (speaking through Neander in the *Essay of Dramatic Poesy*), this was one of the ways of writing that Shakespeare and his contemporaries had not exploited; and, far from implying adverse criticism of what they had done, the attempt to turn to other modes of writing now was a tribute. It involved the recognition that "there is scarce an humor, a character, or any kind of plot which they have not used." Would they themselves, after so rich an expenditure of all that could be done in the art, have been able to "equal themselves, were they to rise and write again?" We "acknowledge them our fathers," but they have already spent their estates before these "came to their children's hand." As a result our present choice is "either not to write at all, or to attempt some other way."

VII

What Dryden is saying here—and all that it implies—is something with which he continued to live throughout his career, and with the good-natured sanity that every later professional man of letters has admired. The thought deepened as the years passed and as he saw his own work, and what the years since the Restoration had been able to do, with increasing perspective. Looking back upon the writers before the Restoration, he describes them now as the "giant race before the flood"—before the great change to the modern formalism. In lines written near the end of his life to his friend William Congreve (1694), congratulating Congreve on a new comedy, he generously pretends that with this new play "the promised hour has come at last; / The present Age of Wit obscures the past." The gentle irony, in so large a claim, is as obvious as the obsession of the period with the achievement of the past. And the fascination of the poem is that the strongest lines, within this formal proscenium arch of conventional compliment, express his own personal condition in his old age, or undercut the clichés of the new formalism ("your *least* Praise is be Regular"), or, above all, speak of the relation of the age itself to that preceding:

> Strong were our Syres; and as they Fought they Writ,
> Conqu'ring with force of Arms, and dint of Wit;
> Theirs was the Gyant Race, before the Flood;
> And thus, when *Charles* Return'd, our Empire stood.

With the Restoration, he goes on, the "stubborn Soil" was "manur'd," and through the new "Rules of Husbandry" the weeds were cut and the rank growth brought into cleaner form:

> Our Age was cultivated thus at length;
> But what we gain'd in skill we lost in strength.
> Our Builders were, with want of Genius, curst;
> The Second Temple was not like the First.

The Second Temple, completed seventy years after the destruction of the First by Nebuchadnezzar, differed in four ways especially from the

Temple of Solomon. Though about the same in area, it was not so high. It was also less of a unit, being divided now into an outer and inner court. In equipment and decoration it was barer. Above all, the Holy of Holies was now an empty shrine, as it was also to remain in the magnificent Third Temple built by Herod. The Ark of the Covenant was gone, and no one felt at liberty to try to replace it with a substitute.

PART THREE

READER AS PARTICIPANT

Critics from Eliot to Bate have traced how individual works and broad traditions shape and reshape each other into new patterns. This interaction between past and present is always in some sense "an influence." Though a troublesome conclusion, it now seems obvious that the present creates the past, that readers at least in part create what they read. Some of the implications of this "audience participation" are easier to accept than others. That audiences have participated in the creation of what "Chaucer" became through five centuries is little contested. But does a poem actually become something new every time it is read? And is influence, then, something that must *necessarily* occur whenever one writer reads another? Does the critic's attempt to understand the reader's fullest subjective response replace his pursuit of "correct" interpretations? As a basis for an entire critical theory, "audience participation" that alters previously fixed categories gets "sticky." Recent links between the study of influence and theories of reading rescue such emphasis on the subjective reader from collapse into nominalism.

Once stated, the connections between literary influence and reader-response theories seem obvious. Louise M. Rosenblatt focuses on the process of reading as transformation, as a transaction between text and reader, Norman N. Holland on the reader's creation of meaning as defense, and Stanley E. Fish on the reader's participation in seventeenth-century literature through what he calls "affective stylistics." Each explores from a different perspective the extent to which the dynamics of the reading process become a part of the literary work. Because they speak to what happens when one writer reads another, reader-response theories have given new energy to literary influence at a time when the historical approach is being called into question in our schools as well as in critical commentaries. Simultaneous emphasis on "influence" as dynamic history and the reader as active participant in the creative process has led many critics to look at the study of influences not as just one more approach but as the basis of an entire critical system. Reader-centered theories have further helped to dispel some of the strongest objections to mechanistic influence study.

In her pioneer study of response to literature (*Literature as Exploration*, 1936) Ms. Rosenblatt described the literary work as "no less than the infinite series of possible interactions between individual minds and individual literary works." While "literary tradition and the crystallization of particular literary forms and techniques of communication" remain important, these considerations primarily underline the extent to which "anything we call a literary experience gains its significance and force from the way in which the stimuli present in the literary work interact with the mind and emotions of a particular reader." This series of interactions again is an "influence."

Current research on the reader's role in the creation of what he reads also draws heavily on Freudian psychology. In *The Dynamics of Literary Response*, Norman N. Holland applies a psychoanalytical approach to the ways in which an audience constructs meaning for a literary work. His aim is "to develop a model for the interaction of literary works with the human mind" in order to explain "the relation between the patterns he finds objectively in the text and a reader's subjective experience of the text."

In *Self-Consuming Artifacts: The Experience of Seventeenth-Century Literature*, Stanley Fish brings critical emphasis on the activity of *reading* literature to one logical conclusion. If literary history itself (and surely, then, "literary influence") is a matter of studying, comparing, and analyzing responses of readers (of course *responses* to works *are* what we come to see as the "works"), then the seemingly "objective" artifact consumes itself as it is absorbed into and transformed by its audience. Traditional confusion between the artifact and the work of art as it exists for any particular reader, tradition, or milieu therefore also disappears. Though Fish does not follow in precisely this direction, a persistent trend in influence studies thus runs its course, and the person being influenced becomes as much an object of study as whatever allegedly had created the influence. For Fish, "affective stylistics" is an accounting of what readers *do* as they respond to literature which is a "kinetic" art.

LOUISE M. ROSENBLATT

TOWARDS A TRANSACTIONAL THEORY OF READING

The task assigned to me in this Seminar on Reading Theory grows out of my interest in the interpretation of literary works of art. The effort to develop a "model" for the kind of reading thought of as aesthetic has led to a view that seems relevant to the whole reading spectrum, aesthetic and non-aesthetic, advanced and elementary. Reversing the usual procedure of beginning at the simpler level, I shall attempt to sketch some emphases that result from consideration of the interpretation of fairly complex literary works of art. This will provide the basis for clarifying resemblances and differences between aesthetic and non-aesthetic reading processes. Some implications may emerge for the dynamics of the reading process in general.

Materials drawn from a study by Rosenblatt (1964) of the responses of a group of men and women to four lines of verse may serve as a springboard for discussion. It should be pointed out that these materials do not offer introspective evidence, about which there is justified skepticism. Before being given the text, the subjects were told that they would remain anonymous and were asked simply to start writing as soon as possible after beginning to read. They were to jot down whatever came to them as they read. These notes turned out to be analogous to "stills" at various stages in a slow-motion picture. Thus it was possible to reconstruct some of the

From *Journal of Reading Behavior* 1 (1969): 31-47. Copyright © 1969 by the National Reading Conference, Inc. Reprinted by permission of the publisher.

kinds of responses and stages involved in the process of arriving at an interpretation. The quatrain (without the name of the author, Robert Frost) and a sampling of the responses follow:

It Bids Pretty Fair

The play seems out for an almost infinite fun.
Don't mind a little thing like the actors fighting.
The only thing I worry about is the sun.
We'll be all right if nothing goes wrong with the lighting.

Typical opening notes in two commentaries reflect a rudimentary literary response, yet they already represent a very high level of organization:

"This seems to me to be bits of conversation between people who are interested in moviemaking or a legitimate play."

"Sounds as if it could be producer of a play giving encouragement to backers."

The effort here is to find a framework into which to fit the meanings of the individual words and sentences. *Who is speaking? Under what circumstances? To whom?* are questions already assumed in these first tentative comments.

The following note reveals another step or kind of awareness; it starts like the others, but quickly makes articulate the realization that this text is to be read as a poem: "This seems to be bits of conversation between people who are interested in moviemaking or a legitimate play. On second thought, the rhymes show it is a poem." This led to a rereading of the text for the purpose of paying attention to rhythm; the lines had evidently first been read as simple conversation, with no effort to sense a rhythmic pattern.

Some of the readers became involved with ideas called up by the first two lines, and neglected the rest. But for most, the third line, with its reference to the sun, created the necessity for a revision in some way of the tentative response to the first two lines. In comment after comment, there occurs a phrase such as "on second thought," "a second look," "another idea." One reader spells out the problem: "The third line seems most confusing. If I stick to my theory of producer talking to backers it really makes no sense."

Many of the readers, having called up such a vivid notion of a director or producer talking about a play, immediately attempted to adapt this to a situation in which there might reasonably be a concern about the sun: "I am reminded of the Elizabethan theatre open to the skies, which indeed was dependent upon the sun (good weather)"; "Seems to be about life in a summer stock theatre"; "Is it a summer theatre? But then there would be worry about the rain, rather than the sun."

Within the brief time given for reading and comment, a number of the readers never freed themselves from the problem of finding such a practical explanation for a play's success being dependent on the sun. One comment ends on this realization: "I'm afraid this is a very literal reading."

Others more quickly became aware of the need for another level of interpretation: "However, after a moment or two, the implied stage begins to represent the world, and the actors, the world's population"; "On second thought, play metaphor—'all the world's a stage'—Life goes on in spite of quarreling, but it won't if the 'lighting' (moral? spiritual?) fails.... Anyway, war, disagreement, etc., don't matter so much—so long as we still have the 'light' (sun—source of light—nature? God?)."

Several readers were alerted, evidently, by the contrast between the word "infinite" and the colloquial tone of the rest of the line. When they were led to wonder about the kind of play for which the sun provides lighting, the notion of infinity had prepared them to think of the great drama being played out through the ages by mankind on this planet. Some tried unsuccessfully to merge with this another level of meaning for the sun.

A few readers sensed the Olympian remoteness of the "I" who could find it possible to view man's life on this planet in the light, almost, of eternity, and who was thus able to see as "little things" such momentous episodes as wars.

For another reader, the reference to something happening to the sun awakened a recollection of Burns's, "Till a' the seas gang dry" as another image of boundless time. This led to a feeling that the persona's "worry" was ironic, a belittling of human conflicts when viewed against the background of the life of the sun.

The following notes illustrate the range covered in one commentary: "Sounds as if it could be producer of a play giving encouragement to backers ... I just got another idea: First line—the world will always be here. Second line—there will always be fighting. We shouldn't worry too much about it. Third line—worries about H-bomb." (Here we see how the reader's fears of an atomic catastrophe were activated by the reference to "worry" about the sun.)

Even these few excerpts demonstrate the need to insist that the reader is *active*. He is not a blank tape registering a ready-made message. He is actively involved in building up a poem for himself out of the lines. He selects from the various referents that occur to him in response to the verbal symbols. He finds some context within which these referents can be related. He reinterprets earlier parts of the poem in the light of later parts. Actually, he has not fully read the first line until he has read the last, and interrelated them. There seems to be a kind of shuttling back and forth as one synthesis—one context, one persona, etc.—after another suggests itself to him.

Moreover, we see that even in these rudimentary responses the reader is paying attention to the images, feelings, attitudes, associations that the words evoke *in him*. It is true that what looks like a certain amount of reasoning went on in the effort to fix on a kind of "play" that would depend on the sun. Actually, however, the notes indicate that, for example, the feeling for the "play" as metaphoric for the life of mankind, and the "sun" as suggesting the backdrop of space and time against which to view it, seems to have been arrived at, not by reasoning, but by paying attention to qualities of feeling due to such things as tonal variations created by the diction, juxtaposed associations, or literary analogies. Notions of mankind as a whole, war, or astronomical time, were part of the reader's contribution to the "meaning."

The preceding discussion may point up the need to eliminate a widespread semantic confusion, the tendency to use the words *poem* and *text* interchangeably. Teachers tell students to "read the poem"; contemporary critics make no distinction between "the poem itself," "the work itself," and "the text itself." This reflects a failure to distinguish between the linguistic symbols (the sounded words, the written or printed marks on the page) and what a listener or reader makes of them. Perhaps it is utopian to hope to change such entrenched confusions in literary or critical usage, but at least in a consideration of the reading process such as the present one, there will be an effort to maintain a semantic distinction: *Text* will designate a set or series of signs interpretable as linguistic symbols: thus, in a reading situation, *text* will refer to the inked marks on the page. *Poem* (or *literary work of art*, and terms such as *lyric, novel, play*) will designate an involvement of both reader and text, i.e., what a reader evokes from a text.

The idea that a *poem* presupposes a *reader* actively involved with a *text* is particularly shocking to those seeking to emphasize the objectivity of their interpretations. Afraid that recognition of the importance of the reader will lead to an irresponsible impressionism, critical theorists such as Wellek and Warren have tended to talk about "the poem itself," "the concrete work of art," or even the ideal and unattainable "real" poem. Yet all that they can point to is an interpretation that has been arrived at by a reader in response to a given text. We cannot simply look at the text and predict the poem. The text is a necessary, but not a sufficient, condition of the poem. For this, a reader or readers with particular cultural and individual attributes must be postulated. The author, at the time of its creation, is the first reader. At a later time, even the author himself has a different relationship with the text; there are many stories about this. So it is with a potentially infinite series of other readers of the text. We may postulate a contemporary of the author with similar education and literary and life experience; a contemporary of the author with different background and experience; other individual readers in specific places and times and at a particular point in their lives, bringing to bear on the text specific linguistic, literary, and social experience.

Always each of the readers has before him only black marks on the page, the text by means of which a poem is to be called forth. These readings may be compared, generalizations may be made about them, some may be considered more generally acceptable by a body of critics, but ultimately specific individual readings must be assumed. Fortunately, the whole problem of the "mode of existence" of the poem need not be debated here, since our concern is necessarily with individual readers in an active relationship with individual texts. To speak of an ideal reading is simply to postulate a relationship between the text and a reader possessing "ideal" attributes, which will need to be specified.

Some critical theorists set up the author as the ideal reader of the text and, especially if it was produced at some remote time, or in another society, use many scholarly aids in order to approximate to the author's hypothetical reading. Yet it is clear that the scholar-reader brings another component to the reading, namely his awareness of the difference between what he brings to the text and what the author or his contemporaries presumably did. (Santayana somewhere tells about the man who built a perfect reconstruction of an eighteenth-century house. There was only one anachronism in it: himself.) Part of the interest of reading any literary work is the sense of participating in another "world."

Wimsatt and Beardsley (1943) and Wimsatt (1954) have noted how twentieth-century criticism has sought to dissociate the interpretation of the text from the author's intention. The author, it is true, may state his intention, or there may be biographical or historical evidence that would indicate his intention. Yet the question still remains. *Did the author succeed in carrying out his intention in the text?* The author may test his creation in the light of his intention, but all that the reader has to fall back on is the text. Any intention of the author's which is not capable of being called forth from the text, or justified by the text, is a matter of the author's biography. Knowledge of the author's intention drawn from other sources may aid in the reading of the text, but only by alerting the reader to verbal cues that he might otherwise overlook. The interpretation, however, cannot validly be "of" anything other than the text itself. The effort to avoid "the intentional fallacy" did not, however, lead to a systematic understanding of the reader's contribution.

The familiar information theory diagram may help us to further clarify the relationship of the reader to the author and the text:

Speaker—encoding—message—decoding—hearer

There is a temptation to substitute *author* for *speaker* and to think of the *reader* simply as seeking to decode the message in a way parallel to the *hearer* decoding the message. But in any actual reading, there is only the text and the reader. The speaker, we know, offers many clues to the listener, through emphasis, pitch, rhythm, pauses—and, if face-to-face, facial expression and gesture. The reader finds it necessary to construct the "speaker"—the "voice," the "persona," the "tone"—*as part of* what he decodes from the text.

Contemporary critical theory has recognized this, but has primarily developed its implications for the author's need to select elements that will produce the effect he desires. Thus T. S. Eliot (1932) developed the notion of the "objective correlative" to refer to elements in the text that would possess the same emotional impact for the author and the reader. There is, however, a tendency to think of the "objective correlative"—whether the structure of a play or the metaphors embedded in it—as somehow eliciting an automatic response from the presumably passive reader. If that were true, the reading of a poem or of a Shakespeare play would be analogous to responding to a red traffic light. Any reading is far more complex than such a simple stimulus-response situation.

In information theory, the listener is said to have "decoded" the "message" when he has reconstructed the sounds and has recognized the patterns of words. This view is understandable when it is recalled that information theory is concerned with such matters as the transmission of utterances over, for example, the telephone. But, of course, workers in this field are quite ready to admit that in any actual communication, the process must be carried through to an interpretation of meaning. And even on the level of recognizing the sounds, evidence exists to demonstrate that the listener's present expectations and past experience are important. For example, Cherry (1957) reports experiments which reveal that once a listener is aware of the general subject matter of an utterance. he is more likely to recognize the words in spite of distorting interference or "noise."

If what the listener brings to even this simple level of listening is important, how much more necessary is recognition of the importance of what the reader brings to a text. The matrix of past experience and present preoccupations that the reader brings to the reading makes possible not only a recognition of shapes of letters and words but also their linkage with sounds, which are further linked to what these sounds point to as verbal symbols. This requires the sorting out of past experiences with the words and the verbal patterns in different contexts.

The readers of the quatrain demonstrated very clearly that, whatever the "model," the reading of a poem is not a simple stimulus-response situation. There was not simple additive process, one word-mear'ng added to another. There was an active, trial-and-error, tentative structuring of the responses elicited by the text, the building up of a context which was modified or rejected as more and more of the text was deciphered.

The fact that a reader of the quatrain might be able to assign "meaning" to each of the verbal symbols and to each of the separate lines did not guarantee that he would be able to organize these into a significant structure of idea and feeling. The reader had to pay attention to much more than the "meanings" of individual words or their syntax before he could relate the four lines meaningfully. He had to respond to many elements, of diction, rhythm, association, possible figures of speech or levels of meaning. In order to sense the particular way of voicing the last line to himself, he had to select a particular implied persona with a particular point of view or tone or attitude toward the subject about which the poem might center.

Thus the text, a pattern of signs, is interpreted as a set of linguistic symbols. But the text serves as more than a set of stimuli or a pattern of stimuli; it is also a guide or continuing control during the process by which the reader selects, organizes, and synthesizes—in short, interprets—what has emerged from his relationship with the verbal symbols. The text is not simply a fuse that sets off a series of responses. As a pattern of linguistic symbols derived from the signs on the page, the "text" also underwent a series of transformations during the process of arriving at the *poem.*

Moreover, the readers of the quatrain were creating a poem through paying attention to what the stimulus of the text was calling forth within them: attention to the sound of the words in the inner ear, attention to the residue of past experiences with these words in different contexts, attention to the overtones of feeling and the blendings of attitude and mood. All of these were needed before even a tentative organization of an interpretation was possible. Hence my [Rosenblatt (1968)] continuing insistence on the idea that the *poem* is what the reader lives through under the guidance of the text and experiences as relevant to the text.

The question remains: Although this view of reading may be important in counteracting the neglect of the reader's contribution and the excessive emphasis on the text of the literary work of art in current criticism and teaching, *What light does this throw on the reading process in general?* How much of what has been said about "the reading of a poem" applies to the reading of other kinds of texts that do not give rise to works of art but that provide, say, information, logical analysis, scientific formulae, or directions for action?

This question leads into the general realm of reading theory where many dangers await the unwary amateur. Having cast discretion to the winds, I shall venture the hypothesis that the reading of a poem probably provides a better basis for a general "model" of the reading process than does the reading of a scientific formula or a recipe for cooking. The tendency of the layman is to assume that the latter forms are simpler modes of reading, and that in the reading that results in a poem, something more has been added. Actually, are not both the aesthetic and non-aesthetic readings different versions of the same basic process? The difference between these two kinds of reading derives ultimately, it seems to me, from a difference in the aspect of the reading process that the reader holds in the focus of his attention.

In a reading that results in a work of art, the reader is concerned with the quality of the experience that he is living through under the stimulus and guidance of the text. No one else can read the poem or the novel or the play for him. To ask someone else to experience a work of art for him would be tantamount to seeking nourishment by asking someone else to eat his dinner for him.

The non-aesthetic mode of reading is primarily instrumental. The differentiating factor is that the reader is not primarily concerned with the actual experience during the time of his relationship with the text. His primary purpose is something that will remain as a residue *after* the actual reading event—e.g., the information to be acquired, the operations referred to or implied in a scientific experiment, or the actions to be carried out in some practical situation.

An illustration of this instrumental type of reading might be a woman who has just discovered a fire in her kitchen, has picked up a fire extinguisher of a type that she has never used, and is frantically reading the directions for its use. Her attention, her whole muscular set, will be directed toward the actions to be performed as soon as she has finished interpreting, i.e., reading, the text. She is not paying attention to the sound of the words, nor to the particular associations that they might evoke. Whether the directions refer to "fire" or "flames" or "combustion" is quite unimportant to her, so long as she grasps what the word points to. The sound, the associations, the relationship of the overtones of these words to those of the rest of the verbal context, would be very important if she were paying attention to this aspect of the reading while evoking a poem; in this instrumental reading they are ignored, are not allowed into the center of attention. The response to the text will be the actual operations to be performed. It would not matter if someone else read the directions and rephrased them for her, so long as the required actions were made clear.

The same text may even provide the occasion for both of these two kinds of reading, depending on the focus of the reader's attention. The young American tourist discovered this when she finished reading the *London Times* weather report, with its "high over Iceland" and its talk of the "Gulf Stream" and found her head full of sonorous phrases and images of snow-peaked mountains and waving tropical palms. She had been paying attention to the sounds and the associations evoked rather than to the practical indications as to whether or not she should carry her umbrella that day. The current "pop" poets who take a sentence from a newspaper article and break it up into free verse are, similarly, inviting the reader to pay attention to the experience evoked even by these seemingly banal words rather than to pay attention primarily to their practical reference. Contrast with this the third-grade textbook in which a poem about a cow in a meadow is headed with the question: "What facts does this poem teach you?" Clearly, the pupil is being instructed to direct his attention to what is farthest from the possibilities of a poetic experience.

The preceding instance undoubtedly spells trouble for that third-grader, since he needs to learn that the visual patterning of the verbal symbols in lines of verse is one of the ways in which the reader is alerted to direct his attention toward the quality of what he evokes from the text. There are, of course, many ways in which the text alerts the reader to adopt one or another stance in his relationship with the text. Courses in poetry are largely concerned with sensitizing the reader to such cues. The more such past experience he brings to the text, it is assumed, the better able he will be to select the appropriate attitude and the more successful he will be in evoking an experience that does justice to the text.

At the other extreme, the mathematical or logical text that is written in a special system of symbols quickly alerts the reader to the fact that he must focus his attention on the operations pointed to by the text and must disregard his sensuous or emotionally colored responses. The reader is further assisted in this by the fact that the special mathematical language is free of irrelevant associations that accrue to ordinary words encountered in a wide range of contexts. But even here the experiential attitude may creep in—as when the mathematician responds to the "elegance" of a proof that he has encountered through a text.

Of course, in much of what we read, both kinds of attitude are brought into play. Our primary purpose may be to gain information, but at the same time we may be aware of the rhythm or the qualitative responses aroused in us by the text, its sound in the inner ear, its appeals to memories involving the senses and the emotions. In fact, it seems not unlikely that such responses are operating even when they are not in the focus of attention. The experienced reader learns to adopt the appropriate stance, and to attend to the aspects of the reading process that are appropriate both to the text and to his own purposes.

The reading process seems to represent a continuum of potential attitudes. A complex literary work of art, such as *Hamlet* or a lyric by Blake, can be placed at one end of the continuum, where the reader's attention is focused squarely on what he is living through in his relationship with the text. Toward the other end of the continuum would be placed the reading of a text with the attention directed toward its instrumental value in terms of information to be assimilated or operations to be performed. The phrasing here is designed to avoid the implication that texts possess absolute "poetic" or "scientific" values, and to suggest a relationship between the reader and the text resulting in one or another kind of reading event. Thus there is not a break between these kinds of reading, but rather a continuum. Any particular reading is situated at a point between these extremes that reflects the nature of the activity and the focus of attention that the conjunction of the reader and text have produced.

Borderline cases, involving both instrumental and "literary" attitudes, illuminate, on the one hand, the importance of the text and, on the other, the fallacy of assuming an absolute character in words themselves. Words, it is usually said, point to sensations, images, ideas, objects, concepts. But this conventional formulation is not a description of the actual way in which these referents are crystallized out. Linguists and psychologists have recognized the existence of this matrix of inner experience or consciousness out of which our common language is ultimately carved. But usually in discussions of reading this matrix has not been sufficiently emphasized. Critics and linguists have been eager to move on to the more easily studied public manifestations of external linguistic behavior, as in analysis of spoken or printed texts.

The problem of the nature of experienced "meaning" is indeed complex and only now beginning to interest the psycholinguists and linguistic philosophers. Some of the entrenched and misleading notions about how we think about the meaning of words are being dispelled. For example, the "picture" theory of meaning is being discarded, as indeed is the idea that the word *think* points to a single activity.[1] Such questions are mentioned here only to indicate awareness of the complexity of the process involved when one talks, as I have so blandly, of the reader focusing his attention "on what the linguistic symbols have called forth within him." Still, is it not becoming generally accepted that when we speak of the reader's sensing the meaning of words from their context, we must broaden the scope of that term? Usually it is the verbal context that is referred to—the lexicographical clues present in the text that indicate which of the alternative dictionary meanings of the words should be selected. And of course the verbal context functions also to indicate to the reader what should be his appropriate stance in relation to this text.

But the context is not limited simply to the interlocking pattern of verbal symbols. The reading even of initial cues, we have seen, is a function of the reader as well as of the text, the result of a two-way process. We can say that the text leads the reader to order segments of his past experience; but it is equally necessary to say that the reader is dependent on past experience, both linguistic and life experience, for the sense of possible modes of order that he brings to the text. (Consider the implications of even so simple an illustration as the following: the sign *pain* will be made a different linguistic symbol by the English and the French reader. Within a common culture and language, individual differences, no matter how subtle, still enter into the process of interpretation.)

Hence we cannot even assume that the pattern of linguistic signs in the text gives us knowledge of the exact nature of the stimuli acting upon a given reader. The living organism, Dewey (1896) pointed out decades ago, to a certain extent selects from its environment the stimuli to which it will respond, and seeks to organize them according to already-acquired principles, assumptions, and expectations. Hence the "meaning" of any element in the system of signs in the text is conditioned not only by its verbal context, but also by the context provided by the reader's past experience and present expectations and purpose. Out of this emerges the new experience generated by the encounter with the text. Thus, the coming together of a particular text and a particular reader creates the possibility of a unique process, a unique work.

In discussion of the reading process, as in other disciplines undergoing revision, we need to free ourselves from unscrutinized assumptions implicit in the usual terminology. The usual phrasing makes it difficult to attempt to do justice to the dynamic nature of the actual reading event. The reader, we can say, interprets the text. (The reader acts on the text.) Or we can say, the text produces a response in the reader. (The text acts on the reader.) Each of these phrasings, because it implies a single line of action by one separate element on another separate element, distorts the actual reading process. This is not a linear relation, but a situation, an event at a particular time and place in which each element conditions the other.

The "transactional" terminology developed by John Dewey and Arthur F. Bentley[2] seems most appropriate for the view of the dynamics of the reading process that I have attempted to suggest. This philosophic approach, for which Dewey developed various phrasings during his long career, has had repercussions in many areas of twentieth-century thought. Dewey and Bentley sought to counteract the nineteenth-century phrasing of phenomena as an *interaction* between different factors, as of two separate, self-contained, and already defined entities acting on one another—in a manner, if one may use a homely example, of two billiard balls colliding. They offered the term *transaction* to designate situations in which the elements or factors are, one might say, aspects of the total situation in an ongoing process. Thus a *known* assumes a *knower,* and vice versa. A "knowing" is the transaction between a particular individual and a particular environment.

The transactional view of the reading process not only frees us from notions of the impact of distinct and fixed entities, but also underlines the essential importance of both elements, reader and text, in the dynamic reading transaction. A person becomes a *reader* by virtue of his activity in relationship to a text, which he organizes as a set of verbal symbols. A physical text, a set of marks on a page, becomes the text of a poem or of a scientific formula by virtue of its relationship with a reader who thus interprets it. The transaction is perhaps similar to the electric circuit set up between a negative and positive pole, each of which is inert without the other.

The transactional view is especially reinforced by the frequent observation of psychologists that interest, expectations, anxieties, and other patterns based on past experience affect what an individual perceives. Dewey rejected the simple stimulus-response notion in which the organism passively receives the stimulus, and pointed out that to some extent the organism selects out the stimulus to which it will respond. This is not limited to situations in which, for example, the perceiver projects his interpretation upon a formless or "unstructured" stimulus as in the projection of meanings onto the blots of ink of the Rorschach Test. Experiments have demonstrated that the perceiver "sees" even a structured environment in the way that his past experience has led him to interpret it.

The transactional point of view has been systematically developed by a group of psychologists mainly through experiments in perception.[3] For example, in one of the Ames-Cantril experiments, the viewer "sees" a room as rectangular although it is in actuality trapezoidal or otherwise distorted. Here, the observer is confronted with a definitely structured stimulus, but the cues are selected and organized or interpreted according to past experience of a room. Simple information that the room is distorted has not necessarily been sufficient to enable the observer to see the room as distorted. Often a disturbing period of readjustment is required. The observer hits walls which he sees or interprets as being elsewhere; he flails about with a stick at non-existent walls. Ultimately, a new set of sensitivities and assumptions is built up, and he learns to respond to or organize those cues than can be interpreted as a room distorted in certain ways. Without the effort at testing his perception, the observer would not have realized that what he saw was largely a projection from past experience. Yet only through such criticism of his own perception could he build up the equipment with which to achieve a more adequate perception. In both instances, what was perceived involved both the perceiver's contribution and the environmental stimulus.

The view of the reading process presented here has not been derived from such experiments. Rather, these offer reinforcement and confirmation for the transactional as a conceptual model. This seems to do greatest justice to the results of prolonged observation of readers encountering texts, and to provide a solution for current confusions in literary theory. Thus, a reader revising his interpretation may be considered analogous to the person looking at the distorted room. In the light of what he brings to the transaction, the reader arrives at a tentative interpretation and then tests it by further study of the text or by comparison with others' interpretations of it. He seeks to find in the verbal symbols the source of his and others' interpretations. He may discover that he ignored some elements or that he projected on it responses irrelevant to the text. Out of this may come a reinterpretation of the text, that is, the structuring of a new kind of experience in relation to it. This simply is a further development of the transactional process that begins with the first effort to derive even the simplest level of meaning from the text.

The transaction involving a reader and a printed text thus can be viewed as an event occurring at a particular time in a particular environment at a particular moment in the life history of the reader. The transaction will involve not only the past experience but also the present state and present interests or preoccupations of the reader. It stresses the possibility that printed marks on a page will become different linguistic symbols by virtue of transactions with different readers.

There is always some kind of selecting out from a matrix of past experiences of language as a phenomenon in particular contexts. Thus the reader draws on this experiential reservoir in even the simplest reading. When only the simplest phonological experience is drawn on, someone has said that the child "barks at the page." As soon as meaning enters, there is not only a recognition of shapes of letters and a linkage with sounds; there is also a sorting out of past experiences with the sounds as symbols or words, and with what the words pointed to in different contexts. "Interpretation," a selective and synthesizing activity, is thus engaged in by the reader even in the most elementary kind of reading.

Does not the transactional point of view suggest that we should pay more attention to the experiential framework of any reading transaction? Is it not extraordinary that major social upheavals seem to have been required to disclose the fact that schools have consistently attempted to teach reading without looking at the language and life experience, the cognitive habits, that the child brought to the text? And should not this same concern be brought to bear on more than the problem of the language or dialect that the child brings? Should not a similar concern for reading as an event in a particular cultural and life situation be recognized as pertinent to all reading, for all children at all phases of their development as readers, from the simplest to the most sophisticated levels?

Nothing that has been said thus far should be interpreted as denying that there must be highly specialized research on many facets of the reading process. But should not both basic and applied research make much more explicit the assumptions concerning the total transaction within which any one element in the reading event may function? The experimenter who is concerned with determining the physical conditions under which spoken utterances may be transmitted by telephone is quite ready to recognize that the physical, linguistic, and general cultural and life equipment that the hearer brings to his listening will condition what he hears, as well as what he interprets. Difficulties arise when these contexts or frameworks are forgotten and the results of narrow experiment are looked upon as significant in isolation. Can it be that many of the efforts to compare various techniques of inducting the child into reading have yielded indeterminate results because elements were being studied without sufficient concern for how these elements fit into the particular reading transactions being studied?

The transactional approach would particularly redress the balance so far as what seems to be a tendency to concentrate on what is most easily measured and analyzed—namely, the signs or, at a somewhat higher level of complexity, the linguistic symbols to which the reader is exposed. This is reflected not only in current controversies about beginning reading, but can also be seen in the zest with which some linguists are applying their particular systems of linguistic analysis to the texts of poems. Such analysis often yields interesting results. But it leaves untouched the question concerning how an individual reader becomes sensitive to the particular linguistic patterns, the parallelisms, the variations from ordinary usage, that often are found to characterize the verbal structure. Statistical analysis of literary styles, for example, must be translated back into terms of sensitivities of the reader in the transaction with a particular text. The difference between statistical or syntactic analysis of a text and the mode of perception of differences within a reading process especially should be recognized.

The importance of the reader in the transaction once established, certain questions become more insistent. What, for example, is the function of the reader's *purpose* in the reading transaction? What are the ways in which the reader develops habits of paying attention to one or another aspect of the highly complex operations generated within this transaction? How, for example, does he develop the habits that enable him to build up from the inked symbols on the page a context within which not only the word order but also the inflections and meaningful cues of the spoken language are embedded?[4] How does he learn when and how to pay attention to the qualitative responses generated by the designated rhythmic patterns and to the past associations with the elements of experience designated by the text? How does he learn when and how to adopt a scientific attitude and pay attention only to the completely public referents of the printed signs? A transactional model of the reading process would not permit neglect of the experiential matrix within which spoken and written language functions. Perhaps this would generate cumulatively meaningful questions, and would provide a framework within which the experimental treatment of aspects of the reading process can be fruitfully carried out.

NOTES

1. Cf. Ryle (1951), Wittgenstein (1953), and Quine (1964).
2. Cf. Dewey and Bentley (1949), Bentley (1950), and Ratner (1964).
3. Cf. Ames (1953), Ames (1955), Kilpatrick (1952), and Allport.
4. Cf. Lefevre (1964).

REFERENCES

Allport, Floyd H. *Theories of Perception and the Concept of Structure.* New York: John Wiley, 1955, p. 271ff.
Ames, Adelbert, Jr. Reconsideration of the Origin and Nature of Perception." *Vision and Action* (ed. Sidney Ratner). New Brunswick, N. J.: Rutgers University Press, 1953.
————. *The Nature of Our Perceptions, Prehensions and Behavior: An Interpretative Manual for the Demonstrations in the Psychology Research Center, Princeton University.* Princeton: Princeton University Press, 1955.
Bentley, A. F. "Kennetic Inquiry." *Science* 112:775–83, December 29, 1950.
Cherry, Colin. *On Human Communication.* New York: John Wiley, 1957, p. 276.
Dewey, John. "The Reflex Arc Concept in Psychology." *Psychological Review* 3:357–70, July, 1896.
Eliot, T. S. "Hamlet and His Problems." *Selected Essays.* New York: Harcourt Brace, 1932, pp. 124-25.
Kilpatrick, Franklin P. (editor). *Human Behavior from the Transactional Point of View.* Hanover, N. H.: Institute for Associated Research, 1952.

Quine, Willard V. "Speaking of Objects" and "Meaning and Translation." *The Structure of Language* (eds. Jerry A. Fodor and Jerrold J. Katz). Englewood Cliffs, N. J.: Prentice-Hall, 1964.
Ratner, Sidney, et al., eds. *The Philosophical Correspondence of John Dewey and Arthur F. Bentley.* New Brunswick, N. Y.: Rutgers University Press, 1964.
Rosenblatt, Louise M. *Literature as Exploration.* New York: Appleton-Century, 1938; rev. ed., New York: Noble and Noble, 1968. (See part 1 for discussion of the problem of the relative validity of different interpretations.)
——. "The Poem as Event." *College English* 26:123–25, November, 1964.
Ryle, Gilbert. "Thinking and Language." *Proceedings of the Aristotelian Society,* supplement 25 (1951), pp. 65-82.
Wellek, René, and Austin Warren. *Theory of Literature.* 3rd ed., New York: Harcourt, Brace and World (n. d.), pp. 146-47 and passim.
Wimsatt, W. K., Jr., and Monroe C. Beardsley. *"Intention." Dictionary of World Literature* (ed. J. T. Shipley). New York: *Philosophical Library, 1943,* pp. 326-29.
——. *"The Intentional Fallacy." The Verbal Icon.* Lexington, Kentucky: University of Kentucky Press, 1954, pp. 3-18.
Wittgenstein, Ludwig. *Philosophical Investigations,* tr. G. E. M. Anscombe. New York: Macmillan, 1953, p. 175ff.

NORMAN N. HOLLAND

LITERATURE AS TRANSFORMATION

The Muse is an enigmatic lady. Ever since Aristotle we have tried to penetrate her mysteries, yet still she eludes us. Still we ask as Aristotle did: What is our emotional response to a literary work? What arouses it? What dampens it? Why do men enjoy seeing mimeses of the real world? How is it that literature can make painful things give pleasure? How does literature affect morality?

Later critics have added to the questions. Coleridge, in particular, raised the most puzzling issue of all: the "willing suspension of disbelief." Somehow, when we are engrossed in a literary work, we lapse into the same state of mind as the embezzler in the joke:

The young executive had taken $100,000 from his company's safe, lost it playing the stock market, and now he was certain to be caught, and his career ruined. In despair, down to the river he went.

He was just clambering over the bridge railing when a gnarled hand fell upon his arm. He turned and saw an ancient crone in a black cloak, with wrinkled face and stringy gray hair. "Don't jump," she rasped. "I'm a witch, and I'll grant you three wishes for a slight consideration."

"I'm beyond help," he replied, but he told her his troubles, anyway.

"Nothing to it." she said, cackling, and she passed her hand before his eyes. "You now have a personal bank account of $200,000." She passed her hand again. "The money is back in the company vault!" She covered his eyes for the third time. "And you have just been elected first vice-president."

From *The Dynamics of Literary Response* by Norman N. Holland. Copyright © 1968 by Norman N. Holland. Reprinted by permission of Oxford University Press, Inc.

The young man, stunned speechless, was finally able to ask, "What—what is the consideration I owe you?"

"You must spend the night making love to me," she smiled toothlessly.

The thought of making love to the old crone revolted him, but it was certainly worth it, he thought, and together they retired to a nearby motel. In the morning, the distasteful ordeal over, he was dressing to go home when the old crone in the bed rolled over and asked, "Say, sonny, how old are you?"

"I'm forty-two years old," he said. "Why?"

"Ain't you a little old to believe in witches?"[1]

The Muse always tricks us that way. Whether she has inspired a joke or a great tragedy, she tricks us as the witch tricked the young executive. In Coleridge's terms, we willingly suspend our disbelief. We agree, as it were, not to doubt that a witch could magically create a bank account—or at least not to doubt that a worldly executive would so believe.

Why do we suspend disbelief? Presumably, for the same reason we do most things in this world, to gain pleasure. Then, behind the question Coleridge raised, How does the Muse induce us not to disbelieve, stands the deeper Aristotelian puzzle, What is the pleasure literature gives us? Curiously, that question takes us to what might seem the least pleasurable part of literature—its moral significance or, more generally, meaning.

Literature means, we would all agree. But how? We might all disagree. A great many critics and philosophers have wrestled with "the meaning of meaning" in ordinary discourse. We can, however, make our question somewhat simpler if we narrow it and ask only what we mean by literary meaning above and beyond the meanings of everyday speaking and writing. Further, a psychoanalytic approach to literary works has, I think, something special to contribute to this gnarled question, because it can describe quite exactly the special pleasure of literature.

"A theme," Frank O'Connor has said, "is something that is worth something to everybody." By "theme," here, I think O'Connor means, roughly, "plot plus meaning of the plot," for he goes on:

The moment you grab somebody by the lapels and you've got something to tell, that's a real story. It means you want to tell him and think the story is interesting in itself. If you start describing your own personal experiences, something that's only of interest to yourself, then you can't express yourself, you cannot say, ultimately, what you think about human beings.[2]

Freud noticed this same limitation on the writer and concluded, "The writer softens the egotistic character of [his] daydream." How? That, said Freud, is the writer's "innermost secret, ... the essential *ars poetica.*"[3]

Freud's answer is at least as mysterious as the Muse herself, but Freud knew no New Critics. He had not been exposed, as, for example, modern college students have, to thirty years' accumulation of academic explications. If he had, he would have been all too aware that literature means, and it means in a general, not a personal way. O'Connor's phrasing leads to a definition: literary meaning is a statement of what in the literary work is of sufficient generality to be "worth something to everybody."

Usually, meaning in this sense takes the form of statements like *"School for Scandal* is a play about the tension between appearance and reality," or "The theme of 'Pied Beauty' is the relationship between the permanent, universal, and ideal and the particular, various, and transitory." Meaning thus becomes a reader's attempt to state a universal proposition derived from the text, not so much a "moral" as an idea or quality that informs and permeates the whole. Northrop Frye, for example, contrasts narrative movement within a poem to "The meaning of a poem, its structure of imagery, [which] is a static pattern."[4] In my own teaching and writing, I have found it helpful to think of literary meaning spatially—as an idea that all the particular details of a work are "about," a "point" to which all the individual words or events in a literary work are relevant, not unlike the "point" of a joke. In a standard handbook for students, Frye suggests a similar procedure as basic to all critical analysis:

The primary understanding of any work of literature has to be based on an assumption of its unity. However mistaken such an assumption may eventually prove to be, nothing can be done unless we start with it as a heuristic principle. Further, every effort should be directed toward understanding the whole of what we read, as though it were all on the same level of achievement.

The critic may meet something that puzzles him, like, say, Mercutio's speech on Queen Mab in *Romeo and Juliet,* and feel that it does not fit. This means either that Shakespeare was a slapdash dramatist or that the critic's conception of the play is inadequate. The odds in favor of the latter conclusion are overwhelming: consequently he would do well to try to arrive at some understanding of the relevance of the puzzling episode. Even if the best he can do for the time being is a far-fetched or obviously rationalized explanation, that is still his sanest and soundest procedure.

The process of academic criticism begins, then, with reading a poem through to the end, suspending value-judgments while doing so. Once the end is reached, we can see the whole design of the work as a unity. It is now a simultaneous pattern radiating out from a center, not a narrative moving in time. The structure is what we call the theme, and the identifying of the theme is the next step ... the theme is not something in the poem, much less a moral precept suggested by it, but the structural principle in the poem.[5]

Meaning in literature—Frye's "poem" is representative of all literature—goes beyond meaning in ordinary discourse to the extent the literary work is shaped and structured by such a central idea.

As a practical matter, it seems to me, most of what we think of as literary analysis is a process of successive abstraction. The skilled reader organizes the details of the text into recurring images and themes. Essentially, he abstracts repeated or contrasted words, images, events, or characters into categories. Some special critics may think in Marxist or psychoanalytic or Swedenborgian terms, but most use categories from everyday discourse. In *Hamlet,* for example, critics will speak of images of disease, incidents of broken rituals, or characters who do as against characters who talk.

If a critic wishes to go as far as he possibly can in this process—many critics, of course, don't—he further re-classifies this first level of abstractions (usually called themes) into a final level consisting of a very few basic terms which the work as a whole is "about." One might, for example, see *Hamlet* as "about" the imperfection that comes between idea and fact. If such a set of terms states the universal intellectual content of the work, if this is its "meaning," then a reader should be able to move from these three very general terms to less general themes like disease, ritual, word-and-deed, and from them back to the text itself. He should be able to see particular manifestations of one or another of the general terms (imperfections, idea, fact) at any point in the text—or else his generalizations from the text left something out.

The technique is a powerful one, as thirty years of "new critical" explications testify. Yet, as anyone knows who has practiced "close reading" or "explication" with students, it often seems overly intellectual, even sterile, certainly far removed from the roots of our pleasure in literature.

By contrast, psychoanalysis seeks out those roots by looking in literary works not so much for a central "point," as for a central fantasy or daydream, familiar from couch or clinic, particular manifestations of which occur all through the text. *Hamlet,* Freud told us sixty-seven years ago, expresses an oedipal fantasy, and all its incidents, imagery, and characters come together around this one issue.

Thus, both a "new critical" reading and a psychoanalytic reading will arrive at something central to a work, some general entity represented at any given point in the text by particular language. What, then, is the relation between these two central entities, one a statement, the other a fantasy? Most critics, I think, would say they are simply two different ways of looking at the text, each valid in its own way, as would be the Marxist or Swedenborgian interpretations. I would like to suggest that, on the contrary, the psychoanalytic reading has a very special relation to any other reading.

Consider, for example, our joke. A modern critic, looking at the joke simply as a literary production, would notice the repeated references to numbers and money. The joke's "incidental imagery" consists of "$100,000," "playing the stock market," "In addition," "slight consideration," "personal bank account of $200,000," the "money," the "company vault." Key phrases are: "What is the consideration I owe you?" "You must spend . . ." "worth it." All these quantifications culminate in the numbering of the young man's years, and one would abstract them as comparing values, distinguishing something from nothing.

The basic metaphor is the bargain. The old woman who can give everything, herself lacks youth and sex. The young man has these two things though he has lost everything else—and they bargain with each other and seem to exchange. As against the motif of exchange stand the un-bargains: the young executive's having "taken $100,000" and lost it "playing"; the witch's not delivering what she promised. Looked at only from the point of view of conscious, intellectual content, the point of the joke seems to be that the young man who thought he would get away with something for nothing or "for a slight consideration," "certainly worth it," finds instead that he has been had for nothing, or for a few magic gestures. More exactly, the joke contrasts what the young executive expected with what he got. He expected to get something (money) for nothing (sex), but he finds he has given something (sex) for nothing (promises of money).

If this analysis of the "point" is correct, if we have found those few terms to which everything else in the joke is related, we should be able to understand the young executive's "character" through this "meaning." Looking at the story realistically, we could say that the young executive's character—to the limited extent we see it in this joke—is that of a man who tries to get what he can of this world's comforts, paying nothing or as little as possible. He is a man who wishes to take into himself what he can. It is fitting, then, that his "punishment" is to be taken in by someone else, for it is a truth well known to confidence men (and artists) that the easiest man to gull is one trying to get something for nothing.

Again, looked at realistically, he is quite sensible to believe and make love to the witch. Having lost everything, he has nothing left to lose. Like a Kierkegaardian knight of faith, he is perfectly right to make the leap into acceptance and trust. His character, in other words, is one particular manifestation of the informing idea of the whole, expecting something for nothing. The joke, in short, is quite moralistic—it punishes the young executive for trying to get something for nothing. And in playing a rather cruel trick on him, it plays a trick on us.

That formulation, however, raises a question more fundamental than meaning. If the joke tricks and fools us, how, then, does it give pleasure? It must give pleasure, or else we would not willingly suspend our disbelief.

I can remember quite vividly, the first time I heard the joke, a fleeting but highly gratifying thought that flashed through my mind when the old lady appeared, did her magic, and made everything right: Oh, if only it were so, if only there were magical people to solve all problems! The punch line quite abruptly deprived me of that fantasy—and yet I laughed and felt pleasure.

What had happened was the feeling from the last line, "I was fooled," had become a reassurance, somehow, not a disappointment. Midway in the joke my feelings toward the old woman changed. At first, she was a powerful parent-figure who would make all well. But then she became quite repulsively seductive. As a result, the feeling "I was fooled" became reassuring: there really are no all-powerful parent-figures who are also frighteningly grabby and seductive and sexual.

It is not hard to recognize a nurturing mother-figure in the crone who usually offers "sonny" all the sustenance he needs at the moment he needs it most. Her repulsiveness in the joke evokes the right feeling, namely, that she is sexually inappropriate, an "old crone on the bed." It is all right to take wish-fulfillment from her, but "distasteful" to make love. The image of taste and her own toothless mouth suggest a fearful fantasy about a mother taking into herself (into her mouth-like genitals) instead of giving into the mouth of her child. The mother-word "sonny" appears at the safe moment—when she lets us know that she is not going to behave like a mother.

In short, the joke gave me pleasure by the way it handled an oedipal fantasy (and I assume that, with appropriate variations, the same mechanism gave pleasure and reassurance to others). This parental reading of the joke gets confirmation from a variant that also went the rounds. Instead of a witch, a devil appears and the "slight consideration" is a night of homosexual love. The variant develops the same conflict between our succoring and our sexual ideas of a parent, but this time it is the father (seen in terms of the negative oedipus complex).

The primary level of the joke's fantasy is oedipal, but underneath that fantasy there is an oral motif. The joke works with a feeling of trusting and expectation that most of us have experienced consciously, but all of us have experienced before we were conscious of ourselves as such. Like Freud and other analysts, Erik Erikson locates its origins in infancy in the period when a child is dependent on its mother for its oral needs, and he shows how that trust leads to "identity." "Basic trust in mutuality is that original 'optimism,' that assumption that 'somebody is there,' without which we cannot live." Identity begins with that nurturing other because the child does not conceive of himself as a separate being until he can trust and await his mother as a separate being.[6] When he accepts her as separate, he has realized he is separate.

In this joke about expectancies and bargains and living or not living up to them, it is surely not difficult to see "mutuality" and "basic trust." We could think of the young executive as suffering oral frustration—his world no longer supports him. When the deprivation the young man suffers makes him feel he can no longer trust his world, he resolves to give up his identity by destroying himself in the engulfing waters of the river. His sense of trust in the old lady leads him instead to an engulfing world of magic, and he becomes a trusting child again. He is "taken in." Figuratively, he is duped; sexually, he is taken into the "toothless" mouth of the crone's genitals. We could even say the hero has a kind of death-and-rebirth through magic: a submerging of his self (from a "bridge") into an underworld of matriarchal magic, then a disillusioning re-emergence into rationality and the real world at the end. He acts out again oral fusion followed by an infant's discovery of his own identity. That is the infantile fantasy the joke works with. On a more realistic level, the young man accepts the witch as real the same way a brainwashed prisoner believes in his keeper; this parent-figure evokes in him the sense of basic trust one associates with a mother at the very moment he most needs that trust to regain his hold on life and his own identity.

At first, the joke reassures us by means of a series of displacements, not unexpectedly, for an exchange or bargain resembles a displacement: both shift attention or concern or, here, valuation from one thing to another. The first words of the joke, for example, shift our attention from the executive's wrongdoing onto his suffering. We pity him rather than condemn him, and we enlist the witch as our aide. At least at first, she, too, seems to pity rather than punish him (just as the story as a whole concerns the seduction of a superego). The "big" concerns of the joke should be the vanished career and the lost money, but these are rendered vaguely and abstractly. The first visual images the joke gives us are the bridge railing and the gnarled hand. In effect, the joke has displaced our attention from the theft and loss to the exchange with the witch. The taboo he broke by stealing becomes quite masked over by the witch's breaking the oedipal taboo.

More exactly, the story displaces the executive's wrongdoing (getting something for nothing) onto the parental witch. Similarly, it displaces our credulity in believing the story at all onto the young executive who believes the witch's story. Then, trust becomes dangerous when the witch becomes sexual. So the punchline undoes both these displacements—we are reassured, we disbelieve again, and we laugh.

To sum up, the story worked with an oral-oedipal fantasy that at first gave pleasure, then anxiety, then pleasure again. The plot and form of the joke served as the defensive ways of handling this fantasy, and the meaning or "point" of the joke turned out to be its intellectual or conceptual transformation. That is, being deprived for expecting something for nothing is simply an intellectual version of the original fantasy: the loss involved in getting mother sexually as against orally. We can call the joke's meaning a transformation analogous to a sublimation, for it makes the unconscious fantasy intellectually, morally, and socially acceptable and even pleasurable; more technically, it makes the fantasy ego-syntonic.

Meaning, then, in one of its aspects, is analogous to the sublimation of an infantile fantasy. Other aspects we shall see in other chapters, but the thesis here is: the meaning of the joke, its point or informing idea, has two levels. The first, conventional literary meaning, states the way the elements of the story are all relevant to an intellectual idea: "getting something for nothing." The second, a psychoanalytic statement, shows how the elements of the story, understood as having unconscious meanings ("toothless mouth" as genitals), are all relevant to a particular unconscious fantasy: being nurtured by a mother as against making love to her. The joke's meaning, then, is not simply a "point" which a static configuration of elements is "about." Rather, its meaning is a dynamic process: the joke transforms the unconscious fantasy at its heart into intellectual terms.

Is this notion of transformation true only for jokes? Or is it true for literature in general? We can test this concept of meaning-as-transformation against a work of literature that bears a striking resemblance to our joke: the Arthurian tale of Chaucer's Wife of Bath.

* * *

[Exposition leading to the conclusions stated below is deleted here. See Holland, pp. 12-20.]

* * *

In short, the Wife of Bath's Tale sets up a fundamental contrast: between masculine, verbal, limiting authority or "maistrie" and feminine submission to the plenitude of experience. In so doing, she sets also the keynote for the three themes of the "Marriage Group" identified by Kittredge: rhetoric, "gentilesse," and, of course, marriage. Rhetoric she identifies with masculine verbalism and "auctoritee," true gentilesse with "experience" and the feminine giving up of "maistrie." And our analysis of the digressions in the Wife of Bath's Tale suggests that a better way than "maistrie" of stating the idea that informs the story is: Which shall have "maistrie"—the imposition of "auctoritee" or submission to "experience"?

This statement of the idea that informs the Tale (and much of the Prologue) gives still another digression relevance: "the wordes bitwene the Somonour and the Frere." Those two worthies represent Mother Church in precisely these two aspects: the Summoner imposes ecclesiastical authority; the Friar begs and is at least supposed to be passive and submissive.

The Wife's Tale purports to prove that if life is to be a contest of authorities, woman will very likely win and man will very likely be unmanned. If, however, man submits to the dominance of a motherly woman, both will gain. The boy-gets-girl ending seems to me a little hard on masculinity, but, all things considered, a happy ending. I am pleased that an old crone becomes a Playmate. And mutual submission and giving seem to be a good thing, even, perhaps, a Christian thing, as hinted by Sir Walter Scott's comment: "What was a mere legendary tale of wonder ... in the verse of Chaucer reminds us of the resurrection of a skeleton, reinvested by a miracle with flesh, complexion, and powers of life and motion."[7] As the loathly lady says when the knight complains of her skeletal qualities,

> I koude amende al this,
> If that me liste, er it were dayes thre,
> So wel ye myghte bere you unto me.

I could amend all this—my poverty, ugliness, low birth, and age—if it pleased me to do so, within three days, provided you bear yourself properly to me. "Dayes thre" suggests to me some doubtful, but perhaps not totally irrelevant associations.

The loathly lady explicitly compares herself to Christ when she claims her "gentilesse" from Christ, not men. She is poor, she says, just like Christ. The analogue that comes most readily to my mind is Flaubert's "The Legend of St. Julian the Hospitaller." There, the saint welcomes a loathsome leper to his hut. When he can love and bed with and embrace this most repulsive of human beings, he finds he is embracing God. The leper is, of course, not the radiant, triumphant Christ of the Transfiguration (not until the end of the story); he is the "man of sorrows" of Isaiah 52 and 53: "His visage was so marred more than any man, and his form more than the sons of men." "He hath no form nor comeliness; and when he shall see him, there is no beauty that we should desire him." "We did esteem him stricken, smitten of God, and afflicted," even as the knight regards his bride. "A fouler wight ther may no man devyse." Her phrase, "dayes thre," would mark the difference between the Christ of the Cross, despised and rejected of men, and the Christ triumphant of the Resurrection. Man's submission to Christ transfigures him, even as the knight's submission transfigures the loathly lady.

If "dayes thre" would have triggered the same associations in the Wife's hearers that it does in me, then her Tale achieved complexities indeed. But it wouldn't have. Professor D. W. Robertson, Jr., has been kind enough to show me how the Tale uses a heroine well known in medieval stories. The loathly lady, he writes,

belongs ... to a common medieval type (also represented by the Wife herself) that can conveniently be described as "The Old Whore," related to Ovid's Dipsas, to La Vieille in the *Roman de la Rose*, and to a number of other figures of the same kind. Specifically, she promises her victim, "I shal fulfille youre worldly appetit" [line 1218] .... The fulfillment she offers, moreover, blatantly disregards the lessons of her preceding discourse, which emphasizes the advantages of (1) virtue, (2) voluntary poverty, and (3) wisdom (the quality honored in old age). The young man is obviously interested in the pleasures of the flesh instead. As soon as the lady has obtained the "maistrie," her victim considers her to be young and fair and true.

To understand this "miracle," it is necessary to know something of medieval moral philosophy. The Old Woman, like the Wife herself, represents the "feminine" element in man (i.e., the senses as distinct from the reason, the flesh as distinct from the spirit, etc.). When this element is given the "maistrie," the victim becomes blinded by his own desires so that he cannot discern even the most obvious truths. Thus, for example, a medieval proverb runs, "He who loves a frog thinks the frog to be Diana." The "miraculous" elements in the story generally should be translated into events that can and do ordinarily take place. We do not, that is, ordinarily encounter "foure and twenty" ladies in a dance who suddenly become a disappointing old hag. We do, however, sometimes discover that the parade of luscious wenches we pursue either in fact or imagination turns out not to be very attractive. To make the "luscious wench" attractive again, all that is really necessary is that we submit to her. That is, whether the "luscious wench" seems to be fair and true or simply another manifestation of fallen Eve, old and ugly, depends entirely on ourselves. The "oldness" of the old whore, incidentally, is not altogether a matter of history, but is related to the "oldness" that Christians are supposed to cast off at baptism (e.g., see Rom. 6:4-6) and periodically thereafter in penance.[8]

In short, to her first audience, the devious Wife has managed to represent as a good thing (and perhaps even as *caritas* itself) a quite un-christian submission to old Eve. If "dayes thre" tipped off a medieval hearer to anything, it was simply that submission to the loathly lady acts as a mocking alternative to and parody of man's proper submission to Christ. The parody, if parody it be, is all the more delicious in that so rigor us a feminist as Dame Alice has quite naturally cast God as a woman.

If the Tale embodies this parody, it becomes one more instance of Chaucer's reinterpreting pagan joys into at least the possibility of Christian values, as in the cruiselike pilgrimage itself or that "aprille" with its amorous birds but restless pilgrims. The Tale as a parody illustrates not only Alisoun's perverse ability to turn conventional churchly views topsy-turvy;[9] it also shows in a larger and less parodic sense a basic pattern of medieval literature. That is, medieval narrative moves not in a pattern of conflict and resolution but in a hierarchy of values:[10] the low—submission to "worldly appetit"—has at least the potential of becoming the high—submission to Christ. After all, lechery was the least of the seven deadly sins.

There is, however, still another dimension of "meaning" in the Wife of Bath's Tale. Chaucer's sources for it are of two types. In the English group, evidently derivative, loving the loathly lady leads to sovereignty in marriage. In the earlier, Irish group, loving the loathly lady leads to a tanist's sovereignty in the kingdom. In either case, the loathly lady would seem to derive from some Persephonic figure deep in the Celtic twilight, some combination of crone and virgin, spring goddess and destroyer, who gives to the year-king who wins her the power to rule.

In the Irish sources, notes Professor Sigmund Eisner, "Her loathly form represents winter." "The original meaning of the marriage. . . . was a seasonal myth—the worldwide belief in marriage between the sun and the earth. The sun, by cohabiting with the earth, insured the earth's customary bounty." In the English sources, the choice is between the lady's being loathly by day or loathly by night, but the implications of day or night match those of spring or winter, and, Eisner concludes, "The prototype of the Wife of Bath's heroine traveled even more widely than Alice herself. Originally, she was the earth goddess who annually married the solar deity."[11]

At a less primitive level, if man submits to the life-and-death power of woman, both gain. If not, both lose. And the Persephonic level fits not only Professor Robertson's reading (submission to the old Eve) and the Wife's concern with phallic loss as against a son's giving in, but also her contrast between imposition of authority and submission to experience—the fertile, giving power of women, be they earth goddesses or just worthy ladies of Bath.

But, as the Friar would surely say at this point, "This is a long preamble of a tale!" Our theme is literary meaning, of which we have seen several different kinds in the Wife of Bath's Tale. From a purely analytic, "new critical" point of view, the story contrasts dominance by verbal or other masculine authority to submission to feminine or other experience. For a modern reader—this modern reader, anyway—that submission seems good: it makes an old crone into a lovely maiden. But as so often for modern readers of medieval literature, what the story means to us ironically reveals our moral and spiritual distance from our forebears. In terms of the traditional allegory pointed out by Professor Robertson, the story contrasts proper Christian values with submission to the Old Whore of "worldly appetit," beautiful (or transfigured) only because man is foolish enough to believe in her. Still more mythically, submission to the Persephonic life-and-death power of woman leads to mutual strength rather than mutual loss (as in the sources studied by Professor Eisner). Psychoanalytically, the reader replaces the danger of phallic woundings, rape, beheading, wearing asses' ears, helplessness, mental impotency or sexual— by submission to a mother's nurturing but also murderously powerful love.

Clearly, meaning is not simply "there" in the text; rather it is something we construct for the text within the limits of the text. And even inconsistent readings may be appropriate: my "modern reader's meaning" may be just as right for some readers as Professor Robertson's interpretation is for Chaucer's first audience.

If you are a critical relativist (as I am on Mondays, Wednesdays, and Fridays), you will simply accept each of these different readings as valid to the extent it brings all the elements of the story together to a single "point." If you are a critical monist (as I am on Tuesdays, Thursdays, and Saturdays), you will carry one step further the process of successive abstraction that led us to these several meanings. You will abstract these various kinds of meaning, the modern reader's meaning, the medieval allegory, the Persephonic myth, and any other interpretations that may turn up subsequently, all together into one abstraction that covers all these possible meanings: perhaps, "Chaucer's Wife of Bath's Tale is a study in authority and submission."*

---

*It is not difficult to demonstrate that any verbal text, taken as a series of discrete words or events, can be recursively classified into a final, single "meaning." Any two things can be logically related: an elephant is like a Rembrandt in that neither is a wastebasket; they are both in the class of non-wastebaskets. One could go on to relate all the elements of a literary text into such classes, and one could classify classes until one arrived at a very small number of classes to one or another of which all elements in the text would be related.

The point is, all these meanings are similar, as we can see if we set them down in a chart:

	AUTHORITY	SUBMISSION
Modern reader's meaning	Masculine, verbal restraint Imposition of "auctoritee" Secular "gentilesse" (restricted to the nobility) Rejected "man of sorrows"	Feminine giving and receiving Submission to "experience" Christian virtues (possible for all) Christ believed in
Medieval meaning	"Worldly appetit" rejected Authority of reason and spirit	The Old Whore adored Submission to senses and flesh
Mythic meaning	Repulsive woman and powerless man	Persephone and the ruler
Psycho-analytic meaning	Phallic wounding	Oral submission

This is, of course, a trivial demonstration. As a practical matter, the elements in a literary text tend to group in classes that represent familiar literary themes: art and nature, appearance and reality, mind and matter, time and eternity, male and female, and so on. As a purely logical matter, however, any number of these traditional themes can be grouped into a unitary "meaning." It is possible. Whether it is desirable is another matter. Most professional critics feel more comfortable with separate themes, not pushing for a final, central statement of meaning to which each and every element of the text is relevant. Either way, however, implicit in any literary text is some grouping, be it full or partial, into meaningful themes. Either way, then, a literary text implies a transformation toward meaningfulness.

The story asks, Which will it be? Which of these two modes shall have "maistrie" over the other? And the story comes out triumphantly for the right-hand side—submission (though that may be good or evil depending on the reader's values). Either way, though, the question and the answer shape and inform the story's incidents and its language. Either way, the story has a theme or themes that are "of sufficient generality to be 'worth something to everybody.'"

Our process of successive abstraction seems sound enough, but it does not explain why Chaucer might have grabbed somebody by his medieval lapels to tell him the story nor why the story has engrossed five centuries of readers (even some modern readers who quite misinterpret it). I claimed at the outset that the psychoanalytic meaning had a special relation to all other meanings. It does so, because the fantasy psychoanalysis discovers at the core of a literary work has a special status in our mental life that moral, medieval, or Marxist ideas do not. These are conscious and adult and intellectual. Fantasies are unconscious, infantile, and fraught with emotion. Fantasies are what make us grab somebody by the lapels. Ideas do so only if they are the later representatives of fantasy. The crucial point, then, in this analysis and in the chart of meanings is: the psychoanalytic meaning underlies all the others.

At the heart of this story we experience a child's fantasy: if I am phallically aggressive and do not submit to my mother, she will castrate me. Fantasies such as this were once all too real to us and a mass of evidence from couch and clinic shows they still provide much of the steam and pattern in our adult lives. If so, then the recognition of the fantasy level in this story points to a very general concept of literary meaning. That is, meaning is not a statement, but a process. The fear, if I do not submit to mother, she will castrate me, becomes in our conscious reading of the story the pleasure of submitting instead of coercing (whether as individual readers we value that pleasure in modern, medieval, or mythic ways).*

The story "means" in that it transforms its unconscious fantasy into social, moral, intellectual, and even mythic terms. Meaning is not a static set of relevancies, but a dynamic process of transforming one kind of relevancy, unconscious, to another, conscious. Sometimes, as in the Wife's Tale, the transformation reverses the unconscious fantasy, making what is

---

*I think, for example, we tend to value experience over Scriptural authority, equal partnership as against authority in marriage, and (some of us anyway) the pleasures of the here-and-now to the traditional values of religion. To a medieval audience, however, Professor Robertson says, "He who allows his wife to dominate him will be served as the Wife of Bath seeks to serve her husbands; he who allows the flesh to dominate the spirit will find it a tyrant like the wife; and, finally, he who disregards the spirit of the Scriptures in favor of experience will find himself enslaved to the Old Law, unredeemed by the 'freedom wherewith Christ hath made us free.'"[12]

fearful desirable. Other stories, like the *Playboy* joke, are more like a sublimation, making illicit wishes conform to moral demands. But all stories— and all literature—have this basic way of meaning: they transform the unconscious fantasy discoverable through psychoanalysis into the conscious meanings discovered by conventional interpretation.

We can represent this transformation, this special status of psychoanalytic "meaning," graphically. We begin with a text which is, ultimately, a discrete collection of words:

x x x x x x x x x x x x x x x x x x x x x x x x x x x x x x x x x x x x x x

The text has a direction; it begins, progresses, and ends. But a skilled reader also gives the text meaning by making connections between all the parts of the text, regardless of direction or position. He makes it, in Frye's phrasing, "a simultaneous pattern radiating out from a center, not a narrative moving in time." As I see it, the skilled reader abstracts recurring images, incidents, characters, forms, and all the rest into certain themes. In the Wife's Tale, for example, he finds themes of male-female, withholding-giving, words-experience, old-young, and so on. We can represent this abstraction into themes as a kind of "stretching" of the text:

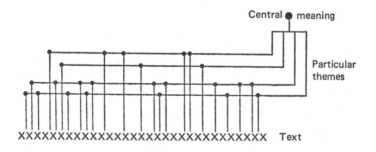

Some readers might then take the final step of abstracting all these several themes into a single, central, nuclear "meaning" such as "authority and submission." If psychoanalytic themes and meaning were like the rest, they would fit simply as one particular grouping into this general picture. But the fantasies the psychoanalytic reading discovers have a special status: infantile, primitive, bodily, charged with fear and desire, we know from clinical evidence they involve the deepest roots of our cumulating lives. Nor can they be abstracted as other meanings can, by the commonsensical, "square" categories of ordinary experience or logic. Rather, they come together by the curious, abrupt groupings known as primary-process thinking: condensations, displacements, symbolizations, projections, splittings, klang associations, and the like. We need therefore to represent the psychoanalytic reading and the primary-process connections among its themes in a special, pre-logical way:

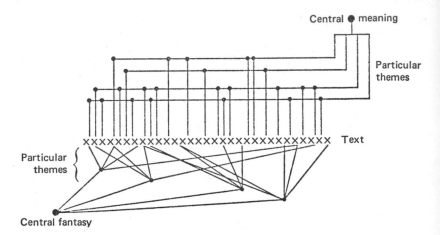

Consciously, we arrive at the psychoanalytic reading by a process not unlike our approach to other kinds of meaning. We abstract images, incidents, characters, forms, and the rest into certain psychological themes: man-woman, mother-child, castration-gratification, coercion-submission, and so on. It is more necessary than in ordinary reading to pull these together into the central fantasy drawn from clinical evidence: if I am phallically coercive, mother will punish me, if I submit, she will gratify me. It is more necessary to think the psychoanalytic reading through to its ultimate form, because it is this ultimate form of the fantasy that generates our response. It is from such deep and fearful roots of our most personal experience that literature gets its power and drive.

We shall return to this picture again and again, for it represents in at least a concise and, I hope, a helpful way "the dynamics of literary response." We shall, however, have to develop it further, for a number of things are missing. Most important, we have been able so far to represent only the text, not the reader. If he appears at all, he is only the invisible agent of this "stretching" of a discrete collection of words. We have talked about meaning, but not form (which will appear in chapter 4). Especially lacking is an account of the role of language (chapter 5).

But we have made a beginning. We have been able to see at least a major force in the pleasure we get from literature. Literature transforms our primitive wishes and fears into significance and coherence, and this transformation gives us pleasure. It is this transformation of deep personal feelings that Freud called "the innermost secret," "the essential *ars poetica*" in which the writer "softens the egotistical character of the daydream." It is this act of meaning that transmutes in laymen's terms, "something that's only of interest to yourself" into "something that is worth something to everybody."

What is worth something to everybody, though, is not the general statement that informs the literary work, the "moral" of the story, but our pleasure in the act of transformation which reaches that moral (or social, intellectual, religious, or philosophical) theme. Fantasy gives force to conscious meaning, but conscious meaning mollifies and manages our deepest fears and drives. If we wish to see literature in its fullness, then, we must deal not with conscious meaning alone or unconscious alone, but the transformation of each into the other. As so often in literary matters, either-or must give way to both-and, the point not only the loathly lady makes, but even the ferociously charitable Wife of Bath herself.

NOTES

1.   Adapted from *Playboy Magazine*, March 1964, p. 94, copyright 1964, reprinted here by permission of the publishers. I am grateful to Mr. Stanley Mackenzie for calling the joke to my attention.
2.   *Writers at Work: The Paris Review Interviews*, ed. Malcolm Cowley (New York, 1958), pp. 180-81.
3.   "The Creative Writer and Day-Dreaming" (1908), Collected Papers, ed. Ernest Jones, trans. Joan Rivière (5 vols. London, 1956-57), IV, 183.
4.   *Anatomy of Criticism: Four Essays* (Princeton, N. J., 1957), p. 158.
5.   *The Aims and Methods of Scholarship in Modern Languages and Literatures*, ed. James Thorpe (New York, 1963), "Literary Criticism," pp. 63-65.
6.   Erik H. Erikson, *Young Man Luther: A Study in Psychoanalysis and History* (New York, 1962), p. 118. See also Sigmund Freud, *Civilization and Its Discontents* (1930 [1929]), ch. I, *Std. Edn.*, XXI, 64-73.
7.   "The Wife of Bath," *The Works of John Dryden*, ed. Sir Walter Scott, 18 vols. (London, 1808), XI, 376.
8.   Personal communication, 25 November 1965.
9.   D. W. Robertson, Jr., *A Preface to Chaucer: Studies in Medieval Perspectives* (Princeton, 1963), pp. 317-31.
10.   *Preface to Chaucer*, ch. I.
11.   Sigmund Eisner, *A Tale of Wonder: A Source Study of the Wife of Bath's Tale* (Wexford, Ireland, 1957), pp. 37, 38, 104, and 141. See also B. J. Whiting, "The Wife of Bath's Tale," in *Sources and Analogues of Chaucer's Canterbury Tales*, eds. W. F. Bryan and Germaine Dempster (Chicago, 1941), pp. 223-68.
12.   *Preface to Chaucer*, p. 330.

STANLEY E. FISH

LITERATURE IN THE READER: AFFECTIVE STYLISTICS

I

Meaning as Event

If at this moment someone were to ask, "What are you doing?" you might reply, "I am reading," and thereby acknowledge the fact that reading is an activity, something *you do*. No one would argue that the act of reading can take place in the absence of someone who reads—how can you tell the dance from the dancer?—but curiously enough when it comes time to make analytical statements about the end product of reading (meaning or understanding), the reader is usually forgotten or ignored. Indeed in recent literary history he has been excluded by legislation. I refer, of course, to the *ex cathedra* pronouncements of Wimsatt and Beardsley in their enormously influential article "The Affective Fallacy":

> The Affective Fallacy is a confusion between the poem and its *results* (what it *is* and what it *does*). . . . It begins by trying to derive the standards of criticism from the psychological effects of the poem and ends in impressionism and relativism. The outcome . . . is that the poem itself, as an object of specifically critical judgment, tends to disappear.[1]

In time, I shall return to these arguments, not so much to refute them as to affirm and embrace them; but I would first like to demonstrate the explanatory power of a method of analysis which takes the reader, as an actively mediating presence, fully into account, and which, therefore, has as its focus the "psychological effects" of the utterance. And I would like to begin with a sentence that does not open itself up to the questions we usually ask.

That Judas perished by hanging himself, there is no certainty in Scripture: though in one place it seems to affirm it, and by a doubtful word hath given occasion to translate it; yet in another place, in a more punctual description, it maketh it improbable, and seems to overthrow it.

Ordinarily, one would begin by asking "What does this sentence mean?" or "What is it about?" or "What is it saying?" all of which preserve the objectivity of the utterance. For my purposes, however, this particular sentence has the advantage of not saying anything. That is, you can't get a fact out of it which could serve as an answer to any one of these questions. Of course, this difficulty is itself a fact—of response; and it suggests, to me at least, that what makes problematical sense as a statement makes perfect sense as a strategy, as an action made upon a reader rather than as a container from which a reader extracts a message. The strategy or action here is one of progressive decertainizing. Simply by taking in the first clause of the sentence, the reader commits himself to its assertion, "that Judas perished by hanging himself" (in constructions of this type "that" is understood to be shorthand for "the *fact* that"). This is not so much a conscious decision, as it is an anticipatory adjustment to his projection of the sentence's future contours. He knows (without giving cognitive form to his knowledge) that this first clause is preliminary to some larger assertion (it is a "ground") and he must be in control of it if he is to move easily and confidently through what follows; and in the context of this "knowledge," he is prepared, again less than consciously, for any one of several constructions:

That Judas perished by hanging himself, *is* (an example for us all).
That Judas perished by hanging himself, *shows* (how conscious he was of the enormity of his sin).
That Judas perished by hanging himself, *should* (give us pause).

The range of these possibilities (and there are, of course, more than I have listed) narrows considerably as the next three words are read, "there is no." At this point, the reader is expecting, and even predicting, a single word—"doubt"; but instead he finds "certainty"; and at that moment the status of the fact that had served as his point of reference becomes *un*certain. (It is nicely ironic that the appearance of "certainty" should be the occasion for doubt, whereas the word "doubt" would have contributed to the reader's certainty.) As a result, the terms of the reader's relationship to the sentence undergo a profound change. He is suddenly involved in a different kind of activity. Rather than following an argument along a well-lighted path (a light, after all, has gone *out*), he is now looking for one. The natural impulse in a situation like this, either in life or in literature, is to go forward in the hope that what has been obscured will again become clear; but in this case going forward only intensifies the reader's sense of disorientation. The prose is continually opening, but then closing, on the possibility of verification in one direction or another. There are two vocabularies in the sentence; one holds out the promise of a clarification—"place," "affirm," "place," "punctual," "overthrow"—while the other continually defaults on that promise—"though," "doubtful," "yet," "improbable," "seems"; and the reader is passed back and forth between them and between the alternatives—that Judas did or did not perish by hanging himself—which are still suspended (actually it is the reader who is suspended) when the sentence ends (trails off? gives up?). The indeterminateness of this experience is compounded by a superfluity of pronouns. It becomes increasingly difficult to tell what "it" refers to, and if the reader takes the trouble to retrace his steps, he is simply led back to "that Judas perished by hanging himself"; in short, he exchanges an indefinite pronoun for an even less definite (that is, certain) assertion.

Whatever is persuasive and illuminating about this analysis (and it is by no means exhaustive) is the result of my substituting for one question—what does this sentence mean?—another, more operational question—what does this sentence do? And what the sentence does is give the reader something and then take it away, drawing him on with the unredeemed promise of its return. An observation about the sentence as an utterance—its refusal to yield a declarative statement—has been transformed into an account of its experience (not being able to get a fact out of it). It is no longer an object, a thing-in-itself, but an *event,* something that *happens* to, and with the participation of, the reader. And it is this event, this happening—all of it and not anything that could be said about it or any information one might take away from it—that is, I would argue, the *meaning* of the sentence. (Of course, in this case there is no information to take away.)

This is a provocative thesis whose elaboration and defense will be the concern of the following pages, but before proceeding to it, I would like to examine another utterance which also (conveniently) says nothing:

Nor did they not perceive the evil plight.

The first word of this line from *Paradise Lost* (I.335) generates a rather precise (if abstract) expectation of what will follow: a negative assertion which will require for its completion a subject and a verb. There are then two "dummy" slots in the reader's mind waiting to be filled. This expectation is strengthened (if only because it is not challenged) by the auxiliary "did" and the pronoun "they." Presumably, the verb is not far behind. But in its place the reader is presented with a second negative, one that can not be accommodated within his projection of the utterance's form. His progress through the line is halted and he is forced to come to terms with the intrusive (because unexpected) "not." In effect what the reader *does*, or is forced to do, at this point, is ask a question—did they or didn't they?—and in search of an answer he either rereads—in which case he simply repeats the sequence of mental operations—or goes forward—in which case he finds the anticipated verb, but in either case the syntactical uncertainty remains unresolved.

It could be objected that the solution to the difficulty is simply to invoke the rule of the double negative; one cancels the other and the "correct" reading is therefore "They did perceive the evil plight." But however satisfactory this may be in terms of the internal logic of grammatical utterances (and even in those terms there are problems[2]), it has nothing to do with the logic of the reading experience or, I would insist, with its meaning. That experience is a temporal one, and in the course of it the two negatives combine not to produce an affirmative, but to prevent the reader from making the simple (declarative) sense which would be the goal of a logical analysis. To clean the line up is to take from it its most prominent and important effect—the suspension of the reader between the alternatives its syntax momentarily offers. What is a problem if the line is considered as an object, a thing-in-itself, becomes a *fact* when it is regarded as an occurrence. The reader's inability to tell whether or not "they" do perceive and his involuntary question (or its psychological equivalent) are events in his encounter with the line, and as events they are part of the line's *meaning*, even though they take place in the mind, not on the page. Subsequently, we discover that the answer to the question "Did they or didn't they?" is "They did and they didn't." Milton is exploiting (and calling our attention to) the two senses of "perceive": they (the fallen angels) do perceive the fire, the pain, the gloom; physically they see it; however they are blind to the moral significance of their situation; and in that sense they do not perceive the evil plight in which they are. But that is another story.

Underlying these two analyses is a method, rather simple in concept, but complex (or at least complicated) in execution. The concept is simply the rigorous and disinterested asking of the question, what does this word, phrase, sentence, paragraph, chapter, novel, play, poem, *do?* and the execution involves *an analysis of the developing responses of the reader in relation to the words as they succeed one another in time.* Every word in this statement bears a special emphasis. The analysis must be of the developing responses to distinguish it from the atomism of much stylistic criticism. A reader's response to the fifth word in a line or sentence is to a large extent the product of his responses to words one, two, three, and four. And by response, I intend more than the range of feelings (what Wimsatt and Beardsley call "the purely affective reports"). The category of response includes any and all of the activities provoked by a string of words: the projection of syntactical and/or lexical probabilities; their subsequent occurrence or non-occurrence; attitudes towards persons, or things, or ideas referred to; the reversal or questioning of those attitudes; and much more. Obviously, this imposes a great burden on the analyst who in his observations on any one moment in the reading experience must take into account all that has happened (in the reader's mind) at previous moments, each of which was in its turn subject to the accumulating pressures of its predecessors. (He must also take into account influences and pressures pre-dating the actual reading experience—questions of genre, history, etc.—questions we shall consider later.) All of this is included in the phrase "in time." The basis of the method is a consideration of the *temporal* flow of the reading experience, and it is assumed that the reader responds in terms of that flow, and not to the whole utterance. That is, in an utterance of any length, there is a point at which the reader has taken in only the first word, and then the second, and then the third, and so on, and the report of what happens to the reader is always a report of what has happened *to that point.* (The report includes the reader's set toward future experiences, but not those experiences.)

The importance of this principle is illustrated when we reverse the first two clauses of the Judas sentence: "There is no certainty that Judas perished by hanging himself." Here the status of the assertion is never in doubt because the reader knows from the beginning that it is doubtful; he is given a perspective from which to view the statement and that perspective is confirmed rather than challenged by what follows; even the confusion of pronouns in the second part of the sentence will not be disturbing to him, because it can easily be placed in the context of his initial response. There is no difference in these two sentences in the information conveyed (or not conveyed), or in the lexical and syntactical components,[3] only in the way these are received. But that one difference makes *all* the difference—between an uncomfortable, unsettling experience in which the gradual dimming of a fact is attended by a failure in perception, and a wholly self-satisfying one in which an uncertainty is comfortably certain, and the reader's confidence in his own powers remains unshaken, because he is always in control. It is, I insist, a difference in meaning.

The results (I will later call them advantages) of this method are fairly, though not exhaustively, represented in my two examples. Essentially what the method does is *slow down* the reading experience so that "events" one does not notice in normal time, but which do occur, are brought before our analytical attentions. It is as if a slow motion camera with an automatic stop action effect were recording our linguistic experiences and presenting them to us for viewing. Of course the value of such a procedure is predicated on the idea of *meaning as an event,* something that is happening between the words and in the reader's mind, something not visible to the naked eye, but which can be made visible (or at least palpable) by the regular introduction of a "searching" question (what does this do?). It is more usual to assume that meaning is a function of the utterance, and to equate it with the information given (the message) or the attitude expressed. That is, the components of an utterance are considered either in relation to each other or to a state of affairs in the outside world, or to the state of mind of the speaker-author. In any and all of these variations, meaning is located (presumed to be imbedded) *in* the utterance, and the apprehension of meaning is an act of extraction.[4] In short, there is little sense of process and even less of the reader's actualizing participation in that process.

This concentration on the verbal object as a thing in itself, and as a repository of meaning, has many consequences, theoretical and practical. First of all, it creates a whole class of utterances, which because of their alleged transparency, are declared to be uninteresting as objects of analysis. Sentences or fragments of sentences that immediately "make sense" (a deeply revealing phrase if one thinks about it) are examples of ordinary language; they are neutral and styleless statements, "simply" referring, or "simply" reporting. But the application to such utterances of the question "What does it do?" (which assumes that something is *always* happening) reveals that a great deal is going on in their production and comprehension *(every linguistic experience is affecting and pressuring)* although most of it is going on so close up, at such a basic, "preconscious" level of experience, that we tend to overlook it. Thus the utterance (written or spoken) "There is a chair" is at once understood as the report either of an existing state of affairs or of an act of perception (I see a chair). In either frame of reference, it makes immediate sense. To my mind, however, what is interesting about the utterance is the sub rosa message it puts out *by virtue of* its easy comprehensibility. Because it gives information directly and simply, it asserts (silently, but effectively) the "givability," directly and simply, of information; and it is thus an extension of the ordering operation we perform on experience whenever it is filtered through our temporal-spatial consciousness. In short it *makes* sense, in exactly the way we make (i.e., manufacture) sense of whatever, if anything, exists outside us; and by making easy sense it tells us that sense can be easily made and that we are capable of easily making it. A whole document consisting of such utterances—a chemistry text or a telephone book—will be telling us that all the time; and *that,* rather than any reportable "content," will be its *meaning.* Such language can be called "ordinary" only because it confirms and reflects our ordinary understanding of the world and our position in it; but for precisely that reason it is *extra*ordinary (unless we accept a naive epistemology which grants us unmediated access to reality—and to leave it unanalyzed is to risk missing much of what happens—to us and through us—when we read and (or so we think) understand.

In short, the problem is simply that most methods of analysis operate at so high a level of abstraction that the basic data of the *meaning experience* is slighted and/or obscured. In the area of specifically literary studies, the effects of a naive theory of utterance meaning and of its attendant assumption of ordinary language can be seen in what is acknowledged to be the sorry state of the criticism of the novel and of prose in general. This is usually explained with reference to a distinction between ordinary language and poetic language. Poetry, it is asserted, is characterized by a high incidence of deviance from normal syntactical and lexical habits. It therefore offers the analyst-critic a great many points of departure. Prose, on the other hand (except for Baroque eccentrics like Thomas Browne and James Joyce) is, well, just prose, and just there. It is this helplessness before all but the most spectacular effects that I would remedy; although in one way the two examples with which this essay began were badly chosen, since they were analyses of utterances that are obviously and problematically deviant. This, of course, was a ploy to gain your attention. Assuming that I now have it, let me insist that the method shows to best advantage when it is applied to unpromising material. Consider for example this sentence (actually part of a sentence) from Pater's "Conclusion" to *The Renaissance,* which, while it is hardly the stuff of everyday conversation, does not, at first sight, afford much scope for the critic's analytical skill:

That clear perpetual outline of face and limb is but an image of ours.

What can one say about a sentence like this? The analyst of style would, I fear, find it distressingly straightforward and non-deviant, a simple declarative of the form X is Y. And if he were by chance drawn to it, he would not be likely to pay very much attention to the first word— "That." It is simply there. But of course it is not simply there; it is *actively* there, doing something, and what that something is can be discovered by asking the question "What does it do?" The answer is obvious, right there in front of our noses, although we may not see it until we ask the question. "That" is a demonstrative, a word that points *out,* and as one takes it *in,* a sense of its referent (yet unidentified) is established. Whatever "that" is, it is outside, at a distance from the observer-reader; it is "pointable to" (pointing is what the word "that" does), something of substance and solidity. In terms of the reader's response, "that" generates an expectation that impels him forward, the expectation of finding out *what* "that" is. The word and its effect are the basic data of the meaning experience and they will direct our description of that experience because they direct the reader.

The adjective "clear" works in two ways; it promises the reader that when "that" appears, he will be able to see it easily, and, conversely, that it can be easily seen. "Perpetual" stabilizes the visibility of "that" even *before* it is seen and "outline" gives it potential form, while at the same time raising a question. That question—outline of what?—is obligingly answered by the phrase "of face and limb," which, in effect, fills the outline in. By the time the reader reaches the declarative verb "is"— which sets the seal on the objective reality of what has preceded it—he is fully and securely oriented in a world of perfectly discerned objects and perfectly discerning observers, of whom he is one. But then the sentence turns on the reader, and takes away the world it has itself created. With "but" the easy progress through the sentence is impeded (it is a split second before one realizes that "but" has the force of "only"); the declarative force of "is" is weakened and the status of the firmly drawn outline the reader has been pressured to accept is suddenly uncertain; "image" resolves that uncertainty, but in the direction of insubstantiality; and the now blurred form disappears altogether when the phrase "of ours" collapses the disinction between the reader and that which is (or was) "without" (Pater's own word). Now you see it (that), now you don't. Pater giveth and Pater taketh away. (Again this description of the reader's experience is an analysis of the sentence's meaning and if you were to ask, "But, what does it mean?" I would simply repeat the description.)

What is true of this sentence is true, I believe, of much of what we hold ourselves responsible for as critics and teachers of literature. There is more to it, that is, to its experience, than meets the casual eye. What is required then is a method, a machine if you will, which in its operation makes observable, or at least accessible, what goes on below the level of self-conscious response. Everyone would admit that something "funny" happens in the "Judas" sentence from Browne's *Religio Medici* and that there is a difficulty built into the reading and understanding of the line from *Paradise Lost;* but there is a tendency to assume that the Pater sentence is a simple assertion (whatever that is). It is of course, nothing of the kind. In fact it is not an assertion at all, although (the promise of) an assertion is one of its components. It is an experience; it occurs; it does something; it makes us do something. Indeed, I would go so far as to say, in direct contradiction of Wimsatt-Beardsley, that what it does is what it means.

II

The Logic and Structure of Response

What I am suggesting is that there is no direct relationship between the meaning of a sentence (paragraph, novel, poem) and what its words mean. Or, to put the matter less provocatively, the information an utterance gives, its message, is a constituent of, but certainly not to be identified with, its meaning. It is the experience of an utterance—*all* of it and not anything that could be said about it, including anything I could say—that *is* its meaning.

It follows, then, that it is impossible to mean the same thing in two (or more) different ways, although we tend to think that it happens all the time. We do this by substituting for our immediate linguistic experience an interpretation or abstraction of it, in which "it" is inevitably compromised. We contrive to forget what has happened to us in our life with language, removing ourselves as far as possible from the linguistic event before making a statement about it. Thus we say, for example, that "the book of the father" and "the father's book" mean the same thing, forgetting that "father" and "book" occupy different positions of emphasis in our different experiences; and as we progress in this forgetting, we become capable of believing that sentences as different as these are equivalent in meaning:

> This fact is concealed by the influence of language, moulded by science, which foists on us exact concepts as though they represented the immediate deliverances of experience.
>
> A. N. Whitehead

> And if we continue to dwell in thought on this world, not of objects in the solidity with which language invests them, but of impressions, unstable, flickering, inconsistent, which burn and are extinguished with our consciousness of them, it contracts still further.
>
> Walter Pater

It is (literally) tempting to say that these sentences make the same point: that language which pretends to precision operates to obscure the flux and disorder of actual experience. And of course they do, if one considers them at a high enough level of generality. But as individual experiences through which a reader lives, they are not alike at all, and neither, therefore, are their meanings.

To take the Whitehead sentence first, it simply doesn't mean what it says; for as the reader moves through it, he experiences the stability of the world whose existence it supposedly denies. The word "fact" itself makes an exact concept out of the idea of inexactness; and by referring backward to find its referent—"the radically untidy ill-adjusted character of ... experience"—the reader performs the characteristic action required of him by this sentence, the fixing of things in their place.

There is nothing untidy either in the sentence or in our experience of it. Each clause is logically related to its predecessors and prepares the way for what follows; and since our active attention is required only at the points of relation, the sentence is divided *by us* into a succession of discrete areas, each of which is dominated by the language of certainty. Even the phrase "as though they represented" falls into this category, since its stress falls on "they represented" which then thrusts us forward to the waiting "deliverances of experience." In short, the sentence, in its action upon us, declares the tidy well-ordered character of actual experience, and that is its meaning.

At first the Pater sentence is self-subverting in the same way. The least forceful word in its first two clauses is "not," which is literally overwhelmed by the words that surround it—"world," "objects," "solidity," "language"; and by the time the reader reaches the "but" in "but of impressions," he finds himself inhabiting (dwelling in) a "world" of fixed and "solid" objects. It is of course a world made up of words, constructed in large part by the reader himself as he performs grammatical actions which reinforce the stability of its phenomena. By referring backwards from "them" to "objects," the reader accords "objects" a place in the sentence (whatever can be referred back to must be somewhere) and in his mind. In the second half of the sentence, however, this same world is unbuilt. There is still a backward dependence to the reading experience, but the point of reference is the word "impressions"; and the series which follows it—"unstable," "flickering," "inconsistent"—serves only to accentuate its *in*stability. Like Whitehead, Pater perpetrates the very deception he is warning against; but this is only one part of his strategy. The other is to break down (extinguish) the coherence of the illusion he has created. Each successive stage of the sentence is less exact (in Whitehead's terms) than its predecessors, because at each successive stage the reader is given less and less to hold on to; and when the corporeality of "this world" has wasted away to an "it" ("it contracts still further"), he is left with nothing at all.

One could say, I suppose, that at the least these two sentences gesture toward the same insight; but even this minimal statement makes me uneasy, because "insight" is another word that implies, "There it is, I've got it." And this is exactly the difference between the two sentences: Whitehead lets you get "it" ("the neat, trim, tidy, exact world"), while Pater gives you the experience of having "it" melt under your feet. It is only when one steps back from the sentences that they are in any way equivalent; and stepping back is what an analysis in terms of doing and happenings does not allow.

The analysis of the Pater sentence illustrates another feature of the method, its independence of linguistic logic. If a casual reader were asked to point out the most important word in the second clause—"not of objects in the solidity with which language invests them"—he would probably answer "not," because as a logical marker "not" controls everything that follows it. But as one component in an experience, it is hardly controlling at all; for as the clause unfolds, "not" has less and less a claim on our attention and memories; working against it, and finally overwhelming it, as we saw, is an unbroken succession of more forceful words. My point of course is that in an analysis of the sentence as a thing in itself, consisting of words arranged in syntacto-logical relationships, "not" would figure prominently, while in an experiential analysis it is noted chiefly for its weakness.

The case is even clearer and perhaps more interesting in this sentence from one of Donne's sermons:

And therefore, as the mysteries of our religions are not the objects of our reason, but by faith we rest on God's decree and purpose (it is so, O God, because it is thy will it should be so) So God's decrees are ever to be considered in the manifestation thereof.

Here the "not"—again logically controlling—is subverted by the very construction in which it is imbedded; for that construction, unobtrusively, but nonetheless effectively, pressures the reader to perform exactly those mental operations whose propriety the statement of the sentence—what it is saying—is challenging. That is, a paraphrase of the material before the parenthesis might read—"Matters of faith and religion are not the objects of our reason"; but the simple act of taking in the words "And therefore" involves us unavoidably in reasoning about matters of faith and religion; in fact so strong is the pull of these words that our primary response to this part of the sentence is one of anticipation; we are waiting for a "so" clause to complete the logically based sequence begun by "And therefore as." But when that "so" appears, it is not at all what we had expected, for it is the "so" of divine fiat—"It is so, O God, because it is thy will it should be so"—of a causality more real than any that can be observed in nature or described in a natural (human) language. The speaker, however, completes his "explaining" and "organizing" statement as if its silent claim to be a window on reality were still unquestioned. As a result the reader is alerted to the inadequacy of the very process in which he is (through the syntax) involved, and at the same time he accepts the necessity, for limited human beings, of proceeding within the now discredited assumptions of that process.

Of course, a formalist analysis of this sentence would certainly have discovered the tension between the two "so's," one a synonym for "therefore," the other shorthand for "so be it," and might even have gone on to suggest that the relationship between them is a mirror of the relationship between the mysteries of faith and the operations of reason. I doubt, however, that a formalist analysis would have brought us to the point where we could see the sentence, and the mode of discourse it represents, as a self-deflating joke ("thereof" mocks "therefore"), to which the reader responds and of which he is a victim. In short, and to repeat myself, to consider the utterance apart from the consciousness receiving it is to risk missing a great deal of what is going on. It is a risk which analysis in terms of "doings and happenings"[5] works to minimize.

Another advantage of the method is its ability to deal with sentences (and works) that don't mean anything, in the sense of not making sense. Literature, it is often remarked (either in praise or with contempt), is largely made up of such utterances. (It is an interesting comment on both Dylan Thomas and the proponents of a deviation theory of poetic language that their examples so often are taken from his work.) In an experiential analysis, the sharp distinction between sense and nonsense, with the attendant value judgments and the talk about truth content, is blurred, because the place where sense is made or not made is the reader's mind rather than the printed page or the space between the covers of a book. For an example, I turn once again, and for the last time, to Pater.

This at least of flame-like, our life has, that it is but the concurrence, renewed from moment to moment, of forces parting sooner or later on their ways.

This sentence deliberately frustrates the reader's natural desire to organize the particulars it offers. One can see for instance how different its experience would be if "concurrences of forces" were substituted for "concurrence, renewed from moment to moment, of forces." The one allows and encourages the formation of a physical image which has a spatial reality; the mind imagines (pictures) separate and distinct forces converging, in an orderly fashion, on a center where they form a new, but still recognizable and manageable (in a mental sense), force; the other determinedly prevents that image from forming. Before the reader can respond fully to "concurrence," "renewed" stops him by making the temporal status of the motion unclear. Has the concurrence already taken place? Is it taking place now? Although "from moment to moment" answers these questions, it does so at the expense of the assumptions behind them; the phrase leaves no time for anything so formal and chartable as a "process." For "a moment," at "of forces," there is a coming together; but in the next moment, the moment when the reader takes in "parting," they separate. Or do they? "Sooner or later" upsets this new attempt to find pattern and direction in "our life" and the reader is once more disoriented, spatially and temporally. The final deterrent to order is the plural "ways," which prevents the mind's eye from travelling down a single path and insists on the haphazardness and randomness of whatever it is that happens sooner or later.

Of course this reading of the sentence (that is, of its effects) ignores its status as a logical utterance. "Concurrence, renewed from moment to moment, of forces" is meaningless as a statement corresponding to a state of affairs in the "real" world; but its refusal to mean in that discursive way creates the experience that is its meaning; and an analysis of that experience rather than of logical content is able to make sense of one kind—experiential sense—out of nonsense.

A similar (and saving) operation can be performed on units larger than the sentence. One of Plato's more problematical dialogues is the *Phaedrus*, in part because its final assertion—"no work . . . has ever been written or recited that is worthy of serious attention"—seems to be contradicted by its very existence. This "embarrassment" has been the cause of a great many articles, often entitled "The Unity of the *Phaedrus*," in which the offending section is somehow accounted for, usually by explaining it away. What these studies attempt to discover is the *internal* unity of the *Phaedrus*, its coherence as a self-contained artifact; but if we look for the coherence of the dialogue in the reader's experience of it rather than in its formal structure, the "inconsistency" is less a problem to be solved than something that happens, a fact of response; and as a fact of response it is the key to the way the work works. Rather than a single sustained argument, the *Phaedrus* is a series of discrete conversations or seminars, each with its own carefully posed question, ensuing discussion, and firmly drawn conclusion; but so arranged that to enter into the spirit and assumptions of any one of these self-enclosed units is implicitly to reject the spirit and assumptions of the unit immediately preceding. This is a pattern which can be clearly illustrated by the relationship between the speech of Lysias and the first speech delivered by Socrates. Lysias' speech is criticized for not conforming to the definition of a good discourse: "Every discourse, like a living creature, should be so put together that it has its own body and lacks neither head or feet, middle nor extremities, all composed in such a way that they suit both each other and the whole."[6] Socrates, in fact, is quite careful to rule out any other standard of judgment: it is the "arrangement" rather than the "invention" or "relevance" that concerns him as a critic. Subsequently, Socrates' own effort on the same theme is criticized for its impiety, an impiety, moreover, that is compounded by its effectiveness as a "piece of rhetoric." In other words, Lysias' speech is bad because it is not well put together and Socrates' speech is bad because it is well put together.

Although neither Socrates nor Phaedrus acknowledges the contradiction, the reader, who has fallen in (perhaps involuntarily) with the standards of judgment established by the philosopher himself, is certainly confronted with it, and asked implicitly to do something with it. What he does (or should do) is realize that in the condemnation of Socrates' speech a new standard (of impiety) has been introduced, one that invalidates the very basis on which the discussion (and his reading experience) had hitherto been proceeding. At that moment, this early section of the dialogue will have achieved its true purpose, which is, paradoxically, to bring the reader to the point where he is no longer interested in the issues it treats; no longer interested because he has come to see that the real issues exist at a higher level of generality. Thus, in a way peculiar to dialectical form and experience, this space of prose and argument will have been the vehicle of its own abandonment.

Nor is that by any means the end of the matter. This pattern, in which the reader is first encouraged to entertain assumptions he probably already holds and then is later forced to re-examine and discredit those same assumptions, is repeated again and again. In the middle section of the dialogue, the two friends agree to explore the subject of "good" and "bad" writing; and Socrates argues against the sophist position that an orator "may neglect what is really good . . . for it is from what seems to be true that persuasion comes, not from the real truth" (p. 46). It is essential, counters Socrates, for a "competent speaker" to know the truth about all things and subjects, for unless he does—and here the reader anticipates some kind of equation between good writing and a concern for the truth—he will be unable to *deceive* ("When a man sets out to deceive someone else without being taken in himself, he must accurately grasp the similarity and dissimilarity of the facts"). While art and truth have been joined in one context—the ruthlessly practical context of manipulative rhetoric—a wedge has been driven between them in another—the moral context assumed at the beginning of the discussion. To the earlier insight that a well-made speech is not necessarily a "true" speech (in the moral sense), the reader must now add the further (and extending) insight that "well-madeness" is likely to be a weapon in the arsenal of Truth's enemies. So that what was a first a standard of judgment to which Socrates, Phaedrus, *and* the reader repaired, is now seen to be positively deleterious to the higher standard now only gradually emerging from the dialogue.

The important word in my last sentence is "seen"; for it suggests that what is being processed by the *Phaedrus* is not an argument or a proposition, but a vision. As an argument, in fact, the dialogue makes no sense, since Socrates is continually reaching conclusions which he subsequently, and without comment, abandons. But as an attempt to refine its reader's vision it makes a great deal of sense, for then the contradictions, the moments of "blurring," become invitations to examine closely premises too easily acquiesced in. The reader who accepts this invitation will find, on retracing his steps, that statements and phrases which had seemed unexceptionable are now suspect and dubious; and that lines of reasoning which had seemed proper and to the point are now disastrously narrow. Of course they—phrases, statements, premises, and conclusions—haven't changes (as Socrates remarks later, "Written words . . . go on telling you the same thing over and over"), but the *reader* has, and with each change he is able to dispense with whatever section of the dialogue he has been reading, because he has passed beyond the level of perception it represents.

To read the *Phaedrus*, then, is to use it up; for the value of any point in it is that it gets *you* (not any sustained argument) to the next point, which is not so much a point (in logical-demonstrative terms) as a level of insight. It is thus a *self-consuming artifact,* a mimetic enactment in the reader's experience of the Platonic ladder in which each rung, as it is negotiated, is kicked away. The final rung, the intuition which stands (or, more properly, on which the reader stands), because it is the last, is of course the rejection of written artifacts, a rejection that far from contradicting what has preceded, is an exact description of what the reader, in his repeated abandoning of successive stages in the argument, has been *doing*. What was problematical sense in the structure of a self-enclosed argument, makes perfect sense in the structure of the reader's experience.

The *Phaedrus* is a radical criticism of the idea of internal coherence from a moral point of view; but identifying the appeal of well-put-together artifacts with the sense of order in the perceiving (i.e., receiving) mind, it provides a strong argument for the banishing of the good poet who is potentially the good deceiver. We can put aside the moral issue and still profit from the dialogue; for if the laws of beginning, middle, and end are laws of psychology rather than form (or truth), a criticism which has as its focus the structural integrity of the artifact is obviously misdirected. (It is the experience of works, not works that have beginnings, middles, and ends.) A new look at the question may result in the rehabilitation of works like *The Faerie Queene* which have been criticized because their poetic worlds lack "unity" and consistency.[7] And a new look at the question may result also in a more accurate account of works whose formal features are so prominent that the critic proceeds directly from them to a statement of meaning without bothering to ask whether their high visibility has any direct relationship to their operation in the reader's experience.

This analysis of the *Phaedrus* illustrates, not incidentally, the ability of the method to handle units larger than the sentence. Whatever the size of the unit, the focus of the method remains the reader's experience of it, and the mechanism of the method is the magic question, "What does this————do?" Answering it of course is more difficult than it would be for a single sentence. More variables creep in, more responses and more different kinds of responses have to be kept track of; there are more contexts which regulate and modulate the temporal flow of the reading experience. Some of these problems will be considered below. For the present let me say that I have usually found that what might be called the basic experience of a work (do *not* read basic meaning) occurs at every level. As an example, we might consider, briefly, *The Pilgrim's Progress*.

At one point in Bunyan's prose epic, Christian asks a question and receives an answer:

Chr. Is this the way to the Celestial City?
Shep. You are just in your way.

The question is asked in the context of certain assumptions about the world, the stability of objects in it, the possibility of knowing, in terms of measurable distances and locatable places, where you are; but the answer, while it is perfectly satisfactory within that assumed context, also challenges it, or, to be more precise, forces the reader to challenge it by forcing him to respond to the pun on the word "just." The inescapability of the pun reflects backward on the question and the world view it supports; and it gestures toward another world view in which spatial configurations have moral and *inner* meanings, and being in the way is independent of the way you happen to be in. That is, if Christian is to be truly in the way, the way must first be in him, and then he will be in it, no matter where—in what merely *physical* way—he is.

All of this is *meant,* that is experienced, in the reader's encounter with "just" which is a comment not only on Christian for asking the question, but on the reader for taking it seriously, that is, simply. What has happened to the reader in this brief space is the basic experience of *The Pilgrim's Progress.* Again and again he settles into temporal-spatial forms of thought only to be brought up short when they prove unable to contain the insights of Christian faith. The many levels on which this basic experience occurs would be the substance of a full reading of *The Pilgrim's Progress,* something the world will soon have, whether it wants it or not.

The method, then, is applicable to larger units and its chief characteristics remain the same: (1) it refuses to answer or even ask the question, what is this work about; (2) it yields an analysis not of formal features, but of the developing responses of the reader in relation to the words as they succeed one another in time; (3) the result will be a description of the structure of response which may have an oblique or even (as in the case of *The Pilgrim's Progress*), a contrasting relationship to the structure of the work as a thing in itself.

III

The Affective Fallacy Fallacy

In the preceding pages I have argued the case for a method of analysis which focuses on the reader rather than on the artifact, and in what remains of this essay I would like to consider some of the more obvious objections to that method. The chief objection, of course, is that affective criticism leads one away from the "thing itself" in all its solidity to the inchoate impressions of a variable and various reader. This argument has several dimensions to it, and will require a multi-directional answer.

First, the charge of impressionism has been answered, I hope, by some of my sample analyses. If anything, the discriminations required and yielded by the method are too fine for even the most analytical of tastes. This is in large part because in the category of response I include not only "tears, prickles," and "other psychological symptoms,"[8] but all the precise mental operations involved in reading, including the formulation of complete thoughts, the performing (and regretting) of acts of judgment, the following and making of logical sequences; and also because my insistence on the cumulative pressures of the reading experience puts restrictions on the possible responses to a word or a phrase.

The larger objection remains. Even if the reader's responses can be described with some precision, why bother with them, since the more palpable objectivity of the text is immediately available ("The poem itself, as an object of specifically critical judgment, tends to disappear"). My reply to this is simple. The objectivity of the text is an illusion, and moreover, a dangerous illusion, because it is so physically convincing. The illusion is one of self-sufficiency and completeness. A line of print or a page or a book is so obviously *there*—It can be handled, photographed, or put away—that it seems to be the sole repository of whatever value and meaning we associate with it. (I wish the pronoun could be avoided, but in a way *it* makes my point.) This is of course the unspoken assumption behind the word "content." The line or page or book *contains*—everything.

The great merit (from this point of view) of kinetic art is that it forces you to be aware of "it" as a changing object—and therefore no "object" at all—and also to be aware of yourself as correspondingly changing. Kinetic art does not lend itself to a static interpretation because it refuses to stay still and doesn't let you stay still either. In its operation it makes inescapable the actualizing role of the observer. Literature is a kinetic art, but the physical form it assumes prevents us from seeing its essential nature, even though we so experience it. The availability of a book to the hand, its presence on a shelf, its listing in a library catalogue—all of these encourage us to think of it as a stationary object. Somehow when we put a book down, we forget that while we were reading, *it* was moving (pages turning, lines receding into the past) and forget too that *we* were moving with it.

A criticism that regards "the poem itself as an object of specifically critical judgment" extends this forgetting into a principle; it transforms a temporal experience into a spatial one; it steps back and in a single glance takes in a whole (sentence, page, work) which the reader knows (if at all) only bit by bit, moment by moment. It is a criticism that takes as its (self-restricted) area the physical dimensions of the artifact and within these dimensions it marks out beginnings, middles, and ends, discovers frequency distributions, traces out patterns of imagery, diagrams strata of complexity (vertical of course), all without ever taking into account the relationship (if any) between its data and their affective force. Its question is what goes into the work rather than what does the work go into. It is "objective" in exactly the wrong way, because it determinedly ignores what is objectively true about the *activity* of reading. Analysis in terms of doings and happenings is on the other hand truly objective because it recognizes the fluidity, "the movingness," of the meaning experience and because it directs us to where the action is—the active and activating consciousness of the reader.

But what reader? When I talk about the responses of "the reader," aren't I really talking about myself, and making myself into a surrogate for all the millions of readers who are not me at all? Yes and no. Yes in the sense that in no two of us are the responding mechanisms exactly alike. No, if one argues that because of the uniqueness of the individual, generalization about response is impossible. It is here that the method can accommodate the insights of modern linguistics, especially the idea of "linguistic competence," "the idea that it is possible to characterize a linguistic system that every speaker shares."[9] This characterization, if it were realized, would be a "competence model," corresponding more or less to the internal mechanisms which allow us to process (understand) and produce sentences that we have never before encountered. It would be a spatial model in the sense that it would reflect a system of rules preceding, and indeed making possible, any actual linguistic experience.

The interest of this for me is its bearing on the problem of specifying response. If the speakers of a language share a system of rules that each of them has somehow internalized, understanding will, in some sense, be uniform; that is, it will proceed in terms of the system of rules all speakers share. And insofar as these rules are constraints on production—establishing boundaries within which utterances are labelled "normal," "deviant," "impossible," and so on—they will also be constraints on the range, and even the direction, of response; that is, they will make response, to some extent, predictable and normative. Thus the formula, so familiar in the literature of linguistics, "Every native speaker will recognize. . . ."

A further "regularizing" constraint on response is suggested by what Ronald Wardhaugh, following Katz and Fodor, calls "semantic competence," a matter less of an abstract set of rules than of a backlog of language experience which determines probability of choice and therefore of response. "A speaker's semantic knowledge," Wardhaugh contends,

. . . is no more random than his syntactic knowledge . . . ; therefore, it seems useful to consider the possibility of devising, for semantic knowledge, a set of rules similar in form to the set used to characterize syntactic knowledge. Exactly how such a set of rules should be formulated and exactly what it must explain are to a considerable extent uncertain. At the very least the rules must characterize some sort of norm, the kind of semantic knowledge than an ideal speaker of the language might be said to exhibit in an ideal set of circumstances—in short, his semantic competence. In this way the rules would characterize just that set of facts about English semantics that all speakers of English have internalized and can draw upon in interpreting words in novel combinations. When one hears or reads a new sentence, he makes sense out of that sentence by drawing on both his syntactic and his semantic knowledge. The semantic knowledge enables him to know what the individual words mean and how to put these meanings together so that they are compatible. (p. 90)

The resulting description could then be said to be a representation of the kind of system that speakers of a language have somehow internalized and that they draw upon in interpreting sentences. (p. 92)

Wardhaugh concedes that the "resulting description" would resemble rather than be equivalent to the system actually internalized, but he insists that "what is really important is the basic principle involved in the total endeavor, the principle of trying to formalize in as explicit a way as possible the semantic knowledge that a mature listener or reader brings to his task of comprehension and that underlies his actual behavior in comprehension" (p. 92). (Interestingly enough, this is a good description of what Empson tries to do, less systematically of course, in *The Structure of Complex Words*.) Obviously the intersection of the two systems of knowledge would make it possible to further restrict (i.e., make predictable and normative) the range of response; so that one could presume (as I have) to describe a reading experience in terms that would hold for all speakers who were in possession of both competences. The difficulty is that at present we do not have these systems. The syntactic model is still under construction and the semantic model has hardly been proposed. (Indeed we will need not a model, but models, since "the semantic knowledge that a mature . . . reader brings to his task of comprehension" will vary with each century or period.[10]) Nevertheless, the incompleteness of our knowledge should not prevent us from hazarding analyses on the basis of what we presently know about what we know.

Earlier, I offered this description of my method: "an analysis of the developing responses of the reader to the words as they succeed one another on the page." It should now be clear that the developing of those responses takes place within the regulating and organizing mechanism, pre-existing the actual verbal experience, of these (and other) competences. Following Chomsky most psychologists and psycholinguists insist that understanding is more than a linear processing of information.[11] This means, as Wardhaugh points out, that "sentences are not just simple left to right sequences of elements" and that "sentences are not understood as a result of adding the meaning of the second to that of the first, the third to the first two, and so on" (p. 54). In short, something other than itself, something existing outside its frame of reference, must be modulating the reader's experience of the sequence.[12] In my method of analysis, the temporal flow is monitored and structured by everything the reader brings with him, by his competences; and it is by taking these into account as they interact with the temporal left to right reception of the verbal string, that I am able to chart and project *the* developing response.

It should be noted however that my category of response, and especially of meaningful response, includes more than the transformational grammarians, who believe that comprehension is a function of deep structure perception, would allow. There is a tendency, at least in the writings of some linguists, to downgrade surface structure—the form of actual sentences—to the status of a husk, or covering, or veil; a layer of excrescences that is to be peeled away or penetrated or discarded in favor of the kernel underlying it. This is an understandable consequence of Chomsky's characterization of surface structure as "misleading" and "uninformative"[13] and his insistence (somewhat modified recently) that deep structure alone determines meaning. Thus, for example, Wardhaugh writes that "every surface structure is interpretable only by reference to its deep structure" and that while "the surface structure of the sentence provides clues to its interpretation, the interpretation itself depends on a correct processing of these clues to reconstruct all the elements and relationships of the deep structure." Presumably the "correct processing," that is, the uncovering of the deep structure and the extraction of deep meaning, is the only goal, and whatever stands in the way of that uncovering is to be tolerated, but assigned no final value. Clues, after all, are sometimes misleading and give rise to "mistakes."

For example, we sometimes anticipate words in a conversation or text only to discover ourselves to be wrong, or we do not wait for sentences to be completed because we assume we know what their endings will be. ...Many of the mistakes students make in reading are made because the students have adopted inappropriate strategies in their processing.

In my account of reading, however, the temporary adoption of these inappropriate strategies is itself a response to the strategy of an author; and the resulting mistakes are part of the experience provided by that author's language and therefore part of its meaning. Deep structure theorists, of course, deny that idfferences in meaning can be located in surface forms. And this for me vitiates the work of Richard Ohmann, who does pay attention to the temporal flow, but only so that he can uncover beneath it the deep structure, which, he assumes, is really doing the work.

The key word is of course experience. For Wardhaugh, reading (and comprehension in general) is a process of extraction. "The reader is required to get the meaning from the print in front of him." For me, reading (and comprehension in general) is an event, no part of which is to be discarded. In that event, which is the actualization of meaning, the deep structure plays an important role, but it is not everything; for we comprehend not in terms of the deep structure alone, but in terms of a *relationship* between the unfolding, in time, of the surface structure and a continual checking of it against our projection (always in terms of surface structure) of what the deep structure will reveal itself to be; and when the final discovery has been made and *the* deep structure is perceived, all the "mistakes," the positing, on the basis of incomplete evidence, of deep structures that failed to materialize, will not be cancelled out. They have been experienced; they have existed in the mental life of the reader; they *mean*. (This is obviously the case in our experience of the line "Nor did they not perceive the evil plight.")

All of which returns us to the original question. Who is *the* reader? Obviously, my reader is a construct, an ideal or idealized reader; somewhat like Wardhaugh's "mature reader" or Milton's "fit" reader, or to use a term of my own, *the* reader is the *informed* reader. The informed reader is someone who

1. is a competent speaker of the language out of which the text is built up;
2. is in full possession of "the semantic knowledge that a mature . . . listener brings to his task of comprehension." This includes the knowledge (that is, the experience, both as a producer and comprehender) of lexical sets, collocation probabilities, idioms, professional and other dialects, etc.;
3. has *literary* competence.

That is, he is sufficiently experienced as a reader to have internalized the properties of literary discourses, including everything from the most local of devices (figures of speech, etc.) to whole genres. In this theory, then, the concerns of other schools of criticism—questions of genre, conventions, intellectual background, etc.—*become redefined in terms of potential and probable response,* the significance and value a reader can be expected to attach to the idea "epic" or to the use of archaic language or to anything.

The reader, of whose responses I speak, then, is this informed reader, neither an abstraction, nor an actual living reader, but a hybrid—a real reader (me) who does everything within his power to make himself informed. That is, I can with some justification project my responses into those of "the" reader because they have been modified by the constraints placed on me by the assumptions and operations of the method: (1) the conscious attempt to become the informed reader by making my mind the repository of the (potential) responses a given text might call out, and (2) the attendant suppressing, in so far as that is possible, of what is personal and idiosyncratic and 1970ish in my response. In short, the informed reader is to some extent processed by the method that uses him as a control. Each of us, if we are sufficiently responsible and self-conscious, can, in the course of employing the method become the informed reader and therefore be a more reliable reporter of his experience.

(Of course, it would be easy for someone to point out that I have not answered the charge of solipsism, but merely presented a rationale for a solipsistic procedure; but such an objection would have force only if a better mode of procedure were available. The one usually offered is to regard the work as a thing in itself, as an object; but as I have argued above, this is a false and dangerously self-validating objectivity. I suppose that what I am saying is that I would rather have an acknowledged and controlled subjectivity than an objectivity which is finally an illusion.)

In its operation, my method will obviously be radically historical. The critic has the responsibility of becoming not one but a number of informed readers, each of whom will be identified by a matrix of political, cultural, and literary determinants. The informed reader of Milton will not be the informed reader of Whitman, although the latter will necessarily comprehend the former. This plurality of informed readers implies a plurality of informed reader aesthetics, or no aesthetic at all. A method of analysis that yields a (structured) description of response has built into it an *operational* criterion. The question is not how good is it, but how does it work; and both question and answer are framed in terms of local conditions, which include local notions of literary value.

This raises the problem of the consideration of local beliefs as a possible basis of response. If a reader does not share the central concerns of a work, will he be capable of fully responding to it? Wayne Booth has asked that question: "But is it really true that the serious Catholic or atheist, however sensitive, tolerant, diligent, and well-informed about Milton's beliefs he may be, enjoys *Paradise Lost* to the degree possible to one of Milton's contemporaries and co-believers, of equal intelligence and sensitivity?"[14] The answer, it seems to me, is no. There are some beliefs that can not be momentarily suspended or assumed. Does this mean then that *Paradise Lost* is a lesser work because it requires a narrowly defined (i.e., "fit") reader? Only if we hold to a universal aesthetic in the context of which value is somehow correlated with the number of readers who can experience it fully, irrespective of local affiliations. My method allows for no such aesthetic and no such fixings of value. In fact it is oriented *away* from evaluation and toward description. It is difficult to say on the basis of its results that one work is better than another or even that a single work is good or bad. And more basically, it doesn't permit the evaluation of literature as literature, as apart from advertising or preaching or propaganda or "entertainment." As a report of a (very complex) stimulus-response relationship, it provides no way to distinguish between literary and other effects, except perhaps for the components which go into one or the other; and no one, I assume, will assent to a "recipe" theory of literary difference. For some this will seem a fatal limitation of the method. I welcome it, since it seems to me that we have for too long, and without notable results, been trying to determine what distinguishes literature from ordinary language. If we understood "language," its constituents and its operations, we would be better able to understand its sub-categories. The fact that this method does not begin with the assumption of literary superiority or end with its affirmation, is I think, one of its strongest recommendations.

This is not to say that I do not evaluate. The selection of texts for analysis is itself an indication of a hierarchy in my own tastes. In general I am drawn to works which do not allow a reader the security of his normal patterns of thought and belief. It would be possible I suppose to erect a standard of value on the basis of this preference—a scale on which the most unsettling of literary experiences would be the best (perhaps literature is what disturbs our sense of self-sufficiency, personal and linguistic) —but the result would probably be more a reflection of a personal psychological need than of a universally true aesthetic.

Three further objections to the method should be considered if only because they were so often made in my classes. If one treats utterances, literary or otherwise, as strategies, does this not claim too much for the conscious control of their producer-authors? I tend to answer this question by begging it, by deliberately choosing texts in which the evidence of control is overwhelming. (I am aware that to a psychoanalytic critic, this principle of selection would be meaningless, and indeed, impossible.) If pressed I would say that the method of analysis, apart from my own handling of it, does not require the assumption either of control or of intention. One can analyze an effect without worrying about whether it was produced accidentally or on purpose. (However, I always find myself worrying in just this way, especially when reading Defoe.) The exception would be cases where the work includes a statement of intention (to justify the ways of God to man), which because it establishes an expectation on the part of a reader becomes a part of his experience. This of course does not mean that the stated intention is to be believed or used as the basis of an interpretation, simply that it, like everything else in the text, draws a response, and, like everything else, it must be taken into account.

The second objection also takes the form of a question. If there is a measure of uniformity to the reading experience, why have so many readers, and some equally informed, argued so well and passionately for differing interpretations? This, it seems to me, is a pseudo-problem.

Most literary quarrels are not disagreements about response, but about a response to a response. What happens to one informed reader of a work will happen, within a range of nonessential variation, to another. It is only when readers become literary critics and the passing of judgment takes precedence over the reading experience, that opinions begin to diverge. The act of interpretation is often so removed from the act of reading that the latter (in time the former) is hardly remembered. The exception that proves the rule, and my point, is C. S. Lewis, who explained his differences with Dr. Leavis in this way: "It is not that he and I see different things when we look at *Paradise Lost*. He sees and hates the very same things that I see and love."

The third objection is a more practical one. In the analysis of a reading experience, when does one come to the point? The answer is, "never," or, no sooner than the pressure to do so becomes unbearable (psychologically). Coming to the point is the goal of a criticism that believes in content, in extractable meaning, in the utterance as a repository. Coming to the point fulfills a need that most literature deliberately frustrates (if we open ourselves to it), the need to simplify and close. Coming to the point should be resisted, and in its small way, this method will help you to resist . . .

* * *

[In two concluding sections, Professor Fish acknowledges some "debts," distinguishes his method "from others more or less like it" and adds "a few final observations" about his own method.]

NOTES

1. *The Verbal Icon* (Lexington, Ky., 1954), p. 21.
2. Thus the line could read: "They did not perceive," which is not the same as saying they did perceive. (The question is still open.) One could also argue that "not" is not really a negative.
3. Of course, "that" is no longer read as "the fact that," but this is because the order of the clauses has resulted in the ruling out of that possibility.
4. This is not true of the Oxford school of ordinary language philosophers (Austin, Grice, Searle) who discuss meaning in terms of hearer-speaker relationships and intention-response conventions, i. e., "situational meaning."
5. I borrow this phrase from P. W. Bridgman, *The Way Things Are.*
6. Ed. W. C. Helmbold and W. G. Rabinowitz (New York, 1956), p. 53.
7. See Paul Alpers, *The Poetry of "The Faerie Queene"* (Princeton, 1967), where exactly this point is made.
8. Wimsatt and Beardsley, *The Verbal Icon*, p. 34.
9. Ronald Wardhaugh, *Reading: A Linguistic Perspective* (New York, 1969), p. 60.
10. That is to say, there is a large difference between the two competences. One is uniform through human history, the other different at different points in it.

11. *Syntactic Structures* (The Hague, 1957), pp. 21-24.
12. See Wardhaugh, p. 55:

Sentences have a "depth" to them, a depth which grammatical models such as phrase structure models and generative-transformational models attempt to represent. These models suggest that if a left-to-rightness principle is relevant to sentence processing, it must be a left-to-rightness of an extremely sophisticated kind that requires processing to take place concurrently at several levels, many of which are highly abstract: phonological or graphological, structural, and semantic.

13. *Language and Mind* (New York, 1968), p. 32.
14. *The Rhetoric of Fiction* (Chicago, 1961), p. 139.

PART FOUR

A SELECT BIBLIOGRAPHY

Altick, Richard D. "Tracing Reputation and Influence," *The Art of Literary Research*. New York: Norton, 1963.

Archibald, Douglas N. "Yeats's Encounters: Observations on Literary Influence and Literary History," *New Literary History*, I (1969), 439-69.

Balakian, Anna. "Influence and Literary Fortune: The Equivocal Junction of Two Methods," *Yearbook of Comparative and General Literature*, II (1962), 24-31.

Baldensperger, Fernand and Werner P. Friederich. *Bibliography of Comparative Literature*. Chapel Hill, N. C.: University of North Carolina Press, 1950.

Bate, Walter Jackson. *The Burden of the Past and the English Poet*. Cambridge, Massachusetts: Harvard University Press, 1970.

Bateson, F. W. "Editorial Commentary," *Essays in Criticism*, 4 (1954), 436-40.

Bateson, Gregory, and Jurgen Ruesch, eds. *Communication: The Social Matrix of Psychiatry*. New York: Norton, 1951.

Beardsley, Monroe C. *Aesthetics: Problems in the Philosophy of Criticism*. New York: Harcourt, Brace and World, 1958.

Block, Haskell M. "The Concept of Influence in Comparative Literature," *Yearbook of Comparative and General Literature*, 7 (1958), 30-37.

Bloom, Harold. *The Anxiety of Influence*. New York: Oxford, 1973.

————. *A Map of Misreading*. New York: Oxford, 1975.

————. *Yeats*. New York: Oxford, 1971.

Borges, Jorge Luis. *Labyrinths: Selected Stories and Other Writings*, eds. Donald A. Yates and James E. Irby. Pref. by André Maurois. New York: New Directions, 1962.

Burke, Kenneth. *Counter-Statement*. New York: Harcourt, Brace, 1931.

————. *The Philosophy of Literary Form*. Baton Rouge, La.: Lousiana State University Press, 1941.

Cohen, Arthur R. *Attitude Change and Social Influence*. New York and London: Basic Books, 1964.

Cohen, Ralph. *The Art of Discrimination.* Berkeley: University of California Press, 1964.

Collingwood, R. G. *The Idea of Nature.* Oxford: Clarendon Press, 1945.

Craig, Hardin. "Shakespeare and Wilson's *Arte of Rhetorique,* an Inquiry into the Criteria for Determining Sources," *PMLA,* (1922), 86-98.

DeMan, Paul. *Blindness and Insight: Essays in the Rhetoric of Contemporary Criticism.* New York: Oxford, 1971.

Eliot, T. S. "Tradition and the Individual Talent," *Selected Essays,* new edition. New York: Harcourt Brace Jovanovich, 1960.

Fish, Stanley E. "Literature in the Reader: Affective Stylistics," *New Literary History,* 2 (1970), 123-61.

————. *Self-Consuming Artifacts: The Experience of Seventeenth-Century Literature.* Berkeley: University of California Press, 1972.

Foerster, N., et al., eds. *Literary Scholarship, Its Aims and Methods.* Chapel Hill, North Carolina: University of North Carolina Press, 1941.

Frye, Northrop. *Anatomy of Criticism.* Princeton, New Jersey: Princeton University Press, 1957.

Gamson, William A. *Power and Discontent.* Homewood, Illinois: The Dorsey Press, 1968.

Ghiselin, Brewster. ed. *The Creative Process: A Symposium.* Berkeley and Los Angeles: University of California Press, 1952.

Greene, T. M. *The Arts and the Art of Criticism.* Princeton, N. J.: Princeton University Press, 1940.

Guillén, Claudio. *Literature as System.* Princeton, N. J.: Princeton University Press, 1973.

Hartman, Geoffrey H. *The Fate of Reading.* Chicago, Illinois: University of Chicago Press, 1975.

Hassan, Ihab H. "The Problem of Influence in Literary History: Notes towards a Definition," *Journal of Aesthetics and Art Criticism,* 14 (1955), 66-76.

Hermerén, Göran. *Influence in Art and Literature.* Princeton, N. J.: Princeton University Press, 1975.

Holland, Norman N. *The Dynamics of Literary Response.* New York: Oxford, 1968.

————. *Poems in Persons.* New York: Norton, 1973.

Jost, Francois, ed. *Proceedings of the Fourth Congress of the International Comparative Literature Association.* 2 vols. Fribourg, 1964. The Hague, 1966.

Kilpatrick, Franklin P., ed. *Human Behavior from the Transactional Point of View.* Hanover, N. H.: Institute for Associated Research, 1952.

Lesser, Simon O. *Fiction and the Unconscious.* Boston: Beacon Press, 1957.

Levin, Harry. *Grounds for Comparison.* Cambridge, Massachusetts: Harvard University Press, 1972.

————. "La Littérature Comparée: Point de vue d'outre-Atlantique," *Revue de Littérature Comparée,* 27 (1953), 17-26.

Lin, Nan. *The Study of Human Communication.* Indianapolis, Indiana: Bobbs-Merrill, 1973.

Lowes, J. Livingston, *The Road to Xanadu.* Boston: Houghton, 1927.

McFarland, Thomas. "Coleridge's Plagiarisms Once More: A Review Essay," *The Yale Review* 63 (1974), 252-86.

————. "The Originality Paradox," *New Literary History*, 6 (1974), 447-76.

————. "The Problem of Coleridge's Plagiarisms," *Coleridge and the Pantheist Tradition*. New York: Oxford, 1969.

Muir, Kenneth. "Editorial Commentary," *Essays in Criticism*, 4 (1954), 432-35.

Peyre, Henri. "A Glance at Comparative Literature in America," *Yearbook of Comparative and General Literature* 1 (1952), 5-7.

Purves, Alan C., and Victoria Rippere. *Elements of Writing about a Literary Work: A Study of Response to Literature*. Urbana, Illinois: NCTE, 1968.

Purves, Alan C., and Richard Beach, eds. *Literature and the Reader: Research in Response to Literature*. Urbana, Illinois: NCTE, 1972.

Richards, I. A. *Principles of Literary Criticism*. London: Routledge and Kegan Paul, 1925.

————. *Practical Criticism*. London: Routledge and Kegan Paul, 1929.

Rosenblatt, Louise M. *Literature as Exploration*. New York: Appleton-Century, 1938; rev. ed., New York: Noble and Noble, 1968.

————. "The Poem as Event," *College English* 26 (November, 1964), 123-25.

————. "Towards a Transactional Theory of Reading," *Journal of Reading Behavior* 1 (1969), 31-47.

Russell, David H. *The Dynamics of Reading*. Waltham, Massachusetts: Ginn and Company, 1970.

Shaw, J. T. "Literary Indebtedness and Comparative Literary Studies," in N. P. Stallknecht and H. Franz, eds., *Comparative Literature: Method and Perspective*. Carbondale: Southern Illinois University Press, 1961, pp. 58-71.

Shrodes, Caroline. "Biblotherapy: A Theoretical and Clinical Experimental Study." Berkeley: University of California dissertation, 1950.

Slatoff, Walter J. *With Respect to Readers: Dimensions of Literary Response*. Ithaca, N. Y.: Cornell University Press, 1970.

Stallman, R. W. "The Scholar's Net: Literary Sources," *College English*, 17 (1955), 20-27.

Trilling, Lionel. "The Sense of the Past," *The Liberal Imagination*. New York: Viking, 1950.

Vico, Giambattista. *The New Science*, Revised Translation of the Third Edition. Thomas Goddard Bergin and Max Harold Fisch. Ithaca, N. Y.: Cornell University Press, 1968.

Wallace, Robert, and James G. Toaffe, eds. *Poems on Poetry*. New York: E. P. Dutton, 1965.

Weimann, Robert. "Past Significance and Present Meaning in Literary History," *New Literary History*, 1 (1969), 91-109.

Wellek, René. "The Concept of Comparative Literature," *Yearbook of Comparative and General Literature* 2 (1953), 1-5.

Wellek, René, and Austin Warren. *Theory of Literature*. New York: Harcourt, Brace, 1942.

Wells, Henry W. *New Poets from Old*. New York: Columbia University Press, 1940.

Wheeler, Ladd. *Interpersonal Influence.* Boston, Massachusetts: Allyn and Bacon, 1970.

Wimsatt, W. K., and Monroe C. Beardsley, "The Intentional Fallacy," *Sewanee Review* 54 (Summer, 1946), 468–88.

Young, Edward. *Conjectures on Original Composition* (1759). Facsimile Edition, Leeds: The Scholar Press, 1966.

INDEX

Note: Italicized names represent authors of articles in this book.

DATE DUE

GAYLORD			PRINTED IN U.S.A